Now That You're Out

Now That You're Out

The Challenges and Joys of Living as a Gay Man

Martin Kantor, MD

 PRAEGER

AN IMPRINT OF ABC-CLIO, LLC
Santa Barbara, California • Denver, Colorado • Oxford, England

Library of Congress Cataloging-in-Publication Data

Kantor, Martin.
  Now that you're out : the challenges and joys of living as a gay man / Martin Kantor.
      p. cm.
  Includes bibliographical references and index.
  ISBN 978–0–313–38751–7 (hard copy : alk. paper) — ISBN 978–0–313–38752–4 (ebook)
1. Gay men. 2. Gay men—Psychology. 3. Male homosexuality. I. Title.
HQ76.K347   2011
306.76′62—dc22   2011001697

ISBN: 978–0–313–38751–7
EISBN: 978–0–313–38752–4

15 14 13 12 11   1 2 3 4 5

This book is also available on the World Wide Web as an eBook.
Visit www.abc-clio.com for details.

Praeger
An Imprint of ABC-CLIO, LLC

ABC-CLIO, LLC
130 Cremona Drive, P.O. Box 1911
Santa Barbara, California 93116-1911

This book is printed on acid-free paper ∞

Manufactured in the United States of America

For Michael

Contents

PART III: THERAPY

Introduction

From day one, some gay men feel entirely comfortable with their being gay and with entering into the gay subculture. But others contact me, a psychiatrist, full of tears and recriminations, either because they are unhappy about being gay or because they are unhappy about being gay in a certain way. They are in conflict about coming out or having difficulty with their relationships—trying to find someone special without success or, having found him, attempting to get over his having rejected or dumped them. They say that they are afraid of their youth passing and middle age approaching. They feel unable to handle their parents who, on the one hand, criticize and reject them and say they never want to see them again and, on the other hand, try to take over their lives and repair them, although nothing about their lives is even remotely broken. The bottom line is almost always the same: they see gay life as an enigma and feel that they need help in sorting things about it out, solving its problems, and resolving its paradoxes; anticipating and dealing with its numerous surprises; and avoiding its predictable complications. And, without this help, they just might throw up their hands and go into retreat, the only way they feel they can avoid the endless pain of what they believe to be the irresolvable uncertainty of getting stuck in personal conflict and being mired in cultural limbo.

Some, turning to peers, parents, educators, and the media for enlightenment, find satisfactory illumination. Others tell me that no matter who they consult, the information they get is unreliable and that the advice they are given as to how best to live their lives is questionable. They say that getting only unsatisfactory answers to sincere questions leaves them with a distorted view of gay life—from friends who lead them astray by repeating entrenched myths, the media that throw them off by viewing them not as individuals but as members of a giant impersonal collective with uniform preferences and problems, and therapists who offer up one-size-fits-all advice that applies more in theory than in practice and suggest solutions to problems that seem to be meant more for someone else than for them personally.

As a result, they constantly feel guilty about being gay; form friendships and relationships that go nowhere, dissolve, or otherwise end up tragically; have difficulty making informed decisions about whether to stay single or get married; if married, vacillate about staying faithful to one special partner or having an open relationship/cheating; can't decide if they should or should not adopt children; suffer unnecessarily from avoidable biomedical complications of gay sex; and continuously experience potentially treatable problems with sexual desire and performance—two in particular: erectile dysfunction and an inability to achieve timely orgasm due to ejaculation that is either way too premature or significantly and seriously retarded.

My goal is to fill the gaps by providing you as a gay man with a resource manual and a survival guide that frankly and fully takes you into realms and domains of being gay and its culture in a way rarely previously explored and almost never written about with such unflinching candor. With this in mind, I address three audiences: gay men just starting out and feeling mystified or confused by what they are finding; more experienced gay men who feel that their lives are nevertheless still missing something and that what they need is help tuning in, tuning up, and turning things around; and parents of gay men, who predictably get drawn into the process at some level and often, just as predictably, mishandle things, creating anxiety all around and unnecessary pain for everyone concerned—mostly for their sons but ultimately as much for themselves as for them.

My method involves passing on information I have obtained and things I have learned from several sources: the many (sometimes desperate) letters I have received from gay men seeking help; therapy interviews/case vignettes of gay men I have seen as patients in my practice; material gleaned from informal contacts/interviews with gay men around town who speak to me, often in an unguarded fashion, as both therapist and friend; and my personal self-observations and experiences as a gay man who has been around for a long time, certainly getting older and, it is hoped, at least a little bit wiser.

Here are some of the letters I received from gay men asking me for advice. Bart wrote to me,

What I want more than anything else is to find a guy I can cuddle with at night, laugh and cry with through the good times and bad, and know that he loves me more than anything.

I'm a 22-year-old college student who has only been out of the closet for one year (as of today). I bought your book, *My Guy*, Thursday night and read it in less than two days. I found it to be very useful and informative. But still, I can't figure out what my problem is, but it's obvious to me that I have one.

Since I've come out, I've dated five guys. Each one seemed to be great guys ... until after we fooled around, when they decided that they wanted to be "just friends." There aren't many gay guys in the area where I live, as I'm from a very conservative, rural place, and I feel trapped there. But at the same time, why haven't I been able to find a DECENT guy here? Instead, I've resorted to meeting guys online, and many of the guys have lived much too far away to actually meet them. As a consequence, I end up liking them, but they can't handle the distance, or just lose interest and stop talking to me.

I have no problem with my physical appearance. I don't mean to toot my own horn, but I AM attractive. Still, I can't find a guy. And I keep having this voice in my head (who I sometimes think is God) telling me that I'm never going to be happy in this life and that I'm going to end up alone, which is my biggest fear.

I definitely want a merger relationship, as I've experienced firsthand the type of relationship where the partners aren't faithful to each other (and I didn't like it).

I don't know what to do. I'm sure you're busy, but if you could take the time to respond, I would greatly appreciate it. Thank you for at least reading this.

Sincerely,
Bart

Richard wrote to me,

Maybe you can help me with this. I am recently dating a guy I met on the Internet, he is adorable and I really like him. He's kind of busy cause of his work and I can see he is interested in me, but I'm not quite sure. My friends all tell me like, "Don't text him, don't call him, let him do that." In short, they say that I should play hard to get. But I worry that that might make me hard to want. So I feel that it won't hurt if I just send like a Hi babyboy!!! text, right? If he doesn't answer me back then I leave it there. He also ended a relationship like two months ago, that's what he told me, and that the guy's being pushy was the reason. I really like this guy, I've never been in a relationship like it in 2 years and I'm freaking out cause I don't wanna lose him. I am 26 and he is 27, I know there are more guys out there, but what do you recommend me plz.

Here are some case vignettes from my practice:

Mark, a depressed patient, said to me that he had just come out as a 20-year-old man, but though he affirmed his identity as a gay man, he still felt anxious, depressed, and suicidal because he feared that his gay life, like all gay life, would end as tragically as it began.

He came to me looking for insights into himself and knowledge of the gay life to guide him both directly and indirectly—the latter by helping him master inner conflicts that overwhelmed him. He wanted to sort things out even if that meant discovering some painful truths about himself.

He hoped to stop buying into all the myths out there about gay men and quit yielding to peer distortions that were diverting him from knowing what kind of life was truly facing him and causing him to make uninformed decisions that might permanently affect him negatively in the years to come. He believed that the gay community in his town was wrong for him because no one in it took his—or any other—relationships seriously, and instead everyone violated his boundaries by trying to make out with all the handsome men he found for himself.

He feared that if he listened too hard to misguided friends he would become a stereotype, as he put it "a satire on himself," and so would never find peace and serenity with someone he loved and who loved him. He would instead be fated to go through one hopeless relationship after another, routinely fail at them all, and in the end be old and lonely—after all the men he truly loved cheated on him, then dumped him for someone younger and better looking.

He wanted to find a man he could love, honor, cherish, and even, when indicated (and in Mark's case it often was), obey. But he feared that because that wouldn't happen he was doomed to go through life by himself, live in a gay ghetto that his family would never visit, spend every night of his life in the bars so that he didn't get enough sleep to be able to do his work effectively the next morning, and get hung up on drugs and sickened by some serious medical disease, only to then go prematurely, and not without guilt and regret that he wasn't straight, to his grave, as, after having been excommunicated by his church, he passed on convinced that during life he had hurt not only himself but also his parents who wanted the grandchildren he could never give them. In other words, as he put it, it was as if a bumper sticker he always used to see around applied to him exactly: the one that said something like, "Life sucks, and then you die."

Matt, another depressed patient, said that he came to me hoping to get some answers to the hard questions about gay life. He wanted to learn not only about coming, *but also about* being, *out; that is, after you come out, what next? For example, when it came to his relationships, he wanted to know, "How aggressive should I be when I really like someone?" and "Exactly how long should I give a relationship to work before deciding it's futile, giving up, and getting out while the getting is still good?" He wanted to know, "How can I develop a sound working permanent relationship that fully expresses my sexuality and satisfies my sexual needs without stifling my partner in those same areas?" and "Can I expect monogamy with fidelity, though all gay men cheat?" He complained that every one of his friendships was transient and that his new marriage was going poorly because no matter what he did he couldn't seem to please, really appease, his guy—a man who was con-stantly picking on him—emphasizing his flaws without simultaneously acknowledging his virtues and putting him in one double bind after another, for example, telling him to go to the gym to firm up his body, only to then complain that because he was always working out, he was never home. Also, he was often depressed because he feared that his gay-unfriendly boss would find out that he was gay; because he felt that his being gay was killing his parents; and because although he was only in his twenties, he was already a victim of ageism on the part of some other gay men in his community who were treating him like a has-been. Too, he was convinced that he would never be able to get along with his family who was giving him a hard time about not getting married and having the grandchildren they so wanted. And he was sad-dened by thoughts about his getting nowhere at work because he feared that he would be unable to mesh his gay life with his profes-sional life without unduly sacrificing one for the other. But to date all he got was advice from friends with their own axes to grind who to boot were unduly swayed by popular trend and political correctness. Also, he had read much of the literature written to help gay men with their deep personal concerns—only to find it didn't satisfy him because it was full of superficialities and because everything he read was too narrowly focused on already well-covered topics now become issues that, though standard, were not particularly meaningful for him, such as the removal of homosexuality from the American Psychological Association's list of mental disorders, the triumph of Stonewall, the virtues of gay activism, the advantages of gay pride, and the benefits of coming cleanly, boldly, forcibly, and honestly out.*

In Chapter 1, "Coming Out," I discuss disclosure, its pros and cons, and its dos and don'ts. In recognition that much of the literature to date has documented the virtues of disclosure, I focus on problem solving related to coming out, emphasizing not the considerable benefits of disclosure but rather ways to resolve the conflicts that sometimes make coming out difficult—so that if you have problems in this respect, you can, by solving them, more fully accept yourself without regrets and avoid the backsliding that can occur due to the inevitable fallout that follows opening up—not only to others but also to yourself.

In Chapter 2, "Lifestyle," I define how I use the term, then focus on ways to become an A-gay while avoiding being a Z-gay—the latter a man who wastes the opportunity of youth to end up tragically old and before his time. Z-gays want life in the mainstream but end up on the fringes. They want to live in a suburban paradise but wind up in a confining ghetto/slum. They seek monogamy but settle for polygamy. They hope to have a satisfactory career but compromise that by sacrificing their work for their gay life. They want to adopt children, but after fighting for the right, they have difficulty with the reality.

In Chapter 3, "Relationships," I put forth my belief that any gay man—rich or poor, handsome or ordinary looking, tall or short, brilliant or of average intellect—has the potential to have a permanent partner *if he wants one*, and if he doesn't get one, it is not because of what he looks like or how much money he has but because of what he does or (mostly) doesn't do. Napoleon notwithstanding, anatomy is only a part of a gay man's destiny. Emotional conflicts determine a lot, for it's these that make gay life hardest when, for example, they cause you to distance yourself from all potential partners and lovers, then spin your fears ("I am afraid of commitment") into preferences ("I prefer to be alone, who needs people?"). So, I first ask you to decide whether you want to be single or married and then, if marriage is your choice, help you break through the commonest barriers to finding your Mr. Right—ranging from holding yourself back due to problematic narcissism that too loudly proclaims "I am too good for him," to equally problematic Ice Princess remoteness associated with a perfectionistic inability to compromise that can lead you to have a compulsively cool response to an in fact innately very hot suitor.

A coolly perfectionistic gay man, still alone at the age of 60, wrote to me,

> I don't believe in being in a rush to find a relationship. I need to explore the possibilities for many more months before I commit. All the men I have already met are doing the same thing, so why not me? I am thinking a lot about what kind of man I want, but haven't yet decided on one. I only want someone like me: a nice man, personable, not manicky, clean, generous, and tall, as well as deep, intellectual, creative and without silly mannerisms like a goofy smirk when something really isn't funny (annoying!), and a need to always have dinner be on me, even when it isn't any more than just a pizza.

Then once you have found him and haven't let him go, I help you decide what kind of relationship you want, particularly focusing on your need to make a decision between one that is open and one that is closed. Then I assist you in pursuing your goal productively—by directing all your attention and efforts to it, facts in hand, and with a brush that paints such emotional impediments as a masochistic need for failure and/or a fear of commitment and success, entirely out of the picture.

In Chapter 4, "Sex and Sexuality," I help you learn what you may need to know about such sexual matters as bisexuality, sexual compulsivity, gender identity disorder, and transsexualism. For example, I believe that sexual compulsivity is often a posttraumatic adult state where old unresolved issues around early abuse, particularly sexual abuse and personal rejection, get repeated in a futile attempt to attain cloture, leaving you with a life not selected *by* you, by your "ego," but *for* you, by your deepest, most primitive impulses, your most horrific fears, and your most detrimental self-abusive needs.

In Chapter 5, "The Paraphilias," I attempt to distinguish "normal" from (what used to be called) "perverted" so that if you are in fact guilty about doing okay things, you can better accept yourself without shame. But if you are not okay but troubled and feel—or should feel—that you need treatment, I help you seek and get the therapy you need and to do so without hesitation and both guilt and shame free.

In Chapter 6, "Identity/Disorders of Identity," I try to help you as a gay man discover who you really are, determine if that is what you truly want to be, and then either self-affirm as necessary or, when indicated, change yourself around to become something else. After defining "gay identity," I discus "identity crises" and "identity disorder" in gay men and offer suggestions as to how to firm up and develop a strong, resolute sexual, gender, and nonsexual identity (terms I go on to define)—avoiding the extremes of excessive paralytic idealism on the one hand (where you only accept becoming something you wish to but can't possibly be) and harmful self-destructive pessimism on the other hand (where you only accept becoming anything *but* you so that you instead turn into a compendium of defenses against yourself.)

In Chapter 7, "Midlife and Beyond: Aging and Ageism," I help you cope and deal with getting older. Coping and dealing with getting older starts with avoiding misspending your youth in a way that devastates your later life. It also involves anticipating and dealing with ageism, such as that ageism that Michael, my partner, still a young man by most standards, encountered when recently he knocked on the door of our downstairs neighbors—two gay men—to ask them to turn the music down, only to hear someone inside looking out through the peephole say, "I don't know exactly who it is at the door other than it's just some old coot making a lot more noise than we are." I offer suggestions on how to avoid feeling that you as an older gay man are somehow on a lower rung of the personal, sexual, and occupational hierarchy just because of your age so that you become convinced that no one wants someone like you around—because your brain has gone soft and your body turned to flab.

In Chapter 8, "You and Your Parents," I discuss dealing with problematic, unsupportive parents. I believe that you should develop and foster a good relationship with your parents no matter how difficult they are, even if they are that too-typical Mom and Dad ashamed of your being gay, responding in a terroristic fashion when you disclose, especially when you open up about some of the details of the gay life that you choose to live. I believe that success here means losing some parent–child battles in order to win the parent–child war, even overlooking a lot to avoid letting petty resentments take over and drive you apart from people who likely do love you—even more than, at least for now, you think they do.

In Chapter 9, "Emotional Disorder in Gay Men," I discuss that typical tendency to confound *DSM-IV* emotional problems with "normal, characteristic, gay behavior," then dismiss troublesome neuroses as typical gay stuff.

Confounding "emotional disorder in troubled gay men" with "all gay men are emotionally troubled" seriously falsifies the picture of what being gay is all about—by stereotyping every gay man as quirky/peculiar/troubled, thus failing to set apart the individual gay man who is in fact having emotional difficulties from the gay man who is fine, thus helping the former obtain a personal diagnosis and get proper, individualized treatment.

In Chapter 10, "Substance Abuse," I discuss problems with alcohol and drugs as they are commonly found in gay men. Many gay men are drinking too heavily and abusing substances, but they don't recognize that they have a problem. And even those who do recognize it generally fail to appreciate its severity and thus its full present and future implications.

In Chapter 11, "Shame, Guilt, and Low Self-Esteem," I go into a basic cause of much emotional disorder in gay men. I offer you a program to help you lessen the self-hatred and self-disdain you might just possibly experience inside yourself and in your gay life. For example, while these days homophobia has gone underground and become more subtle, it is still sufficiently widespread and problematic to create much sadness and self-questioning for you. Responding to it not with anger but with guilt can but further catalyze the homophobia by intensifying homophobic negativity toward gays. For most straights, buying into the bad things gays think and say about themselves, line up with gays' own negative self-views. Then, coming to agree with such of their negative self-assessments as "I am a second-class citizen," they find what they need to condemn them as sinful and bad individuals.

In Chapter 12, "Suicide," I discuss a very serious problem in gay men: suicidality, which in gay men, as in anyone else, may or may not exist in intimate association with emotional disorder. In this chapter, I note that many gay men not only contemplate suicide but also act out feeling suicidal either indirectly, by becoming guiltily self-destructive, or directly, by making an actual suicidal attempt. In the first instance, they might harm themselves through deliberately contracting a disease or destroying their physical health, say, through substance abuse. In the second instance, they might take pills, hang themselves, or jump off a bridge. This is a preventable/treatable problem but only if it is accepted as such, not dismissed as an inevitable complication of being gay and so the wages of (as a homophobe might say and a depressed gay man might think) "that particular sin." This chapter helps you recognize your own suicidal tendencies early on and deal with them by getting at their cause, particularly three: bullying, personal rejections that make for crushing abandonments, and the loneliness that sometimes plagues even those gay men surrounded by good friends and ensconced with a loving partner.

In Chapter 13, "Getting Professional Help," I help you determine if you need to seek professional intervention. I go into the various forms of therapy available to you. Some gay men enter therapy to go straight, but there are few (if any) pros, only cons, here. I also guide you in seeking therapists who are helpful while avoiding those who are potentially harmful, such as those who are unknowledgeable, sadistic, or both. (As Kort says, even lesbian or gay therapists comfortable with being gay themselves can harbor negative thoughts about gay culture[1] to the point of influencing you negatively or actually ruining your life personally and professionally.)

Should you need therapy, I recommend an affirmative-eclectic form of treatment where a positively inclined therapist employing psychodynamic, interpersonal, cognitive, and supportive interventions embedded in a welcoming, inspirational context offers you an accepting supportive holding environment as he or she also goes back in time to your early years to reawaken past sleeping problems and bring them back into the open and into alignment with your present. Now you can live in the here and now, not in some unwelcome, unwanted past, one that continually hovers over you like a specter, ordering you about, taking over your life completely just before scaring you half to death.

If you are without a therapist and choose to continue that way, this chapter can help you develop a self-help approach to changing. You can read into it specific tools to put at your fingertips to help you cope in troubled times; determine and achieve true, valued goals; and find your own way to ultimate peace and happiness—through developing a self in harmony both within and between you and those who share—or soon will be sharing—your life with you.

Finally, the appendix, "Origins," presents FYI material that is both educational and potentially therapeutic. I outline some of the many psychological and biological theories advanced to date as to the causes of homosexuality. It is hoped that after you read this, you will firmly and finally recognize at least one thing for certain: that homosexuality is *not* a choice, and because no one fully understands how men get to be gay, people who have your best interests at heart should stop pointing fingers at you for voluntarily going down some drain and instead retroflex those fingers at themselves for even thinking that you are up to something of which they disapprove and of which you should be anything less than completely, thoroughly proud.

ACKNOWLEDGMENTS

My sincere thanks to Dr. R. A. M., for her considerable help with this text.

PART I

Gay Life

ONE

Coming Out

This chapter attempts to separate the myths from the facts surrounding coming out. I go into the dos and the don'ts, as well as the pros and the cons, of disclosure. One of my goals is to challenge some of the unscientific and potentially harmful advice out there, in particular, those one-size-fits-all suggestions that fail to take into account the considerable differences among gay men, instead lumping them all into one stereotypical collective into which you, as a given individual, may very well not even begin to fit.

For some gay men, coming out is no more difficult than breathing out. Such men eagerly seek to disclose, doing so both unhesitatingly and effectively. From the start, they just accept who and what they are and wouldn't have it any other way. For them, disclosure doesn't create anxiety or guilt. And if—or when—they encounter parental and social disapproval, they respond not with regrets but by ignoring the negativity: facing it down or enhancing pride by ratcheting up defiance.

For other gay men, coming out is sufficiently difficult that they need help both in recognizing and understanding who they are and in making decisions about disclosing that exactly to others. These men, often guilty and ashamed of being gay, anticipate—and likely receive—antigay backlash from parents, friends, educators, and their church. As a result, their openness and honesty restores their integrity less than it increases the damage—diminishing their self-acceptance and respect and shattering rather than enhancing their inner sense of peace. Having equated disclosure with exposure, they wind up feeling not stronger than before but more vulnerable than usual.

DEFINITIONS

The process of disclosure differs among gay men, for each gay man has unique personal needs and individual passions. In addition, each gay man has to deal with his own input from family and friends who most definitely have needs and passions of their own. It follows that advice about disclosure that is right for some gay men is wrong for others. An approach to disclosure that works for gay men who are natively open and voluble works less well for gay men who are natively shy and untalkative. What can be good for the hypomanic can be bad for the avoidant; secretiveness is a relief, not a burden, for gays with paranoid tendencies, and for those wracked by guilt about being gay, disclosure often does not decrease but rather, at least temporarily, increases stress by activating shame. For those in whom the disclosure process itself feeds off serious emotional disorder, coming out can be less a valid affirmation and self-fulfillment than an expression of emotional conflict—as when a hypomanic gay man reveals too much about himself and to the wrong people, a sadomasochistic gay man uses the coming-out process to give his parents grief by disclosing in a spiteful rather than in an empathic way, or a narcissistic gay man comes out even though his partner, reminding him that he is not only coming out himself but also outing a reluctant companion, asks him to stay in. Too often overlooked is that coming out is not a one-way process but an interpersonal event, and that involves—or should involve—delicate interactive negotiations, making it less the "me" happening that so often experts in the field and the reporting media portray than the "us" affair that is so often deemphasized or entirely overlooked. Most importantly, coming out, too often portrayed as a simple one-time event, is really a protracted ongoing process. Though I still call it "coming out," I really mean "becoming out." That's a better term because it encompasses the important things that occur both before and after the moment of truth: leading up to it and including what happens next.

The "becoming-out" process often has some or all of the following phases, any one or several of which can be truncated or skipped entirely:

Phase 1. Subliminal awareness: You suspect that something about you is special, different, and even unique, but you don't know exactly what, perhaps because you don't yet know what "gay" is exactly.

Phase 2. Contemplation with ambivalence about coming out *to yourself*: You determine you are gay, wonder if that pleases more than it displeases you, and consider avowing or disavowing your identity as a gay man. Should you fully acknowledge being gay and then go on to fulfill your destiny by sincerely accepting yourself as good, or should you continue to harbor thoughts of being a shameful, weak, defective individual—someone who hurts himself and his parents by being that way and violates society's expectations of what a real man should be?

Phase 3. Contemplation with ambivalence about coming out *to others*: You hear that full disclosure to others is optimal for members of your (minority) group, but as you think about disclosing publicly you weigh the advantages of being frank and forthcoming against the advantages of keeping your being gay to yourself along the lines of, "If you don't ask, I won't tell," and, sometimes, "I won't even tell should you ask."

> *Mel, one of my patients, was equally troubled both by hiding and fully disclosing his being gay. At times, he felt the urge to come out boldly, proudly, and unambivalently—without caring what others might think or, if they thought ill of him, without worrying about how they might act. At other times, he experienced the urge to stay in because he felt ashamed of being gay, as if it were a bad thing to be, with likely negative consequences involving the doing of physical and emotional, personal and professional, harm to himself and his loved ones. Ultimately, he decided to stay in after all, allowing excessive inappropriate guilt to take over and rule, as he rationalized his keeping being gay a secret along the lines of "For me, coming out is a complete waste of time, for it's just gilding the lily, because people already know all there is to know about me, and probably even more than I think," and "Out or in, there are more important things in this world to worry about than telling people you are, or are not, gay."*

Phase 4. Coming out to others but doing so selectively rather than fully: Many gay men decide to disclose/hide certain aspects of themselves but not everything. If this is you, instead of actively spreading all of the word, you answer only questions that are asked and/or merely drop hints and clues that leave others suspecting but keep them guessing. How open you are is highly dependent on your personality and external circumstances. Some gay men are most comfortable coming out partially by seeking gay relationships openly—but only out of town in places where presumably nobody knows them. At home, they pass for celibates, or hermits, putting on a show of sexual reticence or asexuality, often after telling the world something untrue, for example, that they are divorced and, permanently soured on marriage, never going to get married to another woman again.

Phase 5. Assimilation: In time, following initial disclosure, you change as do external circumstances either on their own or because of your input. Now as you more fully understand yourself and the subculture, you adapt and progressively, it is hoped, develop an authentic guilt-free cohesive sense of self that is synchronized within and with what goes on around you, leading to even more self-authentication along with maximum generativity.

PROBLEM SOLVING

When you come out, come out in a focused, methodical way. Ensure as positive a response to your coming out as possible by refining your presentation. Before you come out, prepare and rehearse what you are going to say. Think through in advance how you are going to respond to any negative reactions your disclosure might produce.

Have specific goals you intend to achieve and do that directly, effectively, and efficiently by developing a narrative that tells others what you want them to know exactly and in a nonconfrontational manner that conveys more information than emotion and that enhances positive relationships rather than becoming a new basis for your distancing yourself from loved ones or professional colleagues.

Never make your coming out the occasion for the expression of built-up rage. This is not the time to hurt your parents by flaunting your being gay in their faces with raw, antagonistic revelations, such as highly realistic, lurid sexual images meant to shock and embarrass them. Avoid attempting to isolate yourself via breaking away from them by devaluing them so that you can dump them without guilt—to allow yourself to go your own way thinking, "I am not a bad person for leaving them, for they deserve to never see me again because of how they treated me up to this point."

Don't make your narrative a vehicle for expressing conflict or reducing/resolving guilt, seeking love and approval from those who have previously withheld it, gaining absolution from those who have until now been critical of you, masochistically invalidating yourself, or narcissistically enhancing your self-image through displaying a personal image burnished just for the occasion or created entirely out of falsehoods. This is not the best time to make a political statement, such as one intended to affirm your antiestablishment views and credentials. Carefully consider the potential downsides of your coming out in inappropriate ways and places just to function as a role model for others; for example, think twice about emulating my patient, a teacher, who came out at school in order to have his students "assist me in my research on homosexuality and to give them courage to come out like me."

Determine who you want to come out to first. Try to make that all-important initial disclosure to people who will predictably be simpatico, not to people who already revile you and you hope to convince to do otherwise.

Be empathic, respecting others' sensitivities just as you hope that they will respect yours. Avoid being so socially autistic that you become immune to the negative feedback that can result when you make other people uncomfortable.

As you come out as a gay man, remind others, as you remind yourself, that you see yourself—and need to be seen—from perspectives other than just being gay. For you are not only a gay man but also a man with many other characteristics who also happens to be a homosexual. Do not allow affirming your gay identity to take over to the point that it has the untended consequence of deaffirming other, just as important aspects of yourself.

Be practical, taking real-life considerations into account, particularly the recognition that you live in a world where honesty should but doesn't always trump spin. Be especially cautious about coming out in situations where significant potential or actual danger looms. There are times when it may be better to dissimulate than to disclose, for ensuring your safety to protect yourself can be as important as telling your truth to affirm your principles. Too many gay men's parents exile their sons when they discover they are gay, throwing them out of the house, even forcing them to go when they are not yet old enough to live on their own, leaving them no choice but to hit the streets and find a way to survive out in the cold. Coming out is not mandatory in those cases where it puts you in danger. And coming out always puts you in some danger. The question is, "How much, and, if a lot, is it worth it?"

Always keep in mind that there is a close interconnection between disclosure and lifestyle. (The next chapter discusses my idiosyncratic use of the term "lifestyle.") A particular advantage of disclosure is that it solves important lifestyle problems such as whether you and a partner should take separate holidays to please your respective parents or live separately to maintain so-called decorum for professional reasons—shopping separately, attending the theater by yourself, and never letting your partner deliver you to or pick you up from work.

Michael, my partner, used to deliver me to and pick me up from my work at a very homophobic medical clinic. A few of the staff kept asking me, "Who is that person?" I was going to lie and say he was my brother or son, but instead, preferring integrity to reputation, I equivocated, with unfavorable results due to others' escalating curiosity-driven homophobia. I often went to the opera with a man whose too-stunning opera jacket was a dead giveaway. On several occasions by chance my boss sat near us, making for a relationship changer between me and him. That became immediately apparent at work the very next

morning after our first encounter, when he went so far as to make it
clear that from the time of this ill-fated nonoperatic recognition
scene/discovery, he had "lost respect for me" and would make certain
that as long as I worked for him, I would never be happy or get pro-
moted. (He told me this some few years before he discovered something
else: that his daughter was a lesbian.)

Do not come out just to please someone who wants you out. And never
unilaterally make coming-out decisions for another person: outing others
who may not yet feel ready to disclose, even though you do so innocently
as you, so caught up in the spirit of the moment, want everyone else out
like you—even those who are not yet ready. If you have a partner, always
consider that your coming is a joint endeavor because your coming out is
likely to affect him too.

A close friend and his wife, neither of whom I had come out to, invited
me over for dinner one evening and I asked if I could bring my new
partner whom I intended to present as "just an old friend." I didn't
want to go alone, my partner had nothing else planned, and I, at the
time somewhat narrow in my criteria for picking love objects, was
so infatuated with this man for his looks that I didn't want to leave
him even for one Saturday night. When he said, grudgingly, "I'll go
if the host is attractive," I, excessively willing to do anything to satisfy
the one I adored and particularly eager to please him, *showed him the*
host's picture on the jacket of a book the host had written and said,
"Yes, he is, very attractive, but let's go and you can decide for your-
self." I didn't give this a second thought partly because I believed
that, like me, my partner was a faithful man who, much as the rest of
us, simply enjoyed being around attractive people. Certainly the far-
thest thing from my mind was pimping for a boyfriend I wanted all
for myself. But I should have known that lover boy, true to what I soon
began to see was his form, would, without my knowing it, out us both
by making a pass at the host. The host's wife was surprised to discover
that I was gay and to boot thought I had put my lover up to seducing
her husband. So, becoming convinced that I wasn't a good person,
she went on to convince her husband that I was the bad guy. Then both
dumped me, after years of our being the closest of friends (I had even
been best man at his wedding). This entire encounter was extremely
painful, yet through denial I managed to let myself think, "I guess
we have just grown apart." The husband didn't care about this pass,
for indeed he had once made a pass of his own at me. Rather, it was

his wife who did all the protesting, leading the charge to throw me out of their lives. Of course, she was working out a problem she had with her husband—with me. She was healing their relationship by berating me to avoid blaming him. I suffered immensely from this experience because I wondered what I did wrong, figured what happened was "just another outcome of my self-defeating behavior," thought that this was my comeuppance for being gay, and became convinced that this incident was just another in a hurtful series of lifetime punishments that properly were my due, to be meted out by all those other people in my life eager to smoke me out of my hiding place, forcing me into the broad daylight all the better to see, in order to condemn, me.

I recently received the following letter laying out my own similar sentiments exactly:

I became friends with a French professor I was assigned to collaborate with on a course last semester. He, only a few years older than me, lives alone and is very cryptic about his life. Claims he has been in therapy for years. Well, just before Christmas, his dog died and he plummeted into depression. I tried to be supportive by encouraging him to come to some stupid university parties, and he did come to oneÐthen he revealed to me that he is gay, but no one knows it, and he would never come out because of his conservative administration (he is non-tenure but has been there for 20 years). I cannot really blame him for wanting to keep his job. He is a very sad soul, though. And lonely. But I don't want to be the one encouraging him to make the decision to come out, even though it may be for his own good.

Never out others to retaliate against them for something they might have done or actually did do to you. Retaliative outing is seriously homophobic—for it sends the message that since this particular disclosure is bound to be embarrassing, by implication being gay is an embarrassment. And never out others opportunistically—for *your* gain in the guise of helping *them*. A patient's sister did just that. She told her mother that her brother was gay to turn the mother against him, hoping that the mother, who was buying herself new car, would give her daughter the old one. The sister got the car. But the mother changed her will to leave everything else to her son!

Do not routinely expect as much benefit from coming out as you hope and may have been led to believe. Being out can do wonders but not everything. It will likely help you develop a sense of inner peace through fostering a cohesive (conflict-free) sense of self to reunite a self divided. It will likely help you be stronger so that you can better cope with homophobia. But by itself, it won't fully solve all serious emotional problems that might plague you. For example, it won't fully correct a flawed core identity based on a deep need for self-devaluation. And as discussed throughout this book, in some ways it can even make things worse for you. The negative fallout from disclosure is almost always anxiety provoking, at the very least. And besides, too much inner peace has its own dark side. It can have a negative homogenizing effect on your personality so that your lack of conflict makes you blurry: more out but less interesting.

Anticipate that you might need to come out more than once.

Professionally, my being gay was definitely holding me back from entering psychoanalytic training. So after years of being out, I decided to go back in. Then, after five years of being celibate to please not myself but my analyst, I came out again. Subsequent professional set-backs turned me back in once more due to reviving my guilt about being gay. Two incidents stand out in my mind: a professor refusing me a staff position on his service because I was gay and a patient dis-covering me in the supermarket with an obvious boyfriend and then quitting therapy because he "didn't want to be treated by a queer."

Just as your parents should understand the son coming out to them, you, in coming out, should understand the parents you are coming out to. No doubt, though they are imperfect, they still tried to do a good job raising you, even if they did, likely unwittingly, fail you in some important respects—generally because their own parents were narrow-minded about homosexuality due to generation-specific cultural norms that existed in their time. So, try to put yourself in your parents' place and see yourself from their point of view—not only from your vantage point of "what are my own joys and burdens?" but also from their vantage point of how you might feel if you were them being confronted with something hard to fully understand that they just want to go away. Let that understanding guide what you say and how you behave. For example, view any undesir-able response on their parts not necessarily as the product of their ill will but as a possible sign of their imperfect humanity. Work with them, be patient, and resolve any differences that come between you and them so that instead of your coming out's opening new wounds and salting them, it closes up old wounds, healing them and avoiding making new ones.

A definite possibility exists that your disclosure will upset them as they come to feel startled, surprised, and even shocked to hear the news and then, like anyone caught off guard, react unpredictably and negatively.

So, view your coming out to them (and to everyone else) not as an incident but as a *process*, one requiring not only initial disclosure (with care) but also follow-up with concern. Work things through until all concerned digest and get comfortable with what just emerged and have the opportunity to rethink and, when necessary, revise their initial reaction and response. If you can, be forgiving of any harsh initial negativity on their parts, hoping that they will come around in time to be more accepting and tolerant. Then try to engineer just that actively. Affirm them as you want them to affirm you and support them as you seek support from them. If they seem upset or worried, find out what is bothering them and help them deal with it. If they feel sadness, regret, depression, and even (some legitimate) fears for your present and future safety and well-being, address that problem, for example, by correcting any of their distortions of what being gay means. Explore their fears in depth. For example, do they fear that the rest of the family will shame, exile, and ostracize *them*? Can you say something about that to relieve at least some of their anxiety?

This said, sometimes, as in the following case, a sanguine outcome may not be forthcoming, and even time may not heal all the resultant wounds.

When a gay man came out to his mother, all she could think of was to respond with, "He is in some sort of trouble," then rewrite her entire will to leave her son everything. His father, however, first went into denial, convincing himself that his son was going through a phase that would soon be over. When his denial subsided, he moved on to condemn his son as a "reprobate in a family known, since they came to this country many years ago, for its propriety, decency and respectability." He then said that his son was clearly trying to hurt him, then sent him off to military school to reform as well as to get away from the new boyfriend that the father thought was making the son gay. Then the father demanded the son go for reparative therapy—and found him a therapist who guaranteed he could turn him straight.

The mother responded the way she did because she was a kindly woman who loved her son unconditionally. The father responded the way he did because he was a depressed man who needed to finger point and affix blame onto others as his way to deal with his own generalized self-blame; a controlling man who saw his son's being gay as defiance, the father having expected everyone in his family to be like him and do what he wanted them to do; an erotophobic man who felt negatively about anything sexual, not only homosexuality; a scrupulously religious man belonging to a sect that disapproved of homosexuality; a chronic worrier who couldn't stop brooding about his son's having unsafe sex and falling in with bad companions; and a lonely man who feared that his son would go off and abandon him, hanging around with his gay buddies, leaving Dad behind at home, alone, and with a wife he no longer found particularly interesting.

The son, while appreciating the mother's support, made no attempt to understand where his father was coming from. Instead, he spent all his energy acting out against the father. He became a contrarian to tell his father, "This isn't your life, it's mine, and I'll live it the way I want." He also expressed defiance by going beyond becoming openly to becoming wildly gay—to the point of becoming deliberately outrageous. In response, his father, defying the mother who now more than ever hoped to heal the divisiveness, cracked down on his son even more by constantly monitoring him and holding back money unless he did his bidding. That, of course, could only enhance the son's rebelliousness and increase his defiance. It took months of family therapy to avoid a complete rift with Dad, but even then there was no full healing reconciliation.

ADVICE TO PARENTS

Parents being come out to have a responsibility to help their sons navigate a situation that can be as difficult for him as it is for them. For, as Denizet-Lewis says, There is a link "between family acceptance or rejection of gay children and their mental health in early adulthood. ... teenagers in 'rejecting families' were significantly more likely to have attempted suicide, used drugs and engaged in unprotected sex than those who were raised in accepting families."[1] As will be evident throughout this book, my own parents' negative attitudes about my being gay left me at odds not only with my homosexuality but also with my forever questioning how much they really loved me. (Relationships with parents is discussed in more detail in Chapter 8.)

You as a parent being come out to also have a responsibility to yourself. You as a parent should always freely ask your son relevant questions without unduly fearing that you will necessarily say the wrong thing and provoke a negative response. Ask for any information you need so that you can respond rationally after considering all the facts. Especially avoid problematic responses that are displacements onto his being gay from other matters entirely—such as issues of parental control or those arising out of a breakthrough of your own pathological erotophobia. Deal forthrightly and head-on primarily—or only—with the actual issue at hand. Ask yourself, "What is my son trying to tell me? What can I learn from him about what being gay means and how it affects us and him?" Then ask him, "Is there anything that I can do for you, any help you might need that I can give you?"

Avoid trivializing his disclosure by going into denial about it and saying, "That's okay," feigning disinterest and lack of surprise, then preoccupying yourself with other things, implying or saying, "So what else is new? I always knew you were gay. You aren't telling me anything special. Now let's move on to something more interesting and relevant." Never trivialize your son's being gay as just a phase he is going through as you ask him to "check back with me in a month, or in a year, or whenever you are over this temporary insanity."

Always avoid a passive-aggressive response consisting of falling into a perplexed silence as your roundabout way to express disapproval. Equally unacceptably passive-aggressive is self-blaming with hostile implications, along the lines of "I am so sorry for having made you this way; I know it's my fault; what can I do to make things up to you?" Not much better is attacking him along similar lines in the guise of excessive altruism ("I'll do anything you want me to do to help you with your problem") associated with patently transparent, cloying, excessive caring and concern along the lines of "I am not mad, only *worried* about your future if you continue in this fashion, for as everyone knows, gays are an unhappy lot who can only look forward to a life of drugging, disease, and endless loneliness, and I want to spare you that."

A patient's parents sublimated their anger and disdain toward their son as unconvincing pity and concern so that "You enrage me for being this way; you are ruining our family" became "I am so sorry for you; I wish I could do something to relieve you of your pain and heal your wounds. Can we pray in church together, and can I pay for a caring therapist who can change you back to normal and fix what is wrong with you, or (suddenly finding the needed funds) send you off to medical school (far from home and your new boyfriend) because "our only wish is to make you happy and see you successful professionally."

Do not criticize/blame your son's boyfriend for making your son gay. Too many parents, instead of being happy that their son has found someone to love, displace their anger and disappointment about his being gay onto the person he has found, along the lines of "you are my son's ruination." You don't want to alienate him from his partner, and you certainly don't want to alienate him from yourself.

Of course, never become openly angry, judgmentally moralistic, and controlling along the lines of "do what I want you to do, or else." *Never* say anything remotely like, "You are ruining our lives, look at what you are doing to us. You disgust us; we can't believe we had a son like that, someone who would do such dreadful things."

The man my parents caught me with in flagrante (see below) became my partner for a few years. I followed him to New Mexico, where he had taken a residency in surgery. Because I had no money of my own, I asked my father for a check to tide me over. But for me to cash the check, my partner had to cosign it. He did, and my father saw this man's name on the back of the check, knew that I hadn't gone quite as straight as he had hoped, and flew into a rage at me for seeing this man again, screaming, "I paid for a therapist to get you over this; now where did all of that get me? You will have to go back into treatment, or you are out of my life and for the rest of it. And in any event, except for your medical care, no more money for you, ever."

Never, never retaliate by withholding love from your son. At first, Michael's mother made it clear that she wanted me to let her son alone and go away. I was banished from the household. I remember having to sit on a park bench on a cold fall day for an hour finishing a badly ending Stephen King novel while Michael, himself reluctantly, went to meet his parents alone because they didn't want me around. Only later, but not until she was on her deathbed, when it was far too late to do much good, did his mother confess that while initially she didn't like me at all, afterward I had mostly won her heart.

Never expect your son to treat himself like a pariah you are ashamed of as you ask him to banish and exile himself from the family and all your friends so that he doesn't ruin you socially should others find out. Thus, "Don't bring your boyfriend home ever, and certainly not for Christmas dinner."

My parents, I, and Michael always ate at the same restaurant every Sunday. My parents, mysteriously, always wanted to eat dinner around lunchtime, and I couldn't figure out why—until I discovered that their best friends also ate dinner at the same restaurant on the same days but at the regular dinnertime, which was two hours after we left. So, my parents were whisking me out of there early so that their friends wouldn't see me with my partner! As a result, not only did I come to resent them, but I lost contact with their friends, whom I liked a great deal but was fated to never see again.

A patient's parents responded to his telling them that he was gay first by becoming more loving to his straight sisters and brothers and then by changing their will. They said, "We are going to leave our entire estate to our grandchildren because they need to have a big wedding and you don't, and also we want your niece to inherit the land in North Carolina so that she can have a place to raise a big family and horses." They then started calculatedly responding to him as if he were a person of little value, not worthy of their time or attention. They also encouraged the rest of the family to ostracize him. To accomplish their end, they made up negative things he supposedly said about them, then passed these on as accurate reporting. Until recently, he never knew why his family's friends, his extended family, and their friends didn't want to have anything to do with him. He always imagined it was because he disappointed them in some way. It never occurred to him that it was because he was a good person and gay, and his parents were bad people though straight.

Parents should never out their sons by tricking them into revealing themselves against their will. When my parents did that to me, they did permanent harm not only to me but also to our relationship:

I was happy being gay, but my parents wanted me, their only son, to be straight: a doctor with a large general practice and an even larger standard family. (True, I was also that typical adolescent more likely to hide my thoughts than to discuss important matters with Mom and Dad.) Ultimately saying that "they had to know," they set up an elaborate ruse. Telling me they were going away on vacation, they dressed up in travel clothes, packed their bags, and kissed me and my new boyfriend good-bye. Only they went to a neighbor's apartment whose windows faced my bedroom. Here they waited until I pulled the shades, at which time they came roaring back to catch me in flagrante. Now they berated me for being a "homosexualist" and forced me into therapy—to take a cure that they, not I, felt was needed.

In summary, this chapter focuses less on the considerable benefits of coming out than on solving disclosure-related problems such as those that exist in a real world that requires you to balance the relief and benefits you obtain from disclosure with the predictable wages of prejudice and discrimination on the part of those you disclose to. So much depends on you—on who you are and your circumstances. Opening up can ultimately bring peace into your life, and almost any gay man can cite the relief and pleasure associated with disclosure. But too many gay men report unpleasantness as the result.

As one of my patients said,

In the main, my revealing that I was gay put me on top overall. I felt freer, more honest, and no longer had to waste time alternating between depressive self-hatred and abandonment of my authentic self and projection of self-criticism to the point of becoming paranoid— evasive, secretive, and isolated, as "I hate myself" became "everyone hates me." Lying took work and sapped energy best reserved for more practical, more creative, and more highly generative matters. Also, it followed that many people became more accepting of me, just because I as a gay man became more accepting of myself. But disclosure by itself didn't solve all of my problems, and it even created some others for me. My family responded by becoming remote, actually almost disowning me. All my cousins dumped me after one of their wives outed me to the whole family. One cousin and her husband even used the occasion of my father's funeral to demonstrate her disapproval: by staring me down in silence, not responding at all when I asked her to tell me if anything was wrong.

Clearly, after most gay men come out, they still have some work to do. After coming out, you will still have to work on your relationship with your family, resolving misunderstandings between you and them, and otherwise developing a valid, personalized, doable game plan based on the immediate and ongoing responses of all concerned. Failing this, at a later date, your joy may turn to anguish, and you very well might want—or have—to go back in again.

TWO

Lifestyle

In this chapter, I discuss the different "lifestyles" (styles of living) available to you as a gay man and offer some suggestions about determining which will be the most healthy, rewarding, enjoyable, stable, and creative for you.

Kort, believing the term "lifestyle" to be misleading, even derogatory, argues against using that term because being gay is not a choice; being gay constitutes not living a lifestyle but having a life.[1] I agree that the term "lifestyle" should not be used to refer to being gay per se. But I see it as acceptable to use the term "lifestyle" to refer to one of the many different patterns of gay living—not "being gay" per se but being gay in a certain way.

In this chapter, I do not favor or push one lifestyle over another. Rather, I attempt to raise your consciousness about the many lifestyles extant so that you can determine for yourself what is right for you without overlooking any options—knowledgeably, carefully, and comfortably selecting the wonderful life you want instead of settling for some life you don't really desire because you don't know better or feel that that is what you should have or all you can get. I also urge you to make the right lifestyle choices as early as possible when there is still time to make changes should you, giving things some thought, come to feel less authentic, happy, fulfilled, stable, altruistic, loving, and accomplished than you can potentially be.

Many of my patients as gay men just starting out or as gay men well into the life and the subculture had doubts and fears about what comes next that weighed on their minds unnecessarily. So ask yourself this: Have you, as a result of distortions of what is to be, become overly pessimistic about what lies ahead? If so, is this because you bought in to negative stereotypes about what being gay involves and drew conclusions about what is to come based on shaky evidence formed from misperceptions about how all gay men live, created not from the reality of what gay life is actually like but from a few anecdotal studies of the lives of atypical gay men on the fringe? Do you as a result of comparing gay to straight life feel that being gay will not be different or better but worse? Do you imagine yourself as always being miserable; constantly alone because you have been unable to find true, lasting love; and forever condemned to live in some underground place soaked with drugs and alcohol, wandering the drafty cruising spots in the middle of the night, regularly getting dumped by those you would love, winding up divorced from those you marry, either having a nonexistent sex life or indulging in one that is a study in excess—your personal world in a shambles because you are devoted less to fulfilling yourself than to making an impression on others and your professional life going nowhere if, which you believe to be unlikely, you are employed at anything meaningful or at all? Do you worry that being gay will be fun for a while but not after what happens next when, paraphrasing Shakespeare and a once popular bumper sticker combined, tomorrow after tomorrow, having run in its frantic pace from night to night, all sound and fury, signifying nothing, you get old, and then you die?

Are you like my friend Frank?

Frank worried that in gay life the only two things that counted were looks and money, and he had neither. He was convinced that because he could never make a great living or look as good as some of his buddies, he was therefore fated to go through life ignored, alone, and lonely.

I had to convince him that anatomy, like wealth, were only a part of his destiny. As I noted, while it was true that in the gay subculture (as in any subculture) good-looking, well-endowed, rich people have some advantages over those not so blessed, most gay men aren't into looks and money as much as the mythology suggests. To prove my point, I invited him down to take a quick look around my town. That convinced him that emotional appeal counted for as much as or more than physical appeal and financial wherewithal. As he concluded, at last agreeing with me, most gay men, including himself, have all they need to succeed, be happy, and have a rewarding, joyful, healthy life, no matter if they are mainstream or untraditional/fringe, what they look like or how much money they have—as long as they are warm, accepting individuals who don't distance themselves from others because of pervasive relational anxiety on the one hand or the influence of constant pressure exerted by compulsive sexuality on the other.

YOUR CHOICES

Out, In, or Somewhere in Between

Those who choose to come out may or may not choose to come out all the way. There are various interim stages in becoming out: shades of gray between being completely in (black) and entirely out (white). A common—and satisfactory—compromise involves being out discretely while still holding back selectively, keeping some aspects of your life to yourself yet remaining fully proud—though less than completely open about what you are and short of being completely truthful about what exactly you do.

The Barroom, the Backroom, or the Bedroom

Hanging out and getting your kicks in today's subculture is different from hanging out and getting your kicks in yesterday's so that the old rules, like "bars are the best, and perhaps the only, places to meet people," no longer apply, but the new rules, like "Internet dating is superior to bar cruising," don't always work. There is no ideal place to meet Mr. Right, so the choice of where to go to find sex/love is up to you, should be based on individual need and unique personality, and ought to evolve based on what you subsequently learn and come to experience. I met Michael in my living room through an introduction from someone I first met in a bar. But a close friend complained that he never had my luck, for *all* the men he met in bars were "losers," just like the following:

I and John, the man I met a few weeks ago at Los Lobos, seemed to hit it off. And then he called me, talked for two hours, and said he hoped to see me around at the gay dance some time. No asking me for a date.

Then a week went by, and he called back, and we made plans to meet and sit with each other at a dance tonight. He showed up, one hour late (so I had to pay for my own entry, of course), said we were just friends and could dance with others, then proceeded to get himself a drink from the bar and not ask me if I wanted anything. We did dance with each other for a while, which was nice, for he is a wonderful dancer and very sexy when he dances. I think I was feeling something, an illusion, that was not there or reciprocated on his part.

When we decided to leave, he let me walk all alone across the parking lot to my car without even asking to accompany me, and he didn't even try to kiss or hug me good-bye, just said we can karaoke sing together sometime.

What a turnoff. I guess he was not interested at all, yet when he sat next to me he would occasionally take my hand in his. A very hard read. I think I am hoping so much that I overlook reality, as I shouldn't.

Chapter 3 deals specifically with solving problems associated with meeting Mr. Right.

The City, the Ghetto, or the Suburbs

With people today much more accepting of gays and gay life than they used to be, gays are no longer marginalized into the ghettos they once fled to, there to exchange the discomforts of mainstream living for the comforts of being with their own kind. There are still towns, such as a few I've lived in, where homophobia reigns, making for unpleasant or dangerous conditions. But with most straight castle walls coming down, today you can become anyone's neighbor and friend. Today you no longer have to choose to go where you fit; you can fit where you choose to go. Many gay men select what they consider to be an ideal compromise: they go to live in funky towns where gays are known as gay and are able to live comfortably side by side with straights who like them just the way they are, the gays pushing their own baby carriages down Main Street, where, though few of the townspeople bat an eyelash, almost none of them bother batting an eye.

Single or Married

Today at least the idea of gay marriage is all the rage, but even if you choose gay marriage, you still have to choose between a partner for a lifetime and a lifetime of partnering—between monogamy and polygamy, between having a faithful marriage that epitomizes "gay family values" and one where infidelity rules with cheating going on. Yours is effectively a choice between sexual freedom/variety and its renunciation for the greater good through constancy. Throughout this book, I make my case for monogamous marriage unapologetically while recognizing that because not every gay man has exactly the same personality structure, needs, preferences, and opportunity, monogamous marriage is right for many gay men but not for all. However, always distinguish a desire for independence from a fear of closeness, never choosing polygamy not because that pleases you but because selecting monogamy scares you.

Your Gender Identity

The choice of a gender identity is strictly yours. In simplistic terms, you should choose your gender identity depending on what makes you most comfortable. Are you more comfortable on the runway or at the raceway? This is an important choice because it determines a very significant aspect of your lifestyle: where you go to look for companionship and sex. For example, your gender identity usually helps determine which bars you frequent, if any. Will it be "The Underground"? or "Boots and Saddle"? or "Rawhide" or "The Manhole"? or "The Anvil"? or "Lickety Split" or "Paradise"? or "The Blue Parrot" or "The Coq D'Or"? or "Swell"? or even "all of the above just depending on my mood of the moment"? Go where the men you like and identify with happen to be, not to a place you don't like because it's where you ought to be, that is, for moral reasons and/or because your inner reformer taking over wants you to make/remake some place over into what you believe it should be ("I'll give this place some class," or "let's go there to give those elegant queens the surprise of their life").

Your Profession

I believe that the happiest, most successful gay men are those who get their wildness out of their system early, have an epiphany sooner rather than later, and, avoiding the extremes of all work and no play (or the other way around), settle down to a quiet married monogamous existence and integrate that with a stable generative career. Growing up without unduly prolonging their adolescence, they attend one Black Party where the entertainment consists of doing onstage circumcisions, then let that grow old fast and way before they do.

Too many people assume that all gays are sexaholic. Too few recognize that many gays are also—or instead—workaholic. Especially if this is you, be very careful to choose your exact profession wisely after deciding between doing what you love and loving what you can do. For not all professions are equally accepting of gay men. It's still true today: gay anesthesiologists require fewer survival skills than gay surgeons. To a great extent, your choice of profession will be determined by and in turn determine your desired degree of disclosure. So, as always, choose to do not only what you love but also what will love you back.

Your Religion

You can scrupulously follow none, some, or all of the precepts of a religion. You can fully embrace the cloth or the blacklist or go from one to the other and back again with regularity—now focusing on your religion's shortcomings and now focusing on its loving messages while overlooking some of its more gay-bashing moments. Always think twice both before using your religion to suppress your homosexuality as you undergo a faith-based redemption and before using your homosexuality to suppress your religion as you undergo a gay-themed downfall.

Your Type of Man

When picking a man, you may prefer to be flexible as to type or prefer—or actually slavishly desire—one type only: rough straight-looking men with muscles or effeminate, perhaps thin and aesthenic men; Wall Street or stevedore types; younger or older men; flat-chested or man-bosomed guys; younger or older men; or men who are homeless versus those who are penthoused. Choice of type in turn generally determines a significant aspect of your lifestyle, for fixed favorite types tend to take you away to places where these congregate, as in, "Because Bert only goes for butch, tattooed, shaggy men with baseball caps on backwards or ponytails coming out the gap in the back of their hats, he swears by and so hangs out with Jersey Boys at the Jersey Shore."

It is okay being fixated on type as long as you recognize two things. First, type *is* a kind of prison that, like any other, at best reduces opportunity, making for fewer men available to you and at worst leaves you with too few candidates to happily and successfully choose from. Second, choosing to be bound by typing that is self-destructive is never the best idea. Never being unable to get beyond a hairy chest to the actual person whose torso you so admire is unrewarding. Seeking only sadists with an inviting dungeon is dangerous.

Substance Abuse or Sobriety

Avoid substance abuse—the biggest detriment to having a healthy, happy lifestyle. Gays often drink and take drugs to excess to treat themselves for a mood disorder, only that predictably worsens the problem should they become downwardly socially mobile as a result, to the point that they develop a subterranean lifestyle because drinking heavily and searching for exotic de rigueur substances commits them to living in a sleazy drug culture; because they think of getting higher and higher to cover feeling lower and lower; and/or because they destroy relationships because of angry outbursts that occur when on stuff if someone, justifiably or not, makes them mad, they overreact, drink more, and take pills, releasing more anger, leading to blowups followed by guilty regrets, making it even likelier that they will overreact to minor provocations, leading to further blowups, followed by promises to reform that go nowhere, leading to explosive personality disorder, and eventuating in a complete breakdown as their healthy lifestyle deteriorates to become a fully unhealthy life.

Your Politics

Generally, when gay men choose a political affiliation, they tend to also choose a personal lifestyle to go along with it. More liberal gays gravitate toward more liberal lifestyles. If liberal gays, paraphrasing what Rita Hayworth says about herself in the movie *Gilda*, "were a ranch they would be called Bar-None."[2] Personally and politically, such men, being more Epicurean than Spartan, tend to espouse freedom of sexual expression with few personal constraints and settle on open marriages ("having an arrangement") where cheating is entirely acceptable and even de rigueur. Believing that their fate is less a product of their own actions than of how society treats them, they tend to downplay the role personal responsibility takes in their lives and instead emphasize how such externals as homophobia are the most—or only—significant determinants of their destiny. Tending to be more idealistic than realistic and more contrarian than mainstream, they lean toward minimizing the importance of professional and financial upward social mobility and instead generally remain content to grow older in their original place without trying too hard to move on up—personally and professionally. Thus, on the job, they tend not to actively seek promotion, often preferring to remain safely in the background to avoid being hassled out there, desperately hoping to steer clear of people likely to call them "Aunty Tom" or worse.

In contrast, more conservative gays tend to favor religious, often morally repressive trends, even—or especially—in their sexuality. They tend to suppress aspects of their sexuality for some greater good, to the point that more liberal gays might call them (as at least some of my critics have called me) "masters of inhibition." Such men tend to be more Spartan than Epicurean and more socialized than contrarian. They downplay the importance of external influences (including the stigmatizing influence of homophobia) in determining their fate and instead emphasize the formative role played in their lives by individual responsibility. They don't favor the nanny state but instead go for a meritocracy where you "get what you earn, which is exactly what you deserve." They are generally highly upwardly social mobile—always looking for a bigger place to live and a higher-paying job with better benefits and more cachet. They are more realists than idealists—except when it comes to love, where they are often extremely idealistic in the belief that gay relationships should be like "classic straight ones" in the sense of being closed and monogamous, where only "death do us part."

The best politico-personal choices are the ones that you make more factually than emotionally and out of inner desire rather than a succumbing to peer pressure. You can be a Democrat, Republican, or an Independent spiritually and/or politically, but it is important for you to make that choice on your own, without letting yourself be pressured or (more likely) shouted down by friends—or those who just claim to be—and even by therapists—and those who in like manner just claim to be.

Your Adoption Decisions

People who say gay men shouldn't adopt children are seriously misguided on several fronts. Some, putting principles before people, actually believe that it's better to let babies wither in an orphanage than to be adopted by a gay man/couple. They remind me of therapists I have known and criticized who say that depressed patients should *not* be prevented from committing suicide—on the grounds that such intervention interferes with their cherished personal freedom.

You as a gay man can adopt unhesitatingly without buying into two myths. The first is that gay adoption doesn't work because gay singles/couples are not psychologically equipped to raise children. There is nothing about being gay/gay psychology that encroaches in any way on your ability to adopt successfully. Being gay exists in a separate part of the brain from being a parent. And it is certainly not true that "two dads will not be able to provide their children with both the father and the mother that all children need to grow up healthy—for all children need a mother to nourish them and a father to guide and provide them with a male identification figure." Rather, it is sexist to assume that men, gay or straight, cannot be as nourishing as women and that women make weaker, less generative identification figures than men. Anyway, there are plenty of fatherly and motherly subordinate identification figures available outside the home. Depending entirely on who they are, what they say, and how they act, teachers, coaches, honorary aunts and uncles, and even comic book characters can partially or wholly fill that bill and suffice.

In addition, *all* the gay men I spoke to who adopted generally wanted to adopt for one or all of the right reasons. Among these were saving a baby from a lack of love and/or poverty, to help a struggling mother out, to enhance their own partnership by extending their personal family, and to do some good in general not only for one man/woman but also, as a modest start, for all mankind.

Adoption more than anything else changes gay life/lifestyle deeply and permanently. I don't know if the more "stable" or "conservative" gays adopt or if those gays who adopt become on that account more "stable" and "conservative." I do know that gays who adopt often choose to work hard on becoming the healthiest role model possible for their children, if need be after the fact, as they make certain, when necessary, to change some of their ways accordingly. Thus, the gay couples who adopt, if they are not remarkably stable in the beginning and if they are not from the start entirely free from emotional problems that might affect their capacity to rear children adequately, generally see to it that they rapidly become emotionally suitable for and up to the task they have set for themselves simply because that is what they want to do. Or, if they remain emotionally disturbed, at least they see to it that they keep what significant emotional problems they have out of their child rearing. They make certain to provide well for their children if only because they know that everyone is looking and so that they can set a good example for other gay men who want to adopt just the way they did.

In turn, all the gay adopters I know had pride, gay and paternal, blossoming in their faces. All of them eagerly embraced and welcomed the burdens and made the necessary sacrifices to give their children everything they could: not only material things but also the shared gift of their own humanity. As a result, so often the children of gay couples didn't merely "somehow escape emotional distress" (a usual homophobic litmus test)—they did very well and even did considerably better than their counterparts in traditional families.

Tom and Jon were selflessly devoted to their two adopted children. Unlike those straight fathers burdened by their having children, they chose to rear them and did so without regret. Their lives revolved around them. They solved the so-called problem of not having a woman in the house by having female friends to serve as mother substitutes. I just recently saw one of these women carrying one of their children, shielding him from the wind by draping her shawl around him, saying, "Don't worry, as long as I'm around you will never feel cold."

Making significant sacrifices for their children, Stan and Robert, two native-born American men, adopted two Latina girls. Not wanting to deprive them of their Latina heritage, they taught themselves Spanish—so that they could move to Mexico and bring their children up in the country of their (the children's) ancestors.

Mothers putting their children up for adoption actually, when given the opportunity to choose, often select gay couples to adopt their children out to. True, in some aspects, theirs is a self-serving decision: the biological mothers don't want to feel competitive with the adoptive mother—as if they are losing out in some sort of contest—so they pick either two men or two lesbians to be the adoptive parents because they see these as being sufficiently different from themselves to stymie significant comparison. But they also know something that detractors of gay adoption seem not to be aware of: most gays who adopt children really want them. And wanting the children, not being of a certain sexual orientation, is close to loving them, and loving one's children is *the* critical element in child rearing and the very thing the children's biological mothers want to make sure is being provided for their kids.

The follow-ups I did of adopted children brought up in a loving home by two loving gay men convinced me that the children were healthy and happy boys and girls. They weren't ashamed of their parents being gay either—for the children themselves put having a loving home way before caring about the sexual preferences of the people who ran the household. If they had any complaints, it was that their parents couldn't stop talking about them to others—loving them so much and so openly that it got embarrassing.

MAKING LIFESTYLE CHOICES

Make as many lifestyle decisions as you can without invoking a preoccupying pro or con cultural or countercultural mindset, and remaining free of excessive guilt, and leaving aside any bent toward self-punishment. Don't put impression management first—before self-realization and personal satisfaction.

Learn not to make, if possible, important irreversible choices before you have the wherewithal to make them entirely sensibly and knowledgeably—which generally is before you have attained full mature self-awareness and a thorough working knowledge of the subculture to make them entirely rationally. First, do what you can to avoid making important lifestyle choices *impulsively* along the lines of "aim, fire, ready." Think about what you are doing before you get too involved in it. Do your research carefully, ask for guidance when necessary, and carefully ascertain *your* motivations and goals as distinct from making plans based on buying into myths and/or yielding to external influences especially just so that you can later blame someone else when things go wrong, along the lines of "I told you that wouldn't work; why did you push me in that direction?"

Try to avoid making important life decisions prematurely when you have not left yourself enough room to experiment and try such different things out as switching from butch to femme, changing from being the leather queen by night into the broker type wearing herringbone stripes by day, going from being a daytime dentist to a dusk-to-dawn drag queen, or, following your mood swings, alternating between being Prince Alarming and Prince Charming. You can—and perhaps should—reinvent yourself as you go along, but to do that you must avoid burning bridges and closing off escape hatches early on and selecting before you are fully ready to settle down. Flexibility also allows you to adapt to an evolving gay subculture, permitting your true self to emerge without slavishly accepting generationally bound strictures so that instead of living a life that suits you, you live a contemporaneous one just so that you can be tops in vogue.

Finally, never make lifestyle choices that are intended primarily to wage war against the establishment. In this respect, always remember that true self-realization generally means being more for than against something and doesn't mean being blindly "you" no matter who and what you happen to be. Depending on your superego structure, it may not be the best idea to let *your* conscience be *your* guide. It might be a better idea to hide or even disavow certain undesirable, negative aspects of yourself—remaining overall authentic and self-fulfilling without necessarily embracing every one of your sides totally. To truly avow yourself, you virtually must disavow one or more of your less-than-stellar parts.

RELATIONSHIPS AND LIFESTYLE

Family

Choose to maintain at least some relationships with your family virtually at all costs. Embrace them even if you can't fully work out all your problems with them. Never become so pissy that you dump them with finality over something unimportant, especially some peccadillo on their part that originates partly or wholly in your imagination.

Friends

Select your close friends carefully, avoiding unreliable men and women who use you when they need you and then dump you when they find someone else, like a new lover. Avoid groups that champion a philosophy that you find foreign to the point of discomfort, and groups strictly glued together by excluding others, for you are likely to be the next man out.

Conversely, should it be necessary, sacrifice for friendships that are solid or that promise to become so in time, putting up with more as you protest less. Never dump a friend for some trivial reason, as I was recently dumped because I remained friendly with one member of a couple who no longer got along between themselves. Most often, the tincture of time takes care of what seem to be insurmountable relational difficulties. So, if you overlook a lot now, later in the long run you will still have your relationship and looking back will wonder, "Why did I allow that to bother me so much back then?"

Dating

I believe that gay men with the most satisfying lives are those who choose close loving relationships over isolation and retain them, sometimes no matter at what cost. I believe that the happiest gay men are those who have many friends, a welcoming family, and one significant other, perhaps even a long-term stable marital partner to regularly come home to. Such men generally avoid loneliness eventuating in sexual acting out, substance abuse, and even suicidal behavior—too often considered to be the inevitable outcome of being gay, even when it has to do less with being gay than with being gay badly. Keeping three basic principles of forming and maintaining relationships in mind can help you have successful relationships: compromise, positivity, and optimism. (Relationships are discussed further in Chapter 3.)

By *compromise*, I mean giving in, especially in the unimportant things, so that you meet your reality (him!) halfway as you align what you will accept to reflect what you can get and what you want with what he wants in and from you. As you compromise and become satisfied with less, you will discover that in life, gay and straight, compromisers actually get more, for the royal road to happiness is paved with giving up something today to get something else, often something better, tomorrow.

By *positivity*, I mean being as loving to others as you can be, even when, for starters, you have to be the loving one. Positivity to generally breeds positivity back from others.

A discontented highly critical patient criticized his friends on the Internet. They found out about it and pressured his whole inner circle to exile him, leaving him little or no choice but to retreat to his house with his four loving cats as his only companions. Ultimately, I convinced him to reemerge, starting with giving other people all the benefit of his doubts. As he later, coming around, told me, revealingly,

"When Bob called me last night, at first I mentioned I found it oddly confusing that until now he chose to communicate with me via text messages/impersonal e-mail and not phone ("I was about to be critical all over again!"). But then I swallowed hard and agreed to meet him for coffee. And a good thing that was, for he shows up with a beautiful bouquet of flowers and explains that he thought not to call so soon because he would be pushing too hard and scaring me away, as he did his last love."

You will find that if you don't say bad things about or do bad things to people face-to-face or behind their backs, friends and a loving family turn your way almost as if by magic. Even homophobes become less homophobic as they come around to laughing not at but with you as they spin your bitchiness into a "put-up-with-nothing assertiveness," your effeminacy into "creative theatricality," and your promiscuity into "emancipation, the true meaning of what it means to be gay."

By *optimism*, I mean not allowing yourself to let temporary setbacks and unavoidable hard times sour you on being gay and especially on gay dating. A sociologist recently advised a friend, "Don't do Internet dating; all the men are desperate." I objected, reminding him that desperation can be a positive force when it involves being available, eager, and willing to do just about anything for love.

Mr. Right

In seeking Mr. Right, be very serious in your quest. Set specific doable goals and work toward fulfilling them, pressing on even in the face of setbacks, which are predictable. Be forthcoming and open about your desire to connect in a meaningful way, that is, without hiding that that's what you really want because you are ashamed of wanting it, in order to play hard-to-get because you think it will be helpful to act disinterested to enhance your allure, or as an acid test of whether your relationship is viable, along the lines of "let him go, and if he comes back to you, he's yours"—perversely and falsely counting on the viability of reverse psychology, only to discover, often too soon and very painfully, that reverse psychology can have the reverse effect and so a disastrous outcome. (Seeking Mr. Right is discussed further in Chapter 3.)

Consider getting married. I strongly believe that most gays really do want a long-term committed monogamous relationship even when, instead of making advances, they make excuses. Some note that marriage isn't right for everybody and convince themselves that they are exhibit A.

But so often, "I don't want marriage" really means "I let my emotional problems, especially my fears, stand in the way of fulfilling that desire." And never give up prematurely on a marriage you already have because you think or hear that "there are more fish in the ocean." Not all fish in the ocean are equally available or desirable, and some are considerably tastier than others. And always resist the influence of destructive outside relationship destroyers, especially people who specialize in making serious boundary violations, particularly in the realm of the cross-cruising that is so common in certain circles in the gay world.

As a fan wrote to me,

Hi Dr. Kantor,

Sorry I didn't get to write last year. Bob and myself just celebrated our 2nd anniversary on January 12th!

We've had lots of changes and adjustments, but with your help (stern, but welcome) we worked out our differences, didn't let them determine the outcome of our relationship, and are now quite happy together.

Thanks to your advice along these lines, I really did find (and keep) My Guy.

Kind regards,
D. B.

THREE

Relationships

Many opportunities for friendship, love, and marriage exist in the gay world. But finding and keeping a friend or a partner can be the single most difficult challenge of gay life. Only some gay men are successful at it. They find what they are looking for through their own effort, through good luck, or with a little help from books they read and therapists they see. But others do not find what they seek. These are the men who don't know how to bond, are beset with fears about connecting, or suffer from serious emotional difficulties that make it hard for them to extend themselves to others while making it just as hard for others to warm up to and love them. So, they shy away from seeking relationships in the first place, seek them only to wind up being rejected, or find someone they like or love, only to end up getting involved in a painful, frustrating, and debilitating liaison. For such men, the issue of gay marriage is moot, for even if it were legally available and they knew exactly how and where to find it, once they had it, they wouldn't quite know what to do with it.

While I recognize that there is much disagreement in the gay community about what constitutes the ideal in relationships both personally and professionally, I believe that the happiest gay men are those in a long-term committed monogamous relationship that supports and nurtures them. Conversely, I do not believe two myths rife in some circles of the gay subculture: that being alone doesn't necessarily mean being lonely (sometimes that is exactly what it involves) and that being alone not only has its advantages but also can be a good way to get through life, for it allows you to grow fully on your own and be yourself. (It is never possible to "be yourself" anyway because all "selves" are "selves divided," and it is never wise to only be "you, yourself" because being "me" isn't generally as good an idea as being "us.") So, I strongly urge you to at least think about the possibility that a long-term monogamous relationship is right for you: not because I say so and not for neurotic reasons—to firm up a shaky identity, make a politically correct statement by carrying the banner for marriage, deny a depression, or live well as the best revenge on someone who rejected/dumped you—but because, after being fair to yourself, open to suggestions, and considering all the alternatives, you yourself conclude that a long-term committed relationship meets your individual needs, is up to your personal standards, and fulfills your wildest dreams.

The goal of this chapter is to guide you accordingly by helping you successfully search for and keep meaningful relationships going in your life. I hope to help you achieve this objective through knowledgeability attained through focus, self-exploration, and learning; hard work; desensitization to anxiety through practice in the field; and the avoidance of the self-destructive putting of obstacles in your own way in order to gratify your masochistic needs by submissively accommodating to others over yourself and/or being obstructionistic by refusing to be conventional, instead insisting on remaining thoroughly peripheral just so that you can be forever and completely disenfranchised, not because that's basically what you desire but because basically you are acting out of spite.

In Table 3.1, I outline what I believe to be the main advantages of a long-term committed loving monogamous relationship over the other possibilities, which are the following:

Going it alone
Being a serial monogamist
Having a committed but open relationship
Being an unabashed polygamist: playing the field while using marriage as a home base
Being a pseudomonogamist: in a relationship that, though manifestly closed, is secretly open—that is, proclaiming marital fidelity while simultaneously cheating behind your partner's back

AN EXAMPLE OF A MODERATELY SUCCESSFUL GAY MARITAL RELATIONSHIP

Jenny and Stu, a straight couple who are friends of mine, were best friends with a gay couple, John and Ron. Jenny and Stu insightfully described the inspirational but cautionary tale of John and Ron's long-term gay marriage as a "paradigm of a gay marriage that lasts and works

Table 3.1   Advantages of Monogamy

1. Avoiding loneliness through built-in companionship.
2. Being admired and accepted not only by the straight people of this world but also by other gays, that is, by the many people who for reasons of their own feel more comfortable with gay men who are involved in a relationship than they do with gay men who are not (whether that's because they have decided to remain single, or because they are looking for love but to date have been unable to find it).
3. Having more money as you become a DINK (double income, no kids).
4. Avoiding sexually transmitted diseases (STD).
5. Avoiding exhaustion syndromes resulting from hanging around in drafty depressing gay haunts at all hours of the night.
6. Avoiding covering up the seediness of your life with forced merriment—grimacing instead of smiling, having just too good a time as your manic way to undo (warranted) doubts that the times are good.
7. Being freed up and able to do other things than constantly having to search for companionship, love, and sex.
8. Having the best sex, for when it comes to sex, familiarity breeds content, because with sex, as with anything else, practice makes perfect.

but is as imperfect as some marital relationships can be." They believed that the relationship illustrated a lifetime of satisfaction as well as personal and family problems that gay men thinking of getting married might want to anticipate and problems that gay men already married might want to resolve.

I, Jenny, first met John, our hairdresser, more than 50 years ago, and my husband, Stu, met him sometime later. We only met Ron, his partner, much later and didn't get to know him well until the tragic years at the end of his life. From photos John showed us, when they were both young they were gorgeous young men. John had always done hair; dabbled, very successfully, in interior design and painting; and was a senior accountant for one of the major Boston firms. Ron at first had an antique shop in Massachusetts, then he too became a big powerful executive. Between them, they did very well financially, and at one time they had an apartment in New York, a house in Massachusetts, a house in the Hamptons, and a house in St. Bart.

What worked the best in their relationship was their division of labor (we think that that is an important component of all prospering relationships, both gay and straight). Ron was entirely and completely in charge of finances—he wrote the checks. Even when he was in the hospital just before he died, he had the checkbook and all the papers brought to his hospital room so that he could take care of the money. John said he did not know how to write a check or anything else about their finances. Whenever we saw them, and especially in St. Bart for a haircut, John always did the cooking, and Ron washed the dishes and cleared up. John prided himself on always having things to eat at the ready. Ron prided himself as always keeping the kitchen clean.

But even though they were together for almost their whole lives—a very long relationship, with both of them in their mid-80s when they died—there were some serious ongoing difficulties here. They were very different people, and the differences were among the things that created some tension between them. For one thing, John was always criticizing Ron for being too laid back and passive, and Ron was always picking on John for being too uptight and tense. Ron was a type B personality. He was extremely polite, for example, to waitresses; always very solicitous about our health; and constantly worried whether after a visit we got home safely. A friend of ours and theirs noted that even at the end when Ron was on his deathbed, he continued to phone her every single Sunday to inquire about her *well-being. But John was brusque and demanding—a type A personality. I will always remember being in John's salon in the city some years ago. It was busy, with a number of people (including me) getting their hair done. One woman who was looking terrific was walking out the door when John stopped what he was doing and turned to her and said in a loud voice, "Simone, don't bother to call again." Apparently, she had irritated him by being late for appointments. Also, John was generally selfish and looked after himself above everything else. While Ron would go out of his way to please John, John would not go out of his way to please Ron or anybody else, including us. For example, John and Ron used to go to New York to the theater and museums every six weeks or so for three days. Ron had programs of every show they ever went to, going back more than 50 years. But relatively early on, John began to complain that he was too tired or that his back hurt too much for them to do anything together. Now he would always say, "Backache prevents me from sitting for more than 30 minutes." We think he was very selfish about that, as it prevented Ron from going to New York. In fact, they even stopped going to a town about 30 minutes away to see televised versions of opera. Near the end, Ron once took a bus to New York by himself, creating some further tension between them.*

Also, for whatever reason, all the years they were together, John saw to it that Ron always played second fiddle to him, creating some bitterness on Ron's part. When they traveled, John always got the main bed, and Ron always got the cot. (In their house, though, they had two beds.) Also, Ron was the one who swept up our hair after John had finished cutting it. John always seemed to be the boss, the leader, and Ron always seemed to be the follower, and we think he resented it.

Too, there were some early infidelities on John's part. They never discussed these with us, but from snippy remarks we occasionally overheard, John's wandering seems to have permanently traumatized Ron, and Ron never let John forget it.

Serious health problems plagued the marriage throughout. Because Ron had been a heavy smoker, he had to have major surgery for lung cancer. That made it hard for him to eat and difficult to understand when he spoke. He was frequently in the hospital, a few days every time, for breathing problems. John was always mad at Ron for "destroying his body."

Adding to the tension between the two men was that ultimately John let himself go. He stopped coloring his hair and stopped exercising, and he gained weight and wore what looked like pajama bottoms (with a sweat-suit kind of top) not only around the house but also when he went out shopping. But Ron, until near the end, insisted that John color his hair for him. And he always looked dashing—cuffs rolled back perfectly and colors beautifully coordinated. Yet during the last few years, John felt that Ron was dressing up for someone else. John also complained that Ron was getting too thin. Ron said it was because he couldn't swallow much after his surgery, but John said it was a mixture of couldn't and wouldn't. John as the cook pulled his hair out thinking of what Ron could (and would) eat and tried very hard to feed him but with only mixed results.

Their relationship with their respective families also made for trouble for and between them. We know little about Ron's family. John had brothers whom he hardly saw because they didn't get along with Ron. Some time ago, John's family had had a family gathering, and they did not invite Ron. Ron has never forgotten that and wanted nothing to do with John's family. This included John's favorite niece. For some reason, Ron never wanted her around and even more so after she and her partner adopted a child. We always asked ourselves, "Weren't these things that could have been resolved?" But they never were, and Ron and John continued to argue about John's family. Worse, when this niece, a health professional dealing with end-of-life patients, heard about Ron being terminal in the hospital, she went to the house to help John. While John was overjoyed and appreciative, for she really was just what he needed with so many things to take care of, Ron deeply resented the relationship and complained about its starting up again.

A final irony was the will. Originally, they had left everything they had to each other since effectively they had no other family. But when Ron got sick and John's favorite niece showed up again, John told Ron he wanted to change the will to give everything to her. He went to the lawyer to do that. Ron was furious, especially since the niece said that she did not want the house anyway and never had. But when the will was opened, it was found that it was never changed! Apparently, John was confused in the lawyer's office and did not make sense to the lawyer, so Ron, whom John had predeceased by a few days, got the house after all. The niece would have been happy to have the house, for she could have used the money to help pay for her daughter's education. And now suddenly, because Ron died so soon afterward, the court is going to give the house to some distant relative neither of them wanted it to go to.

Toward the end, their finances began to deteriorate. Through most of their years together, they had had a very upscale lifestyle, especially that fancy apartment in New York complete with houseboy. And for many, many years, they never missed a Broadway opening—or eating at "their" table at Sardi's afterward. But ultimately, they were becoming more and more impoverished and even a bit seedy. Within the past few years, when we went out to eat with them once or twice, it was our treat because by then they were getting poor and had even sold all their jewelry. It was fun going out with them, but expensive too. We realized what was happening to them financially when for my birthday John sold Stu a wonderful ring that had belonged to Ron's sister and also remade another piece of her jewelry for me for another birthday. (The ring John sold Stu was in the antique shop, which they also had to close because it was losing money.) But at least until near the end, they still through most of it all made a dashing pair—fur coats, jewelry, scarves, and perfume.

Closer to the end, we realized that John and Ron began behaving very negatively toward each other. Though the hospital was not far away, when Ron was admitted during his final illness, John spent no more than a few minutes with him on any given day. He said that Ron did not want more, but we doubted it.

Yet in the end, death did not them part. In spite of all their difficulties, John was so attached to Ron that he could not live without him. When we saw John, after Ron was in the nursing home, he was completely lost and just could not cope and mostly lived on sandwiches and junk food.

John had always said that if Ron went, he would take pills. We last saw John sometime in September, by which time he knew that Ron would never come home again from the nursing home. When we said good-bye to John, he said he would see us again at the next haircut. That was on a Sunday. On Tuesday, John took an overdose of pills. He was rushed to the hospital, having choked on his own vomit, but there was nothing they could do.

They died within four days of each other, John first. We never knew if Ron knew that John was also in the hospital and had predeceased him. But at least in the end, they were both in the same hospital, together, then, as they will be forever.

If you want a partnership/marriage but are having difficulty finding one, consider the following recommendations.

AVOIDING MR. WRONG

I describe a few gay men whom those of you who want a committed relationship might consider staying away from. These are the men about whom a number of my friends and patients said something like, "If you ever see me being this blinded, please speak up, and loudly."

(1) Those who say they want a committed relationship but make it clear and in advance that they really want to wander within its confines.

A patient should have realized that things weren't going to go well with a new lover when "just out of curiosity" he asked his potential partner-to-be, "Who is that man in the gym wearing the too-tight spandex?" only to have his potential partner reply, "I don't know who he is, but I do know that he has a great ass."

Then the man he loved actually asked the man in the spandex with the great ass, "Can we make a date?"

The man replied, "I am already married."

He shot back, "Don't worry, that doesn't bother me."

A few weeks later, not surprisingly, my patient's potential lover dumped him by heading home to a foreign country, the land of his birth, departing in the middle of the night, leaving only a note behind that said, "I went because your behavior meant that our relationship couldn't possibly work."

(2) Psychopaths

I personally was "in love with" and wanted to marry a man who in spite of his personality problems was so good looking that I felt I couldn't resist. I ignored that he used drugs and also sold them to others. He had a business synthesizing poppers from his New York apartment and would get doctors to prescribe valium for him so that he could then sell it on the street. Literally as well as figuratively a hustler, he was already married to another man and so disinterested in me that my desire to pursue him could only have been based on my masochistic need to go after someone I could work on, hoping to turn his "no" into a "yes."

A friend wrote to me, "One of my friends, whom I haven't seen in a while, said he married a European man from his interfaith group only to find he was doing some very secretive things and getting more hostile when I began to ask questions. And that was because he was only looking to get a green card." My friend added, "I went through hell for five years before I could get rid of him." Another friend, an attorney (head of my church group), fell in love on a dating site, sight unseen. He fell so in love that he started to think his dead husband had sent this guy to him so that he wouldn't be alone. But his love couldn't see him right now because he was about to go to Bermuda to do a contract construction job. Well, now Mr. Bermuda ran into some unforeseen circumstances and e-mailed him that he needed money to make it home to him. My friend sent him the money, but he never saw Mr. Bermuda again.

(3) Sadists

A patient was living with a man who, after signing out against advice from the alcohol rehab where he was seeking a cure for his heavy drinking, sneaked back home when his partner was away at work, kidnapped their dogs, and, out of spite and for the money, returned them to the breeder.

(4) Egoistic men

A friend wrote to me,

Dear M:
   Just got in from another date with Darryl. Well, hmmm, let's see. Where to begin. How about the following:

1. Is taking multiple psychotropic drugs for years for voices that tell him he is in the Messiah's inner circle, and about to get a promotion.
2. Tells me he was glad that I didn't look the same in person as my picture with that ethnic smirk on, the one I wore in the picture on my dating site.

3. Tells me he could overlook my artsiness and how sickening it is that I am so positive about everything.
4. Gets paranoid taking walks almost anywhere because he is afraid he will be singled out to get mugged.
5. Shoves his tongue into my throat whenever he kisses and I can hardly breathe.
6. Thinks it's hilarious to take a quick grab at my private parts, then say it was only an accident. NOT.
7. Tells me he tells his brother everything I say and so far his brother thinks I may not be a good enough catch for him.
8. Tells me that when we do finally make love his preference is to make me come several times first and then do oral on him for as long as I still can.
9. Remarks what a good figure I have but that in the beginning he thought I wouldn't do for him because he couldn't tell I had one because until lately everything I had worn was a baggy rag.
10. Says after I told him that I spent all morning at the stylist getting a cut and highlight that he still didn't like my hair.
11. Makes slurs against Latinos, Blacks, Orientals, and even (especially!) Gays.
12. Cackles like a chicken over things that aren't funny, as long as he made the "joke."
13. Loves slapstick. Although the slapstick at first may have been tolerable, I drew the line at the following: his pulling a backward swinging of his leg behind him to kick my crotch as we are walking. That was supposed to be hilarious. Well guess what. I'm not laughing.

Several weeks pass, then I get another letter from the same friend:

I am way too vulnerable, I realize. This week Darryl charmed his way back into my life with apologies and attention that gave me the illusion that I could let my heart go for him. This was Monday and Tuesday. Wednesday and Thursday he had a "cold" and could not see me, so I went out with some friends from school and had my phone off. There were a slew of panicky messages this morning about him being "worried about me." I called him this morning and he demanded to know why I didn't have my phone on, and I told him I just didn't (there really was no "reason"). He accused me of not even having the "decency" to call him back right away last night. I told him I have a lot of decency and resent that statement—to which he said "of course, because you are little miss perfect aren't you?" Then he said, you know what, "YOU GO TO HELL." Then after telling me that, he told me that if I had ever slept with him, he would have to take a shower. Then he hung up in my face.

I was really distraught over this and would never have said this to another human being, let alone a man I was dating.

And I was starting to have real feelings for him and believing that he did for me, too. Bummer.

And then:

Another date gone awry. This one said he was 50 but was so old he couldn't even walk upright. Plus he had velvet soft ladies' hands, which he pointed out and asked me to think of "the possibilities" (GROSS). He kept holding my hand and lunging to kiss me, then telling me to imagine him putting lotion all over his body (YUK) and did I want to know how it felt to be with a circumcised man, such as he? It was AWFUL having to sit there and have dinner with him, and even worse when I wound up having to pay because he left all his money at home. Then he explained his being broke by saying he looked really good and his time was valuable and you only get what you pay for.

Getting VERY discouraged. This is not as easy as I thought it was going to be. Believe it or not, I am still reeling over how much I liked some of these men, even though they mostly only liked themselves.

(5) People who don't appreciate you more or less as you are.

I personally was once having dinner with a gay couple, Bob and Frank. When Bob got up to go out and have a cigarette, Frank, his partner, told me that they had gotten together after he (Bob) had lost his wife during childbirth, and after that Bob was afraid to ever again let his heart go for another woman. Frank said, "Bob is always telling me, 'You don't understand me,'" and still gets sullen even though we have been together now for 16 years. I tell him to get over it and that "I give you everything you need." But Bob says I will never *understand him or be able to give him what he needs because I've never been with a woman.*

AVOIDING COMMON NEGATIVE MINDSETS OF YOUR OWN THAT CAN INTERFERE WITH YOUR RELATIONSHIPS

Need Rationalized as Attraction

As a patient asked me, "I wonder if it is a man thing, a widower thing, or just a lonely thing that makes us not see emotional cripples when we do need to see them as such if only to ultimately protect our feelings?"

Fear Rationalized as Lack of Desire

Instead of recognizing that you have commitment fears, you deny that you have them by convincing yourself that you don't want a relationship, along the lines of "The grapes are sour."

A long-term single gay man I treated said to me, "Why bother getting married? Marriage is a joke; all partners cheat on you or disappoint you in some other way." He had "been dumped" many times but never got used to it. So he isolated himself protectively as his way to say, "I don't care if I never meet anyone." Also, he feared success as much as he feared failure. Turning "I fear having a relationship" into "I don't want one," he avoided getting close by blanking out at moments of truth—denying someone who approached him was really interested in him, causing the other person to pull back in the belief that "He isn't interested in me." Next, having fully externalized the problem, he could, conveniently, entirely ignore his own contribution to it. In truth, he had never resolved the inner conflicts that kept him from relating and instead constantly blamed his relational difficulties entirely on "all those rejecting gay men where I live, and it's no better anywhere else" and continued to insist that it was only "my bad experiences that made me the way I am because those have conditioned me to fear failure."

Excessive Perfectionism So That No One Is Ever Good Enough

A patient, expecting too much, couldn't settle for less because "only the best would do." "All" he wanted was someone who looked like a famous movie star—absolutely gorgeous, young, talented, rich, and willing to support him, whose grammar was perfect and who had a degree of sophistication as reflected in his profession ("no accountants for me!"). When I advised him to rethink his impossibly strict standards, expectations that could but lead him to criticize almost everyone who was actually interested in him and available—and suggested that instead he develop a whole new set of priorities—he quit therapy.

A patient was unable to find the committed long-term relationship he sought for a number of reasons. Particularly destructive was his glomming on to people precisely because he already sensed or knew that they were not his type, which inspired him upward and onward in the hope that he would be able to bring them around. Too, instead of being actively task oriented relationally, he allowed himself to become relationally overly passive. He failed to plan his moves, instead preferring to leave at least the first moves up to others or even entirely to chance. But mainly, expecting too much, he became unable to compromise and accept less. Aiming too high, he got too little, as he demanded what was ideal but rejected what was possible and available. Difficult to please, he complained that he didn't like men with bad grammar, especially construction-worker types unable to talk intelligently about art. Then in an abrupt turnaround, when someone responded to his dating ad by saying, "Let's go for a walk in the woods on the beach and talk," he didn't like that either, saying that he only wanted someone who at least had enough money and interest in him to offer to buy him a lovely dinner.

Excessively type oriented, he eliminated one good man after another. One he eliminated because he didn't have a well-trimmed dark beard, another because his body was less hirsute than what one might have divined from his hairy face, and a third "though he led with his sensibility, his intellect, and his Buddhism—which had him avoid drama, and even brought me a medallion for our first date," he still found him unsatisfactory because he was unkind since "he refused to listen to my troubles one day when I felt I really needed a sympathetic ear."

Unfortunately, on many occasions smoking pot dulled his judgment so that now, going to the opposite extreme, no longer picky, he instead picked up anything, no matter how sleazy. Mostly he snatched straight sleaze off the street and took them directly home. Once he took some-one he picked up in a bar home after ignoring the implication of the man's strange behavior. The pickup, after asking him to get into his (the pickup's) car, drove exactly one block closer to his (my patient's) apartment, a warning sign—one that my patient overlooked—that the man was maneuvering in order to make it easier to put the stuff he was about to steal from my patient's apartment into his car now newly poised for a fast getaway. Then once in his apartment, he actually drank the beer the pickup specified he pour out for himself, ignoring the good possibility that this strange request presaged that he as victim was about to drink a Mickey Finn. When my patient awoke, 12 hours later, he discovered that his apartment had been ransacked and his credit cards stolen and that his jewelry was gone, including, most sadly, a ring that he didn't want his just deceased former partner buried in because he feared that the undertaker might steal it. Ulti-mately, he said, "I can't stand this anymore; dating isn't for me; every-one I meet is such a mess," and, burned out from having been "blown away on all my tries," never attempted dating again.

The False God of Absolute Compatibility

Few couples start out compatible. Mostly true compatibility develops gradually, as in the following examples, generally worth emulating:

A patient looking for exactly Mr. Right only favored websites that emphasized compatibility. But soon he discovered that compatibility is but a theoretical concept that doesn't help much with reality. For he met many men who, though they passed the theoretical compatibility test, were nevertheless thoroughly unlovable. Eventually, he formed a lasting loving relationship with a stranger he met in a bar who in the beginning seemed to be entirely incompatible. *At first, all they had in common was that they were both lonely. But they stuck with the relationship, and as they worked out its problems, their compatibility grew as if spontaneously—really through careful step-by-step nurturing— blossoming through hard work based on motivation to do well. So, though they remained theoretically imperfectly matched forever, they were, in actuality, really happy together—a less-than-storybook relationship but one that nevertheless had a fairy tale ending.*

A man wrote to me,

I decided to put in an ad on a dating site, as I am so lonely, stating what love is to me. Within thirty minutes my ad was removed, but during that time I received fifteen responses, and they were mostly from men. I thank everyone for their reply. Out of all the replies one stood out. From the name, I could not even tell if it was a guy or a girl. We started corresponding every day for two weeks. During this time, I realized we had some things in common and I started thinking this is probably a man. My hunch was correct when this person sent his phone number and I called. We had a great conversation and met for lunch twice. My new friend had been in a long-term gay relationship where he was burned, so he is taking our friendship very slowly, as I am. He knows of my life situation—divorced, kids, broke—and does not seem to care. Here is my problem. I think I am falling in love with him. He even turns me on sexually, although we have done nothing yet. If we did get together sexually, having no experience I would not even know what to do to please him. I am not scared, just a little confused. What now? Where do I go from here? Advice please? Josh.

Destructive Ambivalence ("I can never make up my mind about who, if anyone, is, or is not, Mr. Right for me")

A patient, clear about his identity as a gay man, nevertheless suffered from an inability to decide whether he wanted a relationship and, if he did, who was going to be his Mr. Right. As a result, he let his friends decide for him if any committed relationship at all was appropriate for him and then if a given relationship was worth pursuing. He let too many of his friends discourage him, for he listened to them when they told him, "The advantages of being single outweigh the problems associated with committed relationships." These friends would not only talk specific relationships down before they formed but also discredit them shortly after they had begun without knowing all the particulars. Not surprisingly, he would also foolishly buy into media presentations of gay life that pandered to the most primal, primitive, self-destructive urges through giving unsuccessful relationships—and only those—the widest press, mainly because drama sold. In addition, he bought in to the media's pimping of a "be-me" philosophy even though he dimly understood, and he was correct, that too much self-realization could interfere with relational success and so ultimately with self-fulfillment.

Self-Disavowal

Self-disavowal involves becoming one with all the usual clichés in order to hide/disavow who and what you really are, as in the following ad, which illustrates overly worn material you should consider downplaying or leaving out of your own dating site ads and other personal presentations entirely:

These are some of the things that I really enjoy doing: taking a long walk along the beach and watching the sunset I think we can do that together some day; spending time with good friends which you will be one of; watching movies together; gardening; loving and being loved; laughter; playfulness; touchiness; sincere friendship; honesty; affection; feeling appreciated; sharing life's experiences with someone I care about. I love quiet romantic dinners with deep conversations; yellow candles; musical concerts; theater; experiencing the world through travel and music; having friends over for dinner; and just enjoying trying out new life experiences with a special person. What else to tell you? I'm a genuine, very open and honest person, no hidden agenda.

I like the way we are corresponding. It's going to help us know more about each other. For I think it now time I get someone back into my life to make me complete, to be with me for a lifetime. I am just waiting for the best thing to happen to me. It's a long road when you face the world alone, when no one reaches out a hand for you to hold. I search within my soul to find love with someone who can make me happy. This happiness I will place in him as what I call love. I have a feeling that sometime someday this will come to pass. Everybody is looking for something, that one thing that makes it all complete. We often find it in strange places. I hope you know what I am looking for and are that special person.

This will be it for now, take care, and write back.

Here is a much better entry—real, informative, honest, and personal, without clichés:

A little about me:
I am very down and out. I lost the only person on earth who cared about me and the only one I cared for. I live in a place I hate living in . . . my in-laws think I am a horses a——that is ok I think the same of them.

What are you looking for in a partner? What do I want is a good question, but don't know. I like an old movie called THINGS CHANGE, that is, what I want is for things to change

I'd just like to add:
I was born in Massachusetts, after high school and two years at Boston State I moved to Arizona, for the best years of my life. Retired and moved to Durham the worse move of my life. I just want out of the life I am living now,

FINDING MR. TRULY RIGHT

Here is some practical advice for those of you looking for but having trouble finding someone to be with and love in the sometimes difficult relational environment of today's gay world. The advice may sound clichéd, and no doubt you thought of much of it first, but has it sunk in, and are you actually putting it into practice? (What follows here is heavily weighted philosophically toward self-determination, making you, not other people or your luck, the major mover of your fate in the direction of relational consummation with permanency and fidelity.)

Make Relationships Your Priority

Assuming that relationships don't work and giving up prematurely on them after a few problematic encounters even though they are exactly what you want creates a self-fulfilling prophecy with clearly negative, pessimistic tones.

Dating is often hard work, success should never be left to chance, and who you desire and what you need are not always readily available and to be immediately found out there. The best way to buck the odds and overcome the difficulties is to decide that you want a relationship, make up your mind to do everything to get one, and sacrifice for relationships, giving up something to get something while overlooking trivial negativity and setbacks for the good of your greater overall relational satisfaction and accomplishment. The most relationally successful gay men make finding love a full-time job, as they look for love without succumbing to distractions, not allowing diversions from their goal to take over—such as notching your gun to prove you are adored, excessive volunteerism where you try to leave your mark on the hoards to the detriment of leaving an impression on just one other person, and seeking temporary balms that can ease anxieties and disappointments for now, only to create problems for later—like quick sex that immediately satisfies but diverts you from the better sex ultimately to be found in the context of a long-term commitment.

Always be on the lookout for Mr. Right. Don't confine your search for him only to a few—and the most obvious—places. Try some you might not at first think of as high yield, like the library or, especially not to be discounted, your own living room (where friends and friends of friends you haven't yet met hopefully congregate). Always be aware of and open to others' unanticipated advances. Don't have that fixed mindset where you are ready for love only in specific designated situations that you set aside—times when you are receptive as distinct from times when you are closed to being responsive to others' approaches, as you play by rigid rules that reduce opportunity, like "I won't go for him; he is my friend's best friend" or "I never meet people at work because if a relationship sours I am stuck with it" (this latter "principle" ignores what can be an even worse fate: being stuck but now with no relationship at all).

The following patient succeeded because he had clear, definable goals; pursued them relentlessly; and remained optimistic throughout the entire process:

Dr. Kantor,

I'm a 31 year old gay male and have had one serious relationship that lasted 3.5 years but ended 4 years ago. Over the last year I came to the realization that although I'm very happy with my life (I love my job, my friends, my doggie, and my condo here in Chicago), I want a relationship, and in a way I've been very lonely. After carefully reading many book reviews then going to the bookstore and thumbing through the books, I decided that I have been attracted to the wrong guy so many times and haven't been able to find many people to date although all my friends and co-workers keep telling me what a catch they think I am and don't understand why I'm still single. I consider myself to be pretty emotionally together and intelligent. But I thought that I already knew everything about dating and relationships when I didn't actually. I was seeing a married guy (Richie) and I took your advice and let him know that I pretty much needed a marriage proposal from him right away to continue. We are still friends but don't have sex anymore. I forced myself to go to bars, even alone, and had many failed attempts and rejections, but I kept on instead of being discouraged like before. I am a little introverted but after putting myself out there even my straight trainer at the gym was introducing me to available guys. Then just before Christmas I went to a party and one guy (Mitch) who was very cute and seemed nice looked like someone I knew, but I was afraid to say "hi." Finally towards the end of the night I introduced myself and said that he looked very familiar to me and I think that I met him before. He said that I looked familiar to him too but he couldn't figure out why. After about 10 minutes, I remembered that I had seen him at a gay friendly Church a few years ago. After that, we ended up hanging out nearly every day for a week, then I told him flat out that I was looking for a relationship and hoped that he was interested in the same thing and I really wanted to date him with that intent. He said he was completely interested, and we've been dating ever since. He is different than me in some ways, which forces me out of my comfort zone, but we are the same in other ways. Oh, and did I say he's super cute and lots of fun? We've talked about many serious things and we both have committed to monogamy (the sex is AWESOME); he seems to be just as happy with me as I am with him; and I can't help but cry when I type this, for so far, no-one has ever treated me so well and been so kind to me in so many ways before in my life, EVER. I've solicited advice from many people, including my ex, who have given me suggestions about things I can do to be the best boyfriend possible for Mitch.

I surely hope it lasts and that he is the one I end up with for the rest of my life. I'm hoping that one day Mitch and I will get married; I will email you and let you know when that happens, and invite you to the wedding.

Be Flexible about Type

As noted in Chapter 2, type criteria involving strict preferences such as those relative to age, hair distribution, height, body weight, and/or wardrobe ought to be of little—and only transient—import. The most important type of man for you is the marrying type.

Deal with Your Dating Phobias/Paranoia

Dating phobias typically take the form of defensive isolation due to a fear of relationships that is a product of relational conflicts. Your best bet may be to keep relational conflicts from interfering excessively with your efforts by living *around* them before you actually get *over* them entirely. This involves acting "as if," that is, "as if" they don't exist—proceeding "as if" they do not trouble you or, if they do, "as if" they don't have a major hold on you. Perhaps you can start small, entering the dating arena gradually in order to desensitize yourself to your fears progressively and then, if you have a therapist, taking the next step and bringing your aroused anxieties back into treatment—for discussion and, hopefully, resolution.

Do what you can to avoid creating distance between yourself and others through projection, a process where you deal with your own self-loathing by displacing it onto others so that "I hate myself" becomes "He dislikes me." Then you withdraw further, and "I hate myself because no one likes me" becomes "People don't like me because I dislike myself," something others actively pick up on, then respond to by pulling away.

Change (When Necessary) for Mr. Right

Too many gay men looking for Mr. Right forget that Mr. Right is also looking for them. Make what he sees and wants in you as much a priority as what you see and want in him. Should you show up on dates fitting the following description and behaving in the following manner?

A patient described his last date in the following terms:

He was hunched over, wearing kakis, no belt, a blazer, and a Nike baseball cap (covering a shaggy head of hair full of gel) turned backwards. And he kissed with his lips so tightly closed saying he was afraid of getting herpes—as opposed to my last one, whose tongue forced its way down my esophagus on the first date, making it impossible for me to breathe.

Minimize as Much Negativity toward Others as Possible

Gay men who are positive find that people become positive toward them in turn, as if by magic. Positive gay men minimize other's liabilities and even view them as their assets. For example, they might view perfectionism not as "rigidity" but as "tastefulness." They avoid stereotyping based on faultfinding, leading to premature pissiness—making others feel inadequate to the point that others stay away in order to avoid being emotionally beaten up by someone who thinks he is better than they are.

Self-affirmation predictably enhances positivity to others. Self-affirmative gay men avoid criticizing themselves unduly to the point that they diminish their value even in their own eyes. If you are being overly self-critical, try to give yourself some votes of self-confidence and then become a good self-promoter who avoids selling himself short by putting himself down publicly, say, by making jokes at his own expense. In particular, never be ashamed of being gay, then displace that shame onto something else you dislike about yourself, such as your age or looks. Excessively self-demeaning humor mostly leads others to demean you in turn, which is certifiably unfunny.

Avoid Rejection/Deal with Unavoidable Rejections Adequately

Not all rejections are unavoidable. Not everyone is going to love you. But you must not provoke some of your own rejections, say, by self-destructively undermining your own purposes through actions that satisfy an immediate need—like getting your anger out or having quick sex—but that defeat your long-term purpose—of forming solid relationships that satisfy and last.

Should rejection, unprovoked or provoked, actually occur, deal with it adequately. Resolutely refuse to allow minor rejections to too readily demoralize you, making you so despondent that you withdraw and refuse to ever try relationships again. Clearly recognize that what appears to be a rejection of you is so often a self-statement on the part of the one who seems to be doing the rejecting. Thus, a man who dumped a romantic candidate because he was "too into appearances and insufficiently concerned about social issues, not enough the social reformer for me" was not rejecting the other person for qualities he didn't have/admire (as he said was the case) but enhancing his own self-pride (which he denied) by emphasizing how he himself had those very qualities ("I am a sincere man and to boot a social reformer") that he claimed the other lacked.

Avoid making rejections worse by thinking about them illogically to the point of responding to them catastrophically. Especially avoid thinking of today's rejection as a sign that you are in for a string of inevitable rejections in the future and for the rest of your life.

In conclusion, patients who were the most successful at finding Mr. Right were like this patient of mine:

He recognized that making contact with a good man takes work and is a tough job, not a sideline, or for the faint at heart. Serious about meeting Mr. Right, he gave first priority to finding a relationship, so he avoided getting sidetracked onto drinking, cruising, and trophy collecting. He broadcast his availability so that everyone knew that he wanted a relationship. By avoiding sending mixed messages, he avoided confusing potential admirers to the point that they couldn't tell whether to approach him or to stay away and avoid him entirely.

He looked for relationships not only in designated cruising places like bars or the Internet but everywhere, including gay and lesbian social centers (too often dismissed as the refuge of losers), the public library, and the local coffeehouses. And everywhere he looked, he was receptive and responsive to what he found and to who found him. He also networked—spreading himself thin at first, surrounding himself with a large group, hoping to get the greatest possible exposure within the group through personal introductions that might lead to his ultimately finding a lifetime partner.

He also sought only the truly important qualities in a man. For him, Mr. Right's looks, pedigree, money, possessions, family background, and the circles he ran in were not so important as his personal attributes, such as sincerity, personal and professional stability, interest in him that trumped self-interest; intelligence and flexibility; being neither extremely inhibited nor overly disinhibited; being motivated to make a relationship work; seeking exclusivity and preferably full monogamy; and having a sense of humor about things that included being relaxed enough to avoid catastrophizing those unimportant matters that always crop up even in the best relationships, leading to an inability to overlook the really unimportant things that come along but in the long run have no real impact or staying power.

Always making it a practice to look his very best for that expected and unexpected Mr. Wonderful, he routinely collected others' opinions on how he appeared and behaved and responded to their advice not by challenging it because he was insulted even by their constructive criticism but by changing when indicated. He took special care to fix his back as well as his front (checking how he looked in the mirror from behind), and he took equally special care of his complexion as part of his being attentive to his overall hygiene. Stylish, he fit in with the majority by avoiding looks that were too outlandish or so bland that he disappeared so entirely into the background that nobody noticed him. He also avoided local looks that didn't cross over elsewhere, like the look of "outcast chic" he had once adopted (only to abandon). For he came to understand that letting his hair grow long- ish and then washing it and putting in additives to deliberately make it look skuzzy and scraggily didn't attract everybody (or anybody). He came to recognize that "that look on my part offers less an interper- sonal greeting then it makes an avoidant self-statement."

Not a very young man, he assiduously avoided trying to hide his age in a way that only called more attention to it. He never told self- demeaning old-aunty jokes or any other jokes that got him a laugh at the expense of getting him a date. He maintained a positive self-view, which came through as seeing himself as a valued individual. As a result, others came to value him just as highly as he valued himself.

He was always careful not to let his body language reveal any neg- ativity toward others even when he might be feeling it. He was careful to avoid being like a friend of his—who, when he was talking to one person, always turned his head around—to look about to see if some- one better was coming along.

He avoided getting openly angry whenever possible, and if he did get angry in spite of himself, he tried to limit the fallout by speaking, if complainingly, then at least quietly and softly, while emphasizing the problem at hand but deemphasizing how he felt about it and always remembering to not say something that he could never take back.

As a generally empathic individual, he tried to read a potential partner's mind for the purpose of ascertaining the other's emotional needs so that he could then gratify them, hopefully turning a "no" into a "yes" by figuring out what the man wanted and liked, then giv- ing exactly that to him. For example, he played easy-to-get with men who were depressed to the point of feeling "nobody loves me" but hard-to-get with men who were paranoid to the point that they feared others were closing in on them too fast. Overall, he tried to be moth- erly, for he recognized that warmth and affectionate kindness were the way to a man's heart, figuratively speaking, "through his umbili- cal cord."

He was generally sober, avoiding getting high, both literally and figuratively, to the point that his judgment was affected, making him look unstable and unreliable.

Once into a relationship, he didn't give up on it easily after too readily accepting abandonments, including by spinning them via reassuring himself that "there were more fish in the ocean." He put any relationship he developed first, avoiding doing rash and impulsive things that might negatively affect a relationship he had just started and was in the process of building. He believed in accommodating by putting the need to be "us" first, making it trump the need to be "me." He didn't give first priority to getting things his way and over-looked a lot, keeping silent and not saying what was on his mind in those cases where he anticipated that getting things off his chest would cause others chest pains. If a partner left wet towels on the bed, instead of complaining, he picked them up and hung them up himself. As he said, "Yes, I just bought a hamper, and he never puts anything inside, instead draping his worn underwear over the top as if he is waiting for me, his personal assistant, to make the final disposition. But I told myself, 'so what?' then moved on. And even if we have important dis-agreements like whether to split up for the holidays, I try to ignore them. Because I have learned my lesson the hard way: when I ignore the things that are unimportant in the infinite scheme of things, the really important things never seem to come up, or, if they do, they appear to just resolve themselves as if spontaneously."

GAY MARITAL DIFFICULTIES

Same-sex partnering is associated both with unique pleasures and with special problems. As for the problems, while in heterosexual marriages two people as much biologically different as alike have to find ways to *become compatible*, in gay marriages two people as much biologically alike as different have to find a way to *avoid becoming incompatible*.

Resolving marital problems is especially important because gay divorce can be very hard and even harder than straight divorce. This is because, even though gay marital bonds are informal, and often there are no children, the emotional connections can, without the legal ties and a big family, even, or especially, make gay marriage more intense than straight marriage. As a result, the grief associated with gay separation/divorce can be even greater and harder to bear than the grief associated with straight separation/divorce. In fact, since a gay relationship, being generally informal, is based almost entirely on trust, breaking up is often associated with a sense of unallayed betrayal, and it is that which can make the separation overwhelming through the addition of that devastating and seemingly irreparable dimension. That's why after separation/divorce, many gay men feel like they have a strong bottomless pit in their stomach; truly long, dark, lonely days follow a painfully intense and protracted struggle to emerge from the mire and feel good again; and overwhelming feelings of anxiety about the future threaten, accompanied by self-esteem falling so low that it feels "as if no one would ever want me again, so I won't even bother trying to find someone new."

Paranoia

Paranoia on the part of one or both partners is the most common emotional difficulty that sinks gay marriages leading to gay divorce. To some extent, the more you love a man, the more paranoid you become about him, while, conversely, if you are not paranoid about a man, you may not love him enough or at all. For both intense love and paranoia make people thin-skinned, worried about imminent abandonment, fearful of possible loss to follow, and prone to respond catastrophically when abandoned after first having been seduced.

But too often *excessive* paranoia is not inspirational but destructive. For one thing, it can lead to cheating. Not all gay men who cheat on their partners are paranoid. But paranoia facilitates cheating should paranoid partners project their own guilty sexual desires onto others to the point that their own cheating heart now begins to beat in their partner's breast.

Jasper, a paranoid gay man, jumped to the conclusion that Rob, his partner, was cheating on him because he mistook his partner's male buddies for sexual partners. Then he got depressed, then he got mad, and then he got even—by being unfaithful to Rob. He wanted to be unfaithful all along, only now he had the excuse he needed: "You did it first."

In a typical instance, he and Rob were friendly with Mike, a single man at the gym. Mike (wrongly) assumed that Rob was, more than being just friendly, becoming interested in him sexually. The final straw: when Jasper left the locker room and Rob, still changing, behind, Mike stopped his workout and rushed in hoping to get Rob alone—as Jasper believed (and not entirely without justification) not just to talk to but also to put the make on him.

Jasper, of course, with eyes in back of his head, saw the whole thing. Already feeling vulnerable and threatened, he now started worrying, entirely without reason, that Rob was wandering and that he was about to lose out to a cuter and younger rival. He became convinced that Rob was not just a passive recipient of but was actively encouraging all the attention Mike was giving him. Jasper said nothing about this to Rob. It was, however, his silence that said it all: by producing a charged wary suspicious atmosphere that soon began to pervade the entire relationship. As things developed, after giving Rob the silent treatment, he became openly accusatory while covertly plotting vengeance—his revenge fantasies fueled by tortured images of treacherous sexual infidelity and the belief that all his friends were laughing at him for being a cuckold, bad-mouthing him behind his back, and encouraging Rob to "leave that loser." Now a complete lack of basic trust enveloped the relationship, leading Jasper to misinterpret even Rob's sincerest attempts at self-defense as a cover-up. Soon Jasper found himself starting arguments with Rob, usually about "Where were you last night?" and "Who were you just looking at, and why?" Next he began checking on Rob's whereabouts, stealthily writing down the odometer setting on Rob's car in the morning then checking it out in the evening while secretly monitoring his computer usage. Then it became "Why bother being faithful to him, he's not to me?" Next, he actually began cheating on Rob. There were recriminations, more cheating, and physical abuse, all of which escalated until one night the two broke up, with Jasper suddenly dumping Rod for his infidelities.

That night, Jasper went for a walk. But he never returned home. Instead, he called Rob from the YMCA to say, "I am sleeping over here and will not be coming back tonight or ever again."

Cheating

Cheating never enhances but always potentially disrupts, relationships. Yet gay men often condone their own cheating and encourage others to cheat by claiming it represents the norm—"because everyone is doing it," "does no harm because few gay men expect anything more or less," and "is actually beneficial because it acts as a valve that by releasing pressure can save, not destroy, a relationship." Science takes few strong stands against cheating, perhaps because researchers, afraid of being thought of as masters of inhibition because they discourage gay men from being themselves, ignore the issue of cheating entirely or rationalize it as a healthy manifestation of self-expression.

Thus, a TV commentator, Philomena, responds to a listener's question:

Dear Philomena: I know that men tend to sleep around and gay men have more opportunity to sleep around than straight men. But my boyfriend and I would like to make our relationship work. Can you give us any idea of what's going on here and suggestions for how we can deal with it? Signed, I can't say no.

Dear ICSN:

I'm glad you asked that. In a recent research project it was found that the gay marriages that seemed to last were the ones where the participants were not so rigid about their sexual fidelity. Gay men who enter a relationship expecting to have a 1950s Donna Reed–*style marriage of complete sexual fidelity were frequently disappointed. You know, of course, anonymous sex is one thing, but actually dating other people, which includes the possibility of an emotional involvement, is much more of a threat. And, as always, honest communication is still the key to relationship longevity.*[1]

I personally believe in defining what is a good marriage at least partly in terms of sexual fidelity. I believe that cheating for the sake of transient sexual thrills introduces permanent and sometimes fatal tension into what otherwise might be a smoothly working relationship. For while many open relationships are loving and last for a lifetime, others lack the fullness and completeness associated with being closed—into monogamy—if only because monogamy enhances sexuality through a full, intense focus on one other person and keeps resentful feelings of betrayal out of a relationship. And that is the very feeling that cools sexual heat the most.

ON TAKING OTHERS' ADVICE ON RELATIONSHIPS

Gay men seeking relationships need to be careful about taking relational advice from others, even about what at first seem to be the smallest things. Few people, certainly including me, know you well enough to give intelligent specific advice about what you should do, yet those who don't are often the ones who offer the most suggestions and in the greatest detail, though the suggestions they advance are sometimes more right for themselves than they are for you. This typically includes such advice as the following:

- Stop being a "master of inhibitions" and "just go for it" (never mind setting limits on yourself or curtailing acting out and just cooling it).
- Be yourself (though we all have many selves we can and should potentially affirm or deaffirm).

- Give him freedom, and if he comes back to you, he is yours (this works as poorly with men as it does with parakeets).
- You shouldn't have to put up with that. Instead of trying so hard to work things out and wasting time through discussion and possible compromise, leave him before you get too old and it's too late for you to find someone else.

Be especially careful to ignore advice from toxic friends and misguided advisers out to sink your relationship for reasons of their own: selfish motivations, especially jealousy that leads them to want destroy your partnership.

Thus one man's adviser whenever he sensed one of his friends was about to go off with a new partner instead becoming jealous recommended he avow his gay identity by reveling in his gay sexuality and showed him what to do by personal example—proudly complaining about the pain he had today from the abrasions his boyfriend gave him last night. He responded to friends looking for a long-term committed relationship by warning them that they were being overidealistic, for any gay marriage, while constituting a valid political cause, was inherently an invalid personal venture. He actually undermined relationships that formed by joining up with one of two partners to defeat the other. Thus, undercutting the other in his usual fashion, in secret he lent one of two partners his out-of-town apartment so that the man could shack up there with a series of new lovers.

Don't glean relational advice from the media without cross-checking it with other media resources and other reliable sources. To illustrate, I view Byron Beck's relational advice as an example of the kind of media advice to be taken with skepticism. He implies or suggests that self-help books directed to helping gay men find love are "man-grabbing manual[s]," "hand-job[s] of . . . book[s that] supposedly teach . . . the . . . basic . . . rules every queer dude needs to know to find—and keep—a man" but in fact teach that "single gay men are inherently flawed" and need to "stop being themselves to find happiness" so that you "almost feel like it's not OK to be gay" due to "outrageousness."[2]

And, by supposedly saying that "relationships where two people fall completely in love are something to be involved in when you're not having sex," Kantor, "an apostle of inhibitions," suggests that the whole homo world head in a more repressive direction when he says that "hot is not a relationship."

A man, ultimately burned by such gay relational advice he received, wrote to me,

> I want to mention the problem I have with one of my friends. Of course part of our problems start at home. Most of us lose family support as we come out. Meaning your aunt or uncle fixing you up with so and so. So we need our friends, and it is a network, and thank the heavens for our friends. But sometimes I think you aren't hard enough on all the stupid preconceived ideas passed down to us by bitter queens like that guy who sucked me in, chewed me up, then spit me out with all his suggestions. Looks [to me] like most [of my friends] have major issues that block them to pass along good advice or judgment.

Here is some of my advice one of my patients took then successfully adopted as his own. "I often find it safer, if not always better, to listen to those who guide me in the direction of connecting than to those who advise me to become disconnected. As I look back, I always lament the man who got, but I never self-congratulate for the man I drove, away."

FOUR

Sex and Sexuality

In this chapter, the first of two on the topic, I describe gay sex and sexuality to help you determine if you have a sexual problem that might need your attention. In the present chapter, I focus on typical/normative sexual attractions/fantasies/practices; discuss monogamy and contrast it with polygamy/cheating/promiscuity; discuss promiscuity and whether all gay men are promiscuous, at least more so than straight men; define and discuss bisexuality; go into compulsive sexuality; mention some of the biomedical complications of normative gay sex; describe the sexual dysfunctions—disorders of arousal and performance, especially those due to erotophobia; speak of abstinence; discuss gay love; and conclude with issues involving a parent's input into their son's homosexuality. In the next chapter, I discuss the paraphilias, such as frotteurism (rubbing) and pedophilia as well as gender identity disorder and transexualism (a component of gender identity disorder), all specifically as they occur in gay men. In both chapters, my information comes from the scientific literature filled out by clinical material obtained from patients, friends, and personal experience while not relying entirely on the following:

• Studies based on statistics that come from telephone interviews so constituted with loaded questions that the answers document reality less than they reflect their subject's wishes and need to brag or complain. (These are often the real issues with such reports as those that conclude that a high percentage of gay males over a certain age when asked if they were sexually active said "Yes.")

- Studies that contain scientific/personal biases that routinely find their way into research into homosexual behavior.[1] Typically, admirably but unscientifically, researchers omit data that appear to be unflattering to gay men in order to avoid further stigmatizing a group admittedly already suffering from negative medical labeling that can have the undesirable/unintended effect of branding them as social misfits.

TYPICAL (NORMATIVE) GAY SEXUALITY

Description

Normative sexual functioning for gay men can best be defined by postulating a continuum spanning the extremes of essential/normative to fringe, with mutual masturbation and oral and anal sex at the essential end of the continuum and fisting, urolagnia (water sports), sadomasochism, and bondage at the fringe end. Somewhere between the two, we find behaviors that "merely" push the envelope, such as a paraphilia-like frotteurism (rubbing)—a practice that is often part of foreplay, only to become abnormal when exclusive and/or harmful to others.

Generally, any sexual practices that are safe, pleasurable, and nonexploitative and that offer what should be guilt-free pleasure and gratification for oneself and others fit my definition of gay normative. But though politically correct, it is scientifically inaccurate to presume that everything sexual that gay men do is "normal"—simply because gay men do it.

Key Aspects

- As a gay man just starting out, you will experience strong same-sex sexual urges. You will also long to be in nonsexual situations with other men who may not or may be straight, although you will generally show a preference for individual gay men/gay groups over heterosexual company.
- Some gay men always prefer certain forms of sex over others. Other gay men are more flexible. Often the sex gay men want and perform is somewhat opportunistic—that is, situation (what is available) and object (whomever I momentarily find attractive) dependent, mood dependent (what I feel like today), and altered and generally enhanced by altruistic love along the lines of "I love him so much that I would do anything for him."
- Some—but not all—gay men attach a gender value to what they do sexually. For example, they see being on top as masculine and being on bottom as feminine.

- Individual personality (as much as anatomy) can become sexual destiny because there is some relationship between such personality traits as passivity and such sexual preferences as receptive anal sex.

- One's own body habitus is unreliably associated with one's sexual preference(s) so that one's overt physical "masculinity" or "femininity" is not a good indicator of one's sexual proclivity.

- In determining sexual attraction, emotional yearnings/conflicts often determine/trump physical attributes. Thus, a physical attraction to waifs may reflect compulsive neurotic exogamy, that is, the allure of someone as different as possible from oneself and/or the longing for someone to mother on the basis of an identification with one's own mother and/or a need to mother a childlike man who is in fact *you* so that, this way, you vicariously obtain mothering—*for yourself.*

- Sexual *preferences* are difficult to distinguish from sexual *fetishes* and sexual *compulsions*. Some observers misuse the term *fetish* to pathologize normative (pleasurable, consensual) sex. Others do the reverse so that they say "I like it" to *depathologize* "I can't help myself and keep myself from doing it."

The following patient with a typical sexual preference with fetishistic overtones wanted to know "is this normal, or am I a fetishist?"

> *Hi Martin, my name is Julio. I am a 48-year-old. I only want to meet somebody special with 21 inches biceps very muscular very handsome high class. Caucasian or more specific European descendant. I only like white Italians.*

Monogamy versus Promiscuity/Cheating

Monogamy within gay relationships is not as unusual as some of the literature, particularly the literature from before the turn of the century, might suggest. Thus, Coleman and Rosser, writing in the 1990s, stated that many observers note that "the majority of gay couples have not been [sexually exclusive] within the[ir] relationship."[2] This may no longer hold today.

Along with Coleman and Rosser, who note that "one of the major shifts within gay culture has been the shift in social support away from polygamy toward monogamy,"[3] my relational bias tends strongly toward being monogamous. For me, monogamy means giving up something to get three things even more gratifying and important than sexual variety:

- The undying lifetime affection of one's partner
- A relationship free of that anxiety, tension and the traumatization that I believe is predictably an outcome of triangular or multiangular sex
- The considerable and very powerful aphrodisiacal (sex-enhancing) benefits of exclusivity

In my opinion, the thrills of extramarital sex within the context of an ongoing so-called committed relationship are negatively balanced by the pangs of guilt and real trouble that cheating and promiscuity cause for gay relationships and particularly for those gay men truly in love with their cheating partner. Cheating and promiscuity invariably lead to jealousy, a sense of betrayal, a fear or conviction of loss, and painful tension and confusion on the part not only of one's partner but also of one's friends and family caught up, often unwillingly, in the goings-on, to the point of agonizing over whether they should tell, just drop a hint to see if it gets picked up, or say nothing, thus risking withholding information they possess that could potentially be useful to a person they love.

Yet some gay men, many of whom are in a gay marriage, seeming to have only sex on their brains, take every opportunity to gratuitously turn a neutral conversation into one about sex—their favorite and at times only topic of interest as well as a fair indication of what is happening/soon to come in their relational practices. Here are some examples:

There are a lot of cute looking dogs on the beach.

And a lot of cute men there too.

What does that man who is chairing a literary conference with a Pulitzer Prize winner actually do?

In bed?

Do enjoy your vacation trip to Australia!

Too bad these days you can't still do the flight attendants in the cabin.

Restaurant manager. Our party of 20 is late. We've been holding the reservation for an hour now, and all that time the tables have sat empty on a crowded Saturday night. It's a birthday party, but only the birthday boy is here.

Waiter: That's okay. He's good looking.

Real estate agent: What do you think of the apartment?

Buyer: All it's missing is a sling.

Me: A cop stopped me because I didn't pick up after my dog. But what
   was I supposed to do? All she was doing was peeing!
Him: Maybe he wanted you to lap it up; after all, some people like that,
   you know.
Observation made about and question asked of the owner of a sandwich
   shop delivering food he holds in one hand while for some reason
   holding a leaf blower in his other hand:
Why is he carrying those two things together?
Reply: Lunch and . . .
Statement: The tar balls are ruining our beach.
Reply: (Fill in your own response.)

*One of my more insightful patients in essence said, "I never met a
double entendre I didn't like, and with a little creativity I can turn
anything into a phallic symbol. Words like 'come' and 'do' and
'squirt' are among my favorite triggers, unutterable in my 'impolite
company,' at any rate without eliciting my knowing wink that says,
as one of my bitchiest friends put it, 'You are about to hear my same
old, same old, tired joke once again.' In real life, this patient was
even more all action than talk and with a bark far worse than his bite.
For in his actual behavior, he typified the promiscuous gay man who
exemplified why some people think that all gay men are, like him,
more promiscuous than any straight man could ever be.*

As an article in a column called the "Rainbow Room" puts it, raising the
possibility that overall promiscuity is more of a significant feature of the
gay than it is of the straight life, "Most researchers [do] say that gay
men have more sex than straight men."[4] Certainly, gays have more backroom (orgy) bars than straights, and gays, unlike straights, will sometimes
patronize rest stops on the parkways for sex. At many colleges, there used
to be—and perhaps still are—bathrooms virtually set aside for homosexual liaisons but few if any unisex bathrooms for straight orgies. Straight
pickup bars do of course exist, but these are as often as much for trolling
for relationships (and sometimes drugs) than for cruising for sex. Many
gay ads on the Internet openly admit that the writer is looking for sex. In
contrast, plenty of straight dating sites are either less direct than this or
cover their true intent by saying that what they are really seeking is a
long-term relationship.
   Why might gays be more promiscuous than straights? Often, early trauma
plays a large role. Trolling for sex often involves trauma repetition where

the goal is to newly passively experience or actively force a more sanguine outcome of earlier traumata, still raw in the mind and emotions after many years. Reparative failure is, however, predictable, necessitating further, panicky, compulsive attempts at repetition with the hope of restitution.

Also, some gays go from partner to partner (and seem unable to be completely satisfied by one man) because the sex they seek is not purely sex; that is, it is not so much sex as it is something else, such as a desire to act out old unresolved but still pressing "oral" and "anal" conflicts trying to relieve and resolve by reliving them. In addition, unique interpersonal components drive the behavior, for many gays are really seeking love, not sex, only to find that love is difficult to obtain in their (and perhaps everyone's) world without using sex as at least part of the search—the best or only method that some or most people, gay or straight, know of for immediate communication and connection, the safest and most direct pseudopod that they can extend—and quickly and safely retract, without getting too involved and too seriously hurt. Frequently, interpersonal issues involving dominance and control are active, with a good part of the real sexual need involving less of "what can I do?" than "who can I get to do it to, and with, me?" Also, having multiple sexual conquests can be a kind of pap that contravenes homophobia, with the sex acting like relational methadone. Of course, sex is also recreational, and it's easy for gays to seek this form of recreation because they are not burdened with the constraints of potential pregnancy, the desire/need to procreate, or, at least in many cases, the potential for messy divorce-related lawsuits, making gay promiscuity so often less a matter of inclination than one of opportunity and mobility, as in "why not, what do I have to lose?" Some (particularly Freudian) observers even state that because gay sex closely involves the excretory organs, it can lead to feelings of disgust and a contempt bred by familiarity relievable only by anonymity and the fantasies of being pristine that newness offers. Finally, too many observers, postulating a theory of no merit whatsoever, improbably suggest that gays are primitive people whose animalistic instincts break through, as if all gays are the rough equivalent of the decorticate monkeys I once saw in a movie in medical school where the animals mated nonstop after having experimental brain lesions inflicted on them.

This said, claiming otherwise, Coleman and Rosser suggest that stereotypes of gay men as having thousands of partners may just be artifacts of atypical samples (e.g., early AIDS cases). Quoting Darrow et al., they say that "a more modest estimate of the median number of lifetime male partners for American gay men is fewer than 50."[5] I personally doubt this, for I know of not a few gay men who at the baths or during an orgy like the one I once attended at a San Francisco private home had their aliquot of approximately 50 partners: in a single sitting.

Overall, I personally believe that promiscuity is less common in gays than some epidemiological and demographic studies suggest. This is because monogamous lifetime relationships tend to go unnoticed because they are more hidden from the world than relationships that are promiscuous. Monogamous gays are among the least likely to be research subjects. Promiscuity being open and lurid is more likely to garner all the headlines and be the thing the press describes and widely disseminates, to the point that most people distortively view promiscuous behavior as representative of the actions of the entire gay community. I am strictly monogamous, but to date no one has counted me in in any relevant study.

Probably, gays are only as promiscuous in *fact* as straights are in *fantasy*. And, additionally, gay promiscuity is of little to no significance as long as the sex is safe and the promiscuity doesn't intrude on an established, committed, monogamous relationship. Promiscuity is, however, underproductive to damaging when unsafe things happen as a result and symptomatic when it is associated with poor judgment that leads to personal and professional self-destructiveness or, perhaps its worst aspect, treacherousness to a partner.

Dear Dr. Kantor:

I am a Gay man striving to be in a lasting and honest relationship.

I am a recent immigrant now living in South Dakota. Long story short, I have been here since last year. I met a local on November 6. There are certain details of my situation that I cannot disclose. But I will be as honest as possible. I met this guy and it was love at first sight. The sex was great . . . while it lasted. We got along just fine, one thing led to another, and we were living together.

I have a very good and accurate sixth sense; I have never been wrong when I had a "feeling." And I had one when we stopped having sex after the first month. In the last two months we have only done it twice. The last time was about two to three weeks ago, when he ran out of excuses like physically feeling sick, or just being tired. We had a fight about it. I asked him if there was something wrong with me, and if he needed to have sex with other people. But he kept answering me with a big "no." He says that he wants to have sex with me but his head tells him not to. Like any man he wakes up with a morning glory. He precums. . . . So what the heck? After the last time we discussed our not having sex, he promised to see someone about it. He went about a week ago and he came back feeling confused and negative about the idea of seeing a doctor with this issue. He said that the therapist made him dig up old bones that as far he's concerned are dealt with. He doesn't think it'll help.

I am not a sex addict, I just want to make love with the one that I love. Well, for a while I had the feeling that he was hiding something from me. When we realized that a relationship was what we both wanted we each deleted profiles on sites, well, the kind that we met on. On Monday I was on Facebook and his Yahoo messenger popped up and an immediately sexual conversation was started by someone on the other side. I was in a state of shock and almost disbelief! Immediately I knew I was right all along. I have to add that I had started on antidepressants because I thought I was losing my mind. I thought I was just being paranoid with the suspicions I had. When these weren't helping I even considered antipsychotics.

I then called him immediately and demanded his passwords to both his email accounts. In this way I found two separate sites on which he had been having conversations of a sexual manner with other men. This broke, killed something inside of me, and whatever else there may be. I was hurt that he was doing things behind my back. Talking about having sex with people while he can't bring himself to make love with someone he loves. While I have tried everything—small talk, asking questions about his likes and dreams, buying board games, puzzles for us to have, to talk. Still after all this he was talking, but to other people, not me.

He is a very private person and is not even completely out to everyone he knows, except for people at work, some friends and his family. His sister too is gay. It has been a week and I am still with him.

I asked him to tell me what kind of relationship he wanted. He said that he didn't know. I asked him if he felt like he needed to keep profiles on those sites while we are involved. He said that he deleted the profiles and people in his contacts that were from that sort. I asked him if he needed to sleep with other people and have an open relationship. He said, "no." I asked him if he thought that I moved in too soon. He said, "no." I asked him if he wanted to lose me. He said, "no." Holy moly, how do you get someone to open up? He doesn't talk.

I have never not given anyone a second chance. I feel like this is a relationship that can be a lasting, successful one. Many people will say that a three month involvement cannot be seen as a relationship yet, but I love him. He loves me. He proved it by being willing to try to make things better and not running away from his mistakes. Just too bad that I am the one who is suffering the most. I feel hurt, betrayed, broken, ugly, and just not good enough. Time will heal but it will take a long time. Trust will take a very, very, very long time to redevelop. Men! Sometimes I wish I was straight instead. LOL! But that would hold problems of another kind, huh? So, how does one get over the emotions? I don't hate him. Is that crazy? How do I deal with feelings of guilt? I mean, I have no reason to feel guilty.

Shame, Dr. Martin, you probably wish this email ended up in your junk mail. I have a problem when it comes to writing. I have to brace myself to stop.

Thank you very much for taking the time to read this. I do not expect you to reply with pages of advice. I just needed to tell an outsider about the experience. Someone who doesn't know either of us.

Have a great weekend.
Serge

Fortunately, most often gay men's promiscuity at least doesn't interfere with their work. This is because usually there is a disconnect between sex and job, with each residing in its own separate compartment in the brain. (That is why discouraging gays from being psychoanalysts—a formerly common practice still today extant in not a few professional circles—or preventing gay men from being soldiers and discharging military men for being openly gay makes about as much sense as refusing to listen to the music of Franz Liszt because he was unfaithful to his mistresses.)

This said, there are some gay men who don't do well professionally not because of antigay prejudice but because of their sexual preoccupation/ compulsivity—and that not so much in and of itself but because of the fallout that makes it hard for them to focus on their work. At times, there are undeniably negative professional consequences associated with the promiscuous lifestyle, as when heavy drinking/hangovers go with the bar scene and the long, late hours looking for sex lead to job-killing sleep deprivation accompanied by a day/night reversal of sleeping patterns, making it difficult to be alert on the job and sometimes even to get to work in the morning in the first place.

BISEXUALITY

There are a number of descriptions of and theories to explain bisexuality. These include the following:

- As Fox quoting Troiden says, bisexuality is by itself a "valid sexual orientation [though] the general lack of recognition given to bisexuality and the lack of a supportive community of other bisexual people make it difficult for an individual to sustain a bisexual identity."[6] In this view, bisexuality is a fixed condition representing an actual position, not an ambivalence about taking one, and as such constitutes a set, unique entity: a fourth sex: (1) male, (2) female, (3) homosexual, and (4) bisexual.

- True bisexuality does not exist, for sexual identity as a bisexual is inconstant. What can look like true bisexuality is transient, the equivalent of a temporary adolescent phase of experimentation, or characterizing a transitional state between "being" straight and "becoming" gay. As Cass saw it, "Heterosexual attractions and behavior are only transitional phenomena some individuals experience as they move toward permanent monosexual lesbian and gay identities."[7] Perhaps there is no such thing as bisexuality, for the statement that "I am a bisexual" is only a protest that says, "Look, I am not a homosexual." In 1956, Bergler stated that "those who consider themselves bisexual are denying a homosexual orientation";[8] that is, bisexuality is a lie because people who claim to be bisexual are doing so just to enhance their personal and professional reputation.

- Bisexuality is "mostly" opportunistic—occurring when an individual already so inclined senses and takes advantage of current possibility. (Opportunistic bisexuality presents us with a possible exception to the rule that everything homosexual is not a choice. For men can alter not their basic sexual orientation but rather their immediate sexual behavior, doing so for idealistic or practical reasons, as when they act heterosexual so that they can marry a woman and have children—in order to please/placate their parents and/or advance themselves professionally.)

- Everyone is bisexual (bisexuality is universal). As Mead suggests, "Bisexuality [is] normal [so that] even a superficial look at other societies and some groups in our own society should be enough to convince us that a very large number of human beings—probably a majority— are bisexual in their potential capacity for love."[9] By implication, the blighted seeds of heterosexuality exist in homosexuals and the reverse; therefore, all gay men are as bisexual as all straight men are homosexual. Thus, Fox quotes Freud as having said that "us[ing] the theory of bisexuality to account for homosexuality, which he saw as an indication of arrested psychosexual development,"[10] we are all bisexual. But, presumably, Mead and Freud never met the gay men I know, men who, like me, can safely say that they never truly desired a woman sexually in their entire lives. When I once tried sex with a prostitute to further my psychoanalysis and meet its goal of going straight, I hated every second of it; and, anyway, all I wanted sexually was my neighbor, the one who put me up to my "good" try by saying he would join in, only to stand there impassively and back out at the last minute, leaving me alone and unsupported on this, my first and last such journey.

- Bisexuality is a psychopathological condition. In psychopathological terms, bisexuality is a manifestation of sexual psychopathology so that people who call themselves bisexual are variously (unconsciously) anxious and defensive about sexuality, overly dependent on the validation of and acceptance by others, truly confused and ambivalent about their sexuality, perhaps suffering from obsessional uncertainty and/or a commitment phobia about their sexuality due to excessive moralistic guilt leading to their needing to establish a rigid ethical antithesis to full pleasurable sexuality, and/or self-destructively masochistic and so needing, and even enjoying, the predictable scorn they get both from homosexuals and heterosexuals by being "uncommitted and wavering."

COMPULSIVE SEXUALITY

Description

I recently received the following e-mail:

> Dear M,
> I called Frank back and we were having a nice albeit simplistic conversation and he tells me he's been dating 2 men a week on his match site and doesn't go on a second date unless they have sex with him after being willing to go clubbing with him in the City. Says he's not the kind of guy who sits home and takes a nap in the afternoon, and people have to realize he is used to having sex 3 times a week. The last guy, he said, told him it's better to go slow (after he had only one date with him), to which he replied, "not for me it isn't, and I know what's right for me." And he never called him back.
> He really does live in the fast lane. Which I am wondering if it may be just as lonely there as is my life in the slow-to no-movement lane. So bye, bye, Mr. Slut.

No clear demarcating line can be drawn between normal sexuality, sexual addiction, so-called sexual compulsivity that is merely a disavowed psychopathological trapping/excuse for syntonic (desirable, acceptable) satyriasis, and true sexual compulsivity that is not an excuse for promiscuity but the real thing. This is because the criteria used to determine the distinctions have been to date—and perhaps of necessity will always be—inherently ephemeral: exclusivity, the degree of spillover to and interference in the rest of one's life, and the degree to which others are hurt or harmed. As Levine notes, "Research findings vary because there is no clear description of what constitutes [the] problem and sampling methods vary from study to study."[11]

Some sexually compulsive gay men recognize that something inside leads to their feeling forced into pursuing sex against their will. Some of these men also know why this is happening. But rarely does insight help them achieve desired meaningful self-control. Insight at most helps them suppress their sexual appetites temporarily, only soon enough they again become obsessed with sex and feel seriously pressured to go out and look for more.

Some sexual compulsives feeling guilty and ashamed of themselves keep their sexual escapades a secret from all but their closest intimates—and sometimes even from them—and this can prevent them from seeking help for their problem. Others accept their compulsive sexuality without guilt, for they find it pleasurable, useful, a good way to enhance their self-esteem (a welcome source of triumphal bragging rights), and a method for reducing loneliness. These men, denying they have a problem, refuse to own up to their true difficulty and instead choose to continue in the old ways. These are the men who balk when strongly urged to stop and refuse to go for help even when their need for assistance is clear and when help, should they ask for it, is likely to work.

Compulsive sexuality can become a most serious practical problem when the sexually compulsive man devotes too much of his life to acquiring/having sex. For example, the typically sexually compulsive gay man cannot wait for a pleasant nonsexual social event to be over so that he can go out and cruise. Sex has become his whole existence to the point that he cannot otherwise "get a life." His relationships, both sexual and nonsexual, even suffer because of his being into pornography over people or because of his consorting mainly with strangers he meets after spending too much time in the three Bs of his gay life: the bars, the baths, and the backrooms. Or the problem can be that he is haunting the rest stops on the highways, going through literally tens of men in one evening. Some sexual compulsives are looking for relationships through the making of one sexual contact after another, and they may actually find them using that means. But even here, when they do find the relationships they are seeking, too often they go on to lose them again as their sexual problems continue even after they have seemingly settled down. Costs to their health and professional life can also be great and multiple as the result of such secondary issues as lack of sleep, intensified depression due to numerous rejections and consequent loneliness, alcohol abuse and drug addiction, obesity from excessive drinking, and damage to their body due to such exotic sexual practices as fisting.

Particularly troublesome is that the unresolved negative effects of the emotional difficulties that create the sexual compulsivity in the first place generally affect the complexion of the consequent sexual behavior, leading to hypomanic and obsessive-compulsive distortions of one's sex life. As its name implies, sexual addiction/compulsivity bears an especially strong relationship to obsessive-compulsive disorder. The obsessive-compulsive sexually compulsive gay man cannot rid himself of the preoccupying thought that he hasn't had enough sex lately and needs more. His accompanying *compulsion* consists of an irresistible urge to cruise and find someone for a sexual partner. Because this leads but to transient gratification, a new, dawning awareness that something is missing and sorely needed impels him to repeat the entire cycle once again. After he achieves temporary comfort, via reduction of anxiety and fulfillment of need, the pressure and sexual tension peep through once again and then fully return—along with the compulsion to seek more sex, for relief as much as for pleasure.

Many sexually compulsive gay men do not suffer from other symptoms of obsessive-compulsive disorder. However, some do display associated, nonsexual obsessions and compulsions. There is often a history of tics starting in childhood, such as repetitive shoulder shrugging or touching each of one's fingers in succession with the thumb then starting over again or hair twirling and pulling. Often, recurrent thoughts occur, taking the form of meaningless phrases that waft into the mind to plague the individual—typically, partial fragments, such as "they turn up," or even "dirty-minded," often anally tinged phrases, such as "he eats it." Often, nonstop hypochondriacal worries appear that no doctor can dispel, such as a cancer "phobia" that is in actuality a cancer obsession. Associated full psychological disorders occur, such as attention-deficit/hyperactivity disorder and depression/bipolar disorder with mood swings, from the lows, typically occurring when sex is not available, to the highs, characterized by insatiable sexual hyperactivity seeking constant, nonstop gratification along with the denial of any possible problematic aspects of the promiscuous behavior.

Some "sexual compulsives" look less obsessive-compulsive than psychopathic. Such gay men refuse, even for health reasons (theirs and others), to deprive themselves of sex that they want. They forge ahead without regrets and guilt and often with an accompanying antiestablishment attitude that feeds their absence of constraints. Features of an impulse disorder can add poor judgment to the picture as the gay man makes inappropriate passes at the wrong people or in places where he is likely to get arrested—because his sexual needs trump any fear of negative consequences, including those pursuant on the criminal activity.

A friend wrote,

> Yesterday a boyfriend and I went to a Civic Association Ballroom Dance, lesson included, but no one under 85, but we had a ball, since we were referred to as "fresh young sirloin." I said to one oldster as we were waltzing, "Everyone else looks like they are floating on the uplift—how do we do that?" To which he replied, "Want me to goose you?"

A patient was at the baths when they were raided by the police. Fortunately, the police left without arresting him or anyone else—they were likely just harassing the customers so that the patrons didn't return at some future date. After the police left, all my patient could hear were the bathhouse clients, virtually in unison, lamenting that "now everyone is leaving, and what fun is that?" He then swore that he would stop putting himself at risk by continuing to attend the bathhouse in this, a very dangerous town for gay men. But that resolution dissolved in short order, and he continued going—or actually went more frequently than before—"because of the challenge." Simultaneously, though it would have been more judicious for him to cruise anonymously out of town where no one knew him, he kept on cruising in his hometown, haunting the local parks, rest stops, and other places where he was routinely recognized. Particularly problematic was his hanging around downtown street corners where cars picked men up for assignations—his presence there, under a streetlight, visible to all who drove by, clients and colleagues alike. Equally problematic was his simultaneously pushing for sex even with people he knew were not only unlikely to be uninterested in him but also likely to be actively antagonized by his coming on to them. In particular, he favored rough trade, even after not a few of them threatened him physically and two beat him up for making an unwelcome pass at them.

Cause

Davies postulates that sexual compulsivity constitutes a "delayed adolescence" due to a "'developmental lag' ... where the ... gay man is living out the adolescence [he was] unable to have during [his] teenage years."[12] According to Kort, sexual addiction/compulsion is the reenactment of early trauma and abuse ("sexual and cultural abuse"), with compulsively unsafe sexual behavior the late life consequence of emotional criticism and/or physical neglect or beatings and rapes that occurred early in life.[13] Gay men who have once been traumatized now seek the love and acceptance they were deprived of through obtaining multiple here-and-now sex partners, hoping that the wider their net, the greater their catch.

Thus, I believe that while my homosexuality was inherited/genetic, its specific early-on hypomanic desperate quality was partly due to the persistent effects of early traumata/parental rejection. Certainly, promiscuity occurring in the context of one of my early supposedly committed relationships was at least partly an attempt on my part to make up for my mother's inability to express warmth, affection, and acceptance of me when I was a child.

Like me, many other sexually compulsive gay men don't remember their mother's ever giving them positive feedback for anything they did that they themselves thought to be worthy/virtuous. Instead, they mostly remember their mothers regularly responding openly, vociferously, and negatively to the positive things they did and certainly to the negative things even when those were but understandable reactions to being sorely—and viciously—provoked. Such men are often using sex to work though/replace a past or present loss, fantasized or real. Often, they also suffer from masochistic trends involving a search for self-annihilation as their punishment "for being bad." This was the case for the gay man who dragged tricks home at night through the doorman installed to protect him from himself and the doctor who was repeatedly sued for doing unnecessary examinations of his attractive male patients' genitalia. Self-esteem issues are also often part of the picture as men feeling pressured to elevate their low self-esteem by impressing others with their ability to get one attractive man after another show off what they got—in order to compensate for what they believe they don't have, hoping that others will see them as more appealing, that is, as less of a failure, than the one that they believe themselves to be.

Not surprisingly, then, speaking therapeutically, gay men often relinquish their sexual compulsivity when they find a stable personal/sexual relationship with a sensitive partner who rarely if ever retraumatizes them—refusing to do so even when they masochistically beg him to. Now they settle down and, as if by magic, stop thinking about having to undo their mother's old negativity to them—losing their interest in making up today for a yesterday that is no longer relevant to their present.

Telling the sexually compulsive gay man to "just cut it out" overlooks not only that sexual self-control is always difficult but also that ordering it into being can make things worse by increasing failure anxiety and by enhancing the oppositionalism that often creates the problem in the first place. Gay men so ordered generally become even more rebellious/resistant as they stubbornly counter the proffered sanctions along the lines of "you don't understand that the essence of being gay equals shaking your booty."

In a typical response to my urging decoupling sexuality from compulsivity, once when I suggested that gay men who are sexually compulsive need not encouragement but treatment, Beck, an extremist columnist, in a 2002 column for the Portland Willamette Week, distorting what I said during a live interview with him, denounced me as "teach[ing] something ... dangerous ... that single gay men are inherently flawed [and so they] need to stop being themselves to find happiness [making you] almost feel like it's not OK to be gay [with Kantor] on a one-man mission to 'shake' queer dudes out of their entrenched gay ways," clearly someone who would "like to see the whole homo world head in a more repressive direction."[14]

MEDICAL/MECHANICAL COMPLICATIONS OF SEX

Some gays fear/loathe recognizing that they are gay/being gay because they believe that having gay sex will make them physically ill. Unfortunately, they are sometimes partly right, for medical and mechanical complications of gay sex, such as sexually transmitted diseases and physical injuries, do exist and can cause considerable pain and suffering. Fortunately, some complications can be prevented and others minimized without giving up being sexually active. I believe that the best idea is to maintain a truly trusting monogamous relationship for a lifetime to allow you to enjoy sex without fear of sexually transmitted diseases. Still, solving the problems associated with the mechanics of gay sex even within an ongoing committed relationship requires that you take sensible precautions, especially with regard to anal sex, where injury can occur because of anatomic incompatibility causing tissue damage that has at times required surgical intervention.

THE SEXUAL DYSFUNCTIONS

Because gays suffer from most of the same sexual dysfunctions as straights, the sexual disorders listed in the *Diagnostic and Statistical Manual of Mental Disorders* (4th ed.) generally apply equally to heterosexuals and homosexuals. However, the manual does seem to show a heterosexual bias.[15]

Among the sexual dysfunctions in gay men that I include here are disorders of arousal, such as aversion to sex and hypoactive sexual desire disorder; and disorders of performance, such as difficulties getting or maintaining an erection, too slow ejaculation, too rapid ejaculation, and aversion to and pain during anal intercourse. (Some observers also include compulsive unsafe sexual behaviors in this list.)

A gay man's sexual dysfunction may exist in both anonymous and intimate relationships or be confined to one or the other. For obvious reasons, research studies tend to overlook the sexual dysfunctions as they appear in such anonymous settings as the backrooms of bars. However, personal experience and anecdotal information indicate that these dysfunctions are *extremely* common in such places.

In the realm of sexual avoidance/hypoactive sexual desire disorders, the myth that all gay men are hypersexual overlooks the reality—that cadres of gay men experience *diminished* or *absent* sexual urges. When gay men come to believe that this (hypoactive) state of affairs is normal, welcome, desirable, and acceptable, the problem likely originates in erotophobia, or "love phobia."

Unfortunately, speaking *descriptively*, a degree of erotophobia is so common in gay (and straight) men as to be virtually normal, at least in the sense of being universal. Erotophobia seems to hover over all sexuality and perhaps especially homosexuality, where there is already an overall and otherwise determined inherent tendency to feel guilty. Sadly, too many of us, gay and straight alike, experience a universal negative attitudinal mindset toward having a body and using it, a mindset that makes all sex, especially homosexual sex, into something wicked and sinful.

Erotophobia is generally associated with the mindsets listed in Table 4.1. Some erotophobic gay men becoming celibate seek substitute gratifications, such as hobbies, to divert them as fully as possible from *any* form of sexual involvement. Others have some sex in their lives, only they are cold and frosty and suffer from physical sexual symptoms, such as diminished genital sensation, erectile dysfunction/impotence (inability to get or maintain an erection), and premature ejaculation (too fast) or ejaculatio tarda (too slow). They don't avoid homosexual sex entirely but have some sex, though only

Table 4.1   Mindsets in Erotophobia

- Fear of exposure of one's bodily parts, based on a negatively distorted body image that makes one want to hide one's physicality.
- Fear of exposure of being gay associated with reticence to disclose (come out).
- Fear of yielding because yielding = dissolution, a kind of melting of the self (ego).
- Fear of intimacy as if intercourse is both literally and figuratively interpersonally confining and will soon enough lead to more complete interpersonal incarceration. There is an associated fear of dependency due to a fear of helpless passivity, paradoxically associated with fear of independence due to a fear of incalculable and incurable isolation.
- Fear of becoming too emotional and being flooded by overly strong sexual feelings (and all other feelings swept along on their coattails) associated with a fear of letting loose as if the slightest stirring might cause all emotions to spin out of control and overwhelm the individual, leaving him no longer in charge of himself and prone to behave in a way that might cause others to become shocked and appalled.
- Fear that a demarcating moral line might be crossed.
- Fear of failing and being humiliated, paradoxically associated with the next item.
- Fear of succeeding and then being defeated and punished—by being literally deemancipated and figuratively castrated.
- Fear of rejection that often originates in a hypersensitive readiness to experience even the most positive feedback as shatteringly negative due to too high, often excessively perfectionist self-expectations and overly idealistic anticipations of others.
- Fear of pleasure on the part of ascetic masochistic individuals who so condemn having fun in any form that they make certain not to partake of sexual pleasure and enjoyment or at least to do so as little as possible.
- Fear that self-assertion = aggression = rape.
- Fear of being asked to make too many sacrifices, including or especially being required to change.

while simultaneously putting one or another form of countervailing cleansing prohibition into place. Potential cleansing prohibitions include the following:

- Taking sex back by condemning it immediately afterward with postcoital revulsion manifest as a desire to get away from one's partner quickly (e.g., to shower immediately)
- Keeping tenderness out of sex entirely by favoring rough trade only

- Developing strong attractions but only to cruel people
- Demeaning an available partner by refuting his value and/or the value of sexual exclusivity itself through becoming openly or secretly promiscuous/cheating where the secret intrigue is especially restorative
- Focusing on virtual sex—displaying an excessive fondness for pornography where sex becomes less sinful and instead more acceptable because it isn't bad if it doesn't involve real people

Developmentally, erotophobia is often the result of the thwarting of a boy's healthy sexual development through early discrete sexual traumata that have a great lingering inhibitory effect. Primal scene (overhearing parents having sex) traumata are especially toxic in this regard, for they make boys feel dirty by linking sex and incest. Feeling dirty, they isolate themselves not only from their own family but also from friends and lovers—because they believe themselves to be too unworthy to enjoy their good company and take pleasure from having good sex.

Levine speaks of how "early attachment problems paralyze . . . adolescent sexual capacity."[16] In my patients, I have regularly identified the developmentally significant contribution to erotophobia of unhealthy containment at the hands of rigidly suppressive parents who encourage the boy to carry on the parents' own sexually suppressive tradition, one often supported by repressive elements in the society the parents happen to—and often choose to—belong to. Themselves erotophobic, many mothers and fathers harbor negative feelings about all sexuality, gay or straight, and manifest this mindset either openly, say, by criticizing their sons for masturbation, or covertly, passive-aggressively, by somehow implying, "Don't get involved because that means leaving home and abandoning your parents who need you." Many fathers, fearing that their sons might "grow up to be a sissy," call their sons names like "faggot" to frighten them straight and simultaneously straitjacket them by closing off Internet access through instituting overly strict parental controls, in one case even going to the extent of getting rid of the computer entirely.

Gay sons thus exposed to shaming antierotic messages and punitive antierotic actions generally internalize the parental erotophobia to the point of imploding sexually by becoming self-homophobic. Internalizing their parents' consciences, they come to view their own being gay through the distortive prism of the newly internalized rigid parental punitive superego composed of harsh, shrill, unloving self-destructive messages antithetical to gay desire, love, and sex, with no forgiving nuances anywhere to be found to soften the inner blows. When the boy's newly minted overly severe conscience rains down on him, it inhibits his growth into a sexually comfortable/properly functioning gay adult.

A patient noted,

When I was a child my mother whipped me whenever she sensed I "felt sexual." She meted out one particularly intense whipping when she caught me "playing doctor" with a neighbor's little boy, saying "nice little boys don't play such naughty games." After the beating I "ran away from home"—to a neighbor's apartment—only to be beaten again, this time for disappearing without telling mother where I was going. Next, my mother did everything she could to make certain that I stayed away from all the boys in the neighborhood—so that I didn't "ruin their lives the way I ruined hers."

Levine describes other (nonerotophobic) *interpersonal dynamics of* "acquired" (situational) hypoactive sexual desire disorder (HSDD), a disorder he calls "psychic impotence." According to Levine, there are three possible causes as follows. The first is the pornography used when real people are too respected to be arousing. The second is Don Juanism, where sex is a sport and a source of pride and objects are trophies (phallic narcissists). The third involves the practical marriage, where an ambitious man marries for material, social, or family gain without any genuine enchantment and is impotent because he feels false to himself.[17]

Levine does not discuss HSDD in homosexual men. Instead, he views homosexuality as *causing* HSDD, that is, as something that interferes with heterosexuality—as, in effect, he categorizes homosexuality as a fourth reason for psychic impotence—in straights.

My Recommendations

Here are some ways men suffering from HSDD can maximize their sexual pleasure:

(1) Move all sex out of the backrooms in the wee hours of the morning and into your bedroom at a reasonable hour of the night.

(2) Never use sex strictly as a means to some end: to enhance self-esteem, to create and maintain an identity, to overcompensate for flaws to feel less small and insignificant, to conquer others in order to be the one in control (of yourself, your life, and your destiny), or to enhance your reputation by impressing others with what you can get. This is sex as a substitute for something else, and substitute sex

will never completely satisfy your sexual needs and, the dissatisfaction persisting, will leave you disappointed and unfulfilled because of feeling incomplete.

(3) Ultimately get around to keeping sex in the context of a long-term exclusive monogamous relationship. Exclusivity reduces two of the biggest sexual turnoffs there are for loving partners: separation anxiety and guilt. Monogamy without masturbation ultimately enhances pleasure and improves performance through focus that acts as a powerful aphrodisiac—improving quality by limiting quantity.

(4) Improve your basic relationship with the one person you are having sex with. Especially be motivated to gratify him before you gratify yourself, making his comfort/pleasure/orgasm your primary concern. That furthers positivity toward him, which gets returned to you as positive feedback, and that in turn enhances your own performance. Conversely, never humiliate your partner by being negative to and devaluing of him. Never express disgust with him, accuse him of doing things he did not do, or, overlooking his needs and desires, constantly push him to have sex even on those occasions when you are but he clearly isn't interested.

(5) In your partnered relationship, communicate honestly by telling your partner what you want sexually, doing so without shame. But don't necessarily tell him about everything he does that upsets you. Keep petty problems to yourself to avoid enlivening trivial relational disruptions by giving them your full attention and demanding his.

(6) Avoid introducing too many artificial sexual inhibitions ("beg me!") in order to enhance the excitement that comes from circumventing them, for this approach can ultimately backfire ("I am not a beggar!").

(7) Freely employ nonsexual touching without immediate release, such as massages.

(8) Benefit from two kinds of books. The first, *sex guides*, teach you about the erogenous zones, helping you learn the sexual ropes (e.g., the secrets of sexual stimulation). The second, *intimacy guides*, teach you about closeness and help you diminish interpersonal distancing so that you can put the stimulated zones to the best possible/maximal use. Be certain to avoid poorly conceived material in peripheral sex manuals (e.g., at least skip the section in one popular gay sex manual on how to properly indulge in bestiality). Both sex guides and intimacy manuals have a valuable collateral effect: reducing guilt by giving sex the stamp of approval, thus giving permission, that way countering negative intrinsic internal and internalized parental and societal "messages of don't."

(9) Accept help from those who are trying to be of assistance, including—or especially—your therapist. Don't, as some younger men do, live by the big idea that older people have no relevance for younger ones. That may be selectively true, and you should certainly discard badly worn advice that doesn't currently apply, but thinking globally along such lines is generally a conceit with a serious ageist component. Carefully avoid mistaking constructive for destructive criticism and then condemning those who advise you as being square spoilers or medical establishment killjoys, and don't, as some of my patients have done when I tried to discuss sexual compulsivity, get up from your chair and storm out of the room and, complaining about oppression, go, never to be heard from (at least in a positive way) again.

(10) Treat your inhibitions behaviorally. For example, attempt to overcome ejaculatio tarda by increasing your thrusting force and speed and reducing the frequency of encounters while forcibly blotting out fantasies about other men, fantasies that can too soon become so intrusive that they turn unexciting. Relax using stress reduction/removal methods, such as specific breathing exercises to enhance calm and reduce anticipatory anxious brooding.

(11) Alter/correct maladaptive (particularly depressive) cognitions that lead to self-defeating behaviors in turn associated with overt sexual inhibitions. Examples of such cognitions include "I am a bad person; I am a homosexual; therefore, my homosexuality is bad" or "Homosexuality is bad; I am a homosexual; therefore, I am a bad person"; or "No orgasm = no life," leading you to view each and every sexual encounter as the sole test of whether you are or are not a full man who will or will not be punished, rejected, and exiled because of your latest, believed to be your faultiest, performance.

(12) Overcome an excessively perfectionistic mindset that encourages too high expectations of what constitutes adequate acceptable sexual performance on the part of all concerned. That can lead only to easy disappointment in yourself and others and on to ready retreat due to enhanced self-spectatoring, creating further fear of inadequacy. If you focus overly much on whether sex will work and what will happen in the future if it doesn't, you will become less able to just enjoy what you are doing in the present.

(13) Grow up in the sense of suppressing early memories that creep into your bedroom to affect your performance. Perhaps your parents did traumatize you many years ago, but today they are, hopefully at least, no longer around to do so, at least while you are having sex.

(14) Improve any unfavorable, sexually negative surroundings that may be holding you back. For example, if you have a curious prying roommate, soundproof your bedroom, get a new roommate, or live by yourself.

(15) Do what you can to improve your appearance and manners. Become more attractive and appealing as you avoid doing what makes you less so. Don't assume that now that you have connected and are partnered, you don't have to keep yourself up and stay that way.

(16) After speaking to your doctor, consider using available medical "magic bullets," such as drugs that treat erectile dysfunction, anti-depressants that retard ejaculation, and, if acceptable to you, sexual aids from a pleasure chest store to enhance your and his sexual pleasure.

(17) Treat any ongoing sexual compulsivity. Sexual compulsivity, like many other anxiety-driven and anxiety-reducing behaviors, tends to remit spontaneously with increasing age or at least to become less intense and preoccupying. But don't wait. Instead, right now embrace a helpful mindset consisting of self-control, even when that stifles some self-affirmation, and self-discipline, even when that stifles some self-expression—in both cases even though or especially when anxiety builds as a result. Try to achieve a measure of inner peace and quiet by savoring the ordinary, nonsexual enjoyments of life as the inherently valid supplementary equivalent experiences to good sex that they can be. As one of my patients put it, "One of the most pleasurable experiences I had in my life was going to a plant store with my partner to buy gloves for transplanting cacti. Didn't beat sex with him, but it came close." Especially, make your work in addition to your sex a source of deep personal satisfaction.

(18) Pick friends who put the right kind of peer pressure on you. Especially helpful are friends willing to tell you constructive truths. One such important truth is that the more you demand out of life, the more disappointed you can become, so at some point, you may get more by expecting less. Another important truth is that all of life contains vagaries, disappointments, and narcissistic injuries so that you should be prepared to respond with equanimity, not retreat, to as many as possible that come your way.

My best friends told me something I never forgot: try not to react to each new birthday by upping your required daily dose of fountain-of-youth sexual conquests or to each rejection by having to immediately find new, more accepting substitutes for what you believe you just lost.

ABSTINENCE

Speaking teleologically, because sex is meant to be irresistible to ensure procreation, abstinence, though possible for short periods of time, will likely over the long run be sustainable only by individuals with a Spartan bent associated with an enhanced capacity for masochistically driven self-abnegation. For many people, abstinence is just too painful and draining to last, and suppressing something so emotionally satisfying and physically unstoppable as sex takes and wastes a lot of energy whose constant output is needed to ensure that the resistance will be both unyielding and unending.

The *Wall Street Journal* writes about a *form of therapy* intended to help gays reject their same-sex attractions in favor of abstinence through living in accordance with their faith.[18] Some find that such an approach works for them, but for other individuals, such as those whose faith itself begins to be symptomatic (e.g., representing guilty scrupulously), the abstinence presents less a pathway to health than a manifestation of extant illness consisting of an unhealthy tendency toward self-abnegation/punishment for having in some way transgressed. I strongly believe that homosexuality is an alternate sexual orientation that requires self-expression, not a bad habit that requires self-suppression—as if it were an addiction that could and should, like any other, be renounced. To me, this "self-control" cure can uncomfortably resemble cleansing through fasting, purging, or going on a bread-and-water diet. When this is the case, the faith-based cure for homosexuality can be profitably viewed as the spiritual equivalent of bulimic vomiting up a prior feast or obsessive disavowal (undoing) of one's forbidden pleasures—as if one is performing 100 genuflections a day in order to cancel out some presumed and generally imaginary wrongs/evil deeds done.

GAY LOVE

The very concept of gay love tends to elicit skepticism and cynicism especially in those inclined to be homophobic. Many acknowledge only gay love's sexual side. As they see it, gay love is nothing but the infatuation of physical attraction, and that rapidly vaporizes as looks fade and familiarity breeds contempt. Many such individuals view gay love as an "erotic neurosis" as they align it with an emotional disorder that is akin to obsessive brooding, hysterical theatrics, borderline overvaluation followed by devaluation of the partner, and/or psychopathic opportunistic manipulativeness meant to attain one's nefarious nonsexual and sexual ends. As an example of the latter, a foreign-born man becomes the "loving partner" of an American citizen to get his "partner" to pay for an immigration lawyer to represent him in his application for citizenship. Only after he gets his green card he leaves for the green of greener pastures.

It is incorrect, as a number of observers do, to cite the "erotic neurosis" concept to point to how gay love is merely a reprocessing of the past with someone in the present. I loved a man with a limp. My analyst said it was to reprocess and ultimately integrate the trauma of being victimized by my father's hypochondriacal worries about my getting polio. (My father actually dressed me in polio shoes because now, fait accompli, he no longer had to worry about what *might* happen.) In my analyst's view, my love was more like an adoption, based on an identification with my lover, a way to allow me, this time around, to treat myself, as my own child, better than my father treated me. She overlooked a few things, such as that he was physically stupendous and made a great identification figure not because he was my mother but because he was the musician I always secretly wanted to be.

What is important is for you to remain nonneurotic in whom you choose to love. Certainly avoid masochism to the point of rigidly and self-destructively falling in love with the same problematic lover over and over again. I went through a phase of making one less-than-elevating (actually sleazy) choice after another. Not working very well was one relationship with a bathhouse attendant already partnered (generally several times on any given night) and another with a rotating nurse, one of whose rotations was between me—and someone both younger and better looking.

FOR THOSE WHO ARE PARENTS

Parents have a job to do: to do what they can to prevent sexual problems occurring and persisting in their sons. They can accomplish a great deal here by not looking through their son's peephole either figuratively or literally, being so intrusive that they set their sons off on a journey characterized not by having fun and giving others pleasure but by avoiding displeasing and shocking mother and father.

And if you have a son hanging around the house with little or no motivation to go forth and make his own gay family, stop complaining about his being gay and start strongly urging him to cut the cord, move on, and develop his outside gay relationships and life: not only for his own good but also for yours.

FIVE

The Paraphilias

NORMAL VERSUS PARAPHILIAC

Gay men, concerned that they might not be normal, ask me if what they do sexually is abnormal, and, if so, are they just slightly out of the gay mainstream, are they overtly troubled, or are they actually "sexually perverted"? They then want to know if they should change—for practical reasons—because they are hurting someone or because they could be getting more pleasure out of sex and life. And they ask whether, if they do need to change, they can do so by a simple act of will or whether they must enter therapy to get better/do things differently?

In response, I provide some guidelines, although I do so in recognition that they are necessarily imperfect. For first, when it comes to gay sex, there are so few holds barred that in a gay context it becomes especially difficult to know when one crosses the line from "normal" to "paraphiliac." Second, my research in this area is unsatisfactory because much of the formal literature on the subject fails to make a clear distinction between homosexual and heterosexual paraphilias and is often derived from men confined as criminals. Third, political correctness always introduces scientific bias in the form of reluctance to call any paraphilia in gay men, other than pedophilia, exactly what it is—lest that become the basis for further stigmatization of an already marginalized group so that the literature and the therapists with whom I have consulted frequently use creative but simplistic alternative lifestyle self-realization-heavy rationalizations to spin paraphiliac sex in the direction of normalcy. Those concerned might, for example, label exhibitionistic sex in semipublic places like the backrooms of bars or in fully public places like a street in New York City at 5:30 in the morning before the neighborhood gets really crowded not as "exhibitionism" but as "self-affirmation" or view nonconsensual sadomasochism not as an example of paraphiliac sex but as an exemplary instance of laudatory self-expression. The PDM Task Force, hedging, says the following: "It becomes easy to pathologize behavior that may simply be idiosyncratic [overlooking] subjective factors, meanings, and contexts of variant sexualities [without considering the important parameters of] drivenness, rigidity of sexual pattern, and inability to feel sexual satisfaction via any other route. [But] some expressions of sexuality may be reasonably considered disorders."[1]

It is true that compassionate spin like this spares men who have already been sufficiently stigmatized from further marginalization. But it is equally true that laudatory sensitivity can make for shaky science, possibly leading to inadequate treatment when sexuality, even that which occurs in a gay context, is pathological and as such requires not spin but proper diagnosis and the institution of causally based therapy.

Here, without implying precision, full accuracy, or scientific finality, are my own practice guidelines based on my professional experiences and personal contacts over the years with gay men who might be paraphiliacs. These guidelines, though imperfect, reflect the most accurate theoretical formulations I know and incorporate the best therapeutic recommendations I believe to be currently available.

DEFINITION OF PARAPHILIA

As a gay man, you suffer from a paraphilia if you constantly want and require unusual, extreme, or dangerous sexual stimulation and/or your primary/exclusive/frequently sought pattern of sexual gratification is through an act and/or your primary/exclusive/frequently sought pattern of sexual arousal is with an object that deviates from an informal norm established within certain circles in the gay community itself: creative foreplay culminating in mutual masturbation and/or oral/anal sex with one (and, stretching the concept of normality somewhat, possibly two) consenting adult, where no serious harm is done to self or others; where in having sex you seek primarily to get and give pleasure and only secondarily, if at all, seek to reduce anxiety and depression and enhance low self-esteem; and where overall your general mental state is healthy because you are mostly free from serious relevant emotional difficulties and thus without significant relevant psychopathology.

CLASSIFICATION

To differentiate among disorders within the paraphiliac spectrum, *psychodynamically oriented* therapists classify the paraphilias *developmentally* according to *developmental tags*. They postulate fixation points, typically "primitive oral, anal, or phallic fixations," then go on to understand the clinical picture as the result of regression to these various fixations points and categorize the different clinical patterns accordingly. Thus, a gay man had a clearly *anal* paraphilia: he constructed a special toilet (adding a translucent divider between user and observer and putting the entire apparatus up on a platform so that he as observer could look up into it) that allowed him to watch a cohort—in the act of defecating.

They further classify the paraphilias according to the *degree of egosyntonicity* (self-comfort/acceptance) as revealed in the patient's answer to the question, "Does what you do bother you?" In addition, they consider *dangerousness* to self and others as well as the nature and severity of any *associated personality disorder* in the recognition that the likes of an associated sadomasochism or histrionic exhibitionism tends to reinforce the primary paraphiliac psychopathology. Also counting are the *quality* of the paraphiliac's general *interpersonal relationships*—whether these relationships are essentially normal or whether the individual has difficulty forming close ties with others. Also, they consider the degree of *encapsulation* of the paraphiliac fantasies and behavior: whether the paraphilia appears only during sexual activity or spreads to contaminate the full personality, as when a man is sadistic both sexually and personally. Thus, a sadomasochistic patient was a fist f——er who suffered from fecal incontinence due to a patent anus that resulted from sphincter damage; was simultaneously a heavy drug user; kept an attack dog he would sic on others, including once on me; and ultimately killed his lover by setting him on fire for his mere four-figure life insurance policy. This man markedly contrasted with other gay men whose paraphilia did not affect either them or others personally because they managed to contain it and keep it from doing harm to themselves and others to the point that most people would never have guessed that these individuals were paraphiliac.

Significant variations can occur within one established diagnostic entity. For example, some transsexuals are socially well adjusted, while others are social misfits, being seriously interpersonally disturbed because of the presence of associated psychopathology. (Being a transsexual neither enables nor protects one from being, to cite just two examples, histrionic or psychopathic.) Many transsexuals lead quiet, healthy lives either alone or coupled. But others are more like the following individual:

> *A disproportionately tall and lanky male-to-female (MTF) transsex-*
> *ual in a neighboring state calls herself a lawyer but actually makes*
> *her living giving release massages. She doesn't pay her rent but uses*
> *the money to keep up her drug habit. Yet she cannot be evicted by her*
> *desperate landlord because, as he complains, "as a member of a*
> *minority group, the judiciary protects her." The electric company*
> *turns off her electricity because she doesn't pay the bill. So to get*
> *money, she sells the landlord's kitchen appliances for a paltry sum*
> *and tampers with the lines to get free power. She also disrupts the*
> *entire neighborhood by playing loud music in the early hours of the*
> *night only to tell the neighbors when they complain, "Tough, suck it*
> *up, this is a musical town, and I am a musical person." And she fights*
> *constantly and noisily with men she brings up to her place in the*
> *middle of the night. When one of her landlords spoke to her to ask*
> *her to set limits on her antisocial behavior, in reply, she hit him with*
> *her fist, then bit him so severely that he had to have 12 stitches.*

Some paraphiliacs are neither troubled themselves nor trouble others and so according to that criterion alone do not suffer from an emotional disorder. I find it useful to classify other paraphiliacs (those where some-one does suffer) into hot red pepper, garlic, and onion paraphiliacs, depending on the specific interpersonal implications and consequences of their paraphilia.

- *Hot red pepper* paraphiliacs figuratively upset only their own stomachs while other people in their lives escape distress. Therefore, these individuals are generally healthier on an interpersonal level than garlic disorder paraphiliacs.
- *Garlic* disorder paraphiliacs figuratively trouble others through "bad breath" while they themselves escape the suffering of "emotional dyspepsia."
- *Onion* disorder paraphiliacs figuratively trouble both others and themselves so that not only do they suffer but so do those around them from the "interpersonal bad breath" that accompanies their "personal dyspepsia."

As examples, while compulsive onanism, or urolagnia (water sports), are hot red pepper disorders, interfering if at all only with one's own functioning and pleasure, sadism without masochism is a garlic disorder, and sadomasochism is an onion disorder that hurts others as it simultaneously affects the individual's personal well-being and happiness. The friction queen's private behavior leads at most to incomplete sexual gratification and possibly unfulfilling relationships, but no one otherwise gets hurt. So it merits a separate classificatory niche from pedophilia, which can destroy the lives of all it touches, often ultimately including the pedophile's own.

Making determinations like these involves developing a sense of how others respond to the paraphilia. Do they see it as an asset, as a mere annoyance, or as offensively intrusive or dangerous to them or to society as a whole? Thus, most people react to transvestic fetishists who entertain others without harming anyone as if they are merely a source of amusement simply parading themselves to seek approval. As such, they see them either as an asset to society, as just there, or, at most, as merely a minor social annoyance. In contrast, most people see exhibitionists who have sex in backrooms as merely having a good if tasteless time—unless and until they become intrusive by having sex on the beach in front of waterfront vacation homes, posing a danger to children who might be watching. And while most people see sadists as being on a continuum from merely playful to scary to hurtful, they routinely see pedophiles as always harmful to all concerned—both to their individual victims and to society at large.

Unfortunately, the parameter of "how others react" is very difficult to standardize, for we need to correct for personal prejudice and alter our determinations on the basis of ever-shifting social norms.

A complicating consideration is that social approval *enables* paraphilias, thus enhancing the paraphiliac's comfort and so reducing his need to seek help. Knowing that there are numerous shops on Christopher Street in Greenwich Village in New York City that specialize in fetishistic toys and sadomasochistic paraphernalia ameliorates a paraphiliac's guilt through social consensual validation. Naturally, as social attitudes change/evolve, society can enhance or entirely withdraw its validation. This is the situation that pertained with a one-time bar in New York City where the entertainment consisted of a display of fist f——ing onstage and an active backroom at the rear of the bar. The newspapers wrote the place up, and it became part of the downtown "straight" scene. When a transvestic fetishist dentist died in the 1950s, his relatives rushed to his apartment to clean the drag out of his closet to spare the family public, humiliation. Today, few would care enough to think of making the trip or to even bother calling him a "transvestic fetishist." Two decades ago, one lawyer settling the estate of a gay man was horrified to discover a shoebox full of pornography hidden at the back of his closet. Then, the gay man would have been diagnosed as a voyeur or worse; today, the box would be trashed or its contents divided among friends, relatives, ex-lovers, and any interested passersby. However, pedophiles are never acceptable on any level—for they always scar their victims emotionally and/or physically. Therefore, few in society condone pedophilia—though there still is disagreement as to how exactly to respond therapeutically. For some, treating it as a disease and advocating psychotherapy makes sense, while for others treating it as a criminal act and advocating incarceration, castration, and even execution is indicated.

The importance of classification is that to some extent it determines prognosis. In large measure, prognosis is dependent on ego-syntonicity: the degree to which a given paraphilia by troubling the individual propels him to seek help. Pedophiles plagued by ego-dystonic forbidden temptations that they feel helpless to control are more likely to seek and benefit from assistance than those who like loving young boys and, unrepentant, sophistically defend their actions, citing anecdotes about how sex doesn't actually hurt children, backed up with tales of the normalcy of childhood masturbation and how pedophilia was socially accepted in ancient Greece.

Some paraphiliac behaviors seem to occur exclusively in gay men and are virtually unknown in straight men, straight women, or lesbians. I have never heard of a straight man fisting a woman or lesbian orgies in the ladies' room. At least according to legend, straight exhibitionists routinely flash in public places, while gay men "flash" mostly in the privacy of dimly lit backrooms in bars. Yet other paraphiliac behaviors are remarkably similar in gays and straights and, on occasion, lesbians. For example, all concerned who want to dominate others might whip or handcuff their partners in essentially the same way and for essentially the same reasons. There is very little difference between the gay exhibitionist/voyeur who, attempting to involve/impress the crowd, sits on a leather sling under a spotlight in the center of the basement of a bar in New York City and performs and has various sexual acts performed on him while the crowd watches and joins in, hoping to find just the right attachment point, and the straight exhibitionist/voyeur who does exactly the same thing with his or her partner(s)—in the same building but at the club right next door.

CAUSE

Psychodynamically oriented therapists connect specific developmental/dynamic patterns with subsequent specific paraphiliac occurrence. They might connect early sexual abuse of the child with later *sadomasochism* involving the compulsion to repeat the early abuse; maternal distancing with *exhibitionism* where the adult's goal is to gain a mother substitute's attention and recognition; early thwarted dependency needs with adult *pedophilia* involving, as that supposedly does, an identification with the boy victim, loving him as one might want oneself to be loved; and oedipal castration anxiety with adult *fetishism* where the fetish is a phallic symbol that acts as a kind of reassuring performance-enhancing sexual prosthesis.

Object-relations theorists emphasize the interpersonal value and function of a paraphilia. For example, they view a clothing fetish as a (troublesome) attraction to a part object, the piece of clothing representing an anxiety-free substitute for a threatening, forbidding whole object—the person who wears the clothing.

Behavioral theorists, emphasizing learned patterns, view paraphilias as pleasure-seeking behaviors in the here and now that repeat an early, still-viable behavioral link forged between infantile sexual fantasy and masturbatory gratification.

I believe that in any given instance of paraphilia, some or all of these psychodynamics apply. But there are also other significant causative factors as yet unidentified, requiring ongoing research.

THE SPECIFIC PARAPHILIAS

The following is a clinical description of the paraphilias to help you as a gay man determine if you suffer from one and so might want or need help. You should *always* seek help if you find yourself seriously hurting others or uncontrollably attracted to children/minors.

I divide the paraphilias into two groups as follows.

Group I Paraphilias

Group I paraphilias, being reflected in ordinary foreplay, therefore occur as part of the normal sexuality of gay men, giving pleasure without doing harm. In this category, I include some types of exhibitionism, some forms of fetishism, frotteurism in private, and certain examples of sadomasochism.

Exhibitionism

Exhibitionism (often associated with voyeurism) may be an occasional, opportunistic, and immature behavior, as when a teenager gets drunk and flashes or moons an anonymous audience. Or it may be compulsive and either an end in itself or a requisite prelude to masturbation or oral or anal sex to orgasm, adding the gratification of watching and being watched to the orgasmic pleasure. Most gay men who exhibit themselves do so in private places, such as in the context of threesomes, or in places set aside as private enclaves for those purposes, such as meat racks on Fire Island and the bushes at the rear outdoor places of gay bars. A few exhibit themselves in semipublic places not specifically designated for sex, as they masturbate, perhaps to orgasm, in the urinals in men's rooms or at rest stops on the highway, sometimes enticing others to watch/join in. Only a few exhibit themselves in fully public places where sexual display is entirely inappropriate/ constitutes criminality, such as in subway cars or on public streets.

Dynamically speaking, in paraphiliac exhibitionism, early unresolved conflicts and never-relinquished old—though no longer entirely appropriate—pleasurable relationships/activities linger now to alter present-day functionality. Some gay men expose themselves shamelessly in the here and now to deny how ashamed they were long ago when caught "with their pants down," effectively repeating this traumatic scenario in an attempt at final mastery. Such was the case for the gay man who exhibited himself freely now to deal with how humiliated he felt long ago when his mother bathed him well into puberty and caught him masturbating while he was observing her and his father having sex.

Also dynamically speaking, exhibitionistic behavior reduces anxiety and guilt by substituting permitted gratifying foreplay for forbidden guilt-ridden, full sex to orgasm. In addition, exhibitionists are often individuals with low self-esteem aching to turn uncaring, disapproving, critical people around to loving them by showing them something they will hopefully admire.

Fetishism

According to the American Psychiatric Association, fetishism involves the need to use an inanimate object (e.g., a piece of clothing) or a part object (e.g., a foot) to achieve sexual arousal, maintain potency, and reach orgasm. It should be distinguished from behaviors that merely episodically augment sexual response, such as the use of a vibrator.[2]

Some fetishistic gay men do not conceptualize and use the fetish as a significant part of their identity/self-image. They do not employ the fetishistic object primarily to alter or enhance their identity. They simply wear, hold, use, or expect their partner(s) to wear, hold, or use a given object in order to enhance their own pleasure/orgasm. For them, the fetishistic object either merely supplements and enhances the sexual attractiveness of the whole object—the penis-enhancing whip or pistol—or serves as a full substitute for (as a "guilt-reducing displacement from") the whole object.

Other "fetishistic" gay men (who, according to the *Diagnostic and Statistical Manual of Mental Disorders* [4th ed.; *DSM-IV*],[3] are not true fetishists but *transvestic* fetishists), such as some leather queens and some drag queens, assume a new total image to reevoke an old and regretfully lost identity or develop a new, more desirable one. With some leather queens, the goal is to enhance their masculinity (by denying their feminine side); with some drag queens, the goal is to enhance their femininity (by denying their masculine side). Sadomasochistic fetishists often alternate between these two goals. Wearing the same outfit consisting of leather cap, jacket, pants, and boots bedecked with chains, they switch, both conceptually and physically, from tying a partner up and whipping him (being a top, for some denoting masculinity) to being tied up and whipped by him (being a bottom, for some denoting femininity.)

Frotteurism

Some frotteurists rub, usually not to orgasm, in public places against anonymous passive clothed partners. (In my experience, this behavior is rare in gay men.) Other frotteurists, known in the vernacular as "friction queens," rub at home in bed against someone they know, at least superficially, hoping to achieve orgasm. When pressured by an eager partner, they may agree to mutual masturbation but rarely if ever to full oral or anal sex.

The frotteurists I have encountered often suffered from a degree of characterological infantilism marked by selfishness characterized by thinking mainly of their own pleasure while overlooking that of their partner. Frotteurists who rub against strangers in public places certainly take without giving. Frotteurists who rub against partners in private may give a little (e.g., some semen for the partner to use as a lubricant with which to masturbate himself). But other than that, they generally do what they can to ensure that, both literally and figuratively, they will always be the ones to come first.

Sadomasochism

A degree of sadomasochism is part of the sexual behavior of a large proportion of gay (and straight) normal men. Here, consenting partners perform mildly sadomasochistic acts in the form of foreplay subsumed under mutual masturbation, oral sex, or anal sex. Examples of such foreplay include giving a hickey and play spanking. In contrast, sadomasochistic paraphiliacs go further to inflict deep emotional and/or physical wounds on a partner/victim, overwhelming, raping, torturing, or killing him. Two men in the next town invited a third man down to their dungeon/torture chamber—then refused to let him go for a few days. When he was finally released, he sued them for kidnapping—and won. Bizarre hurtful acts like fisting or overly intrusive and/or demeaning acts like water sports involving drinking urine may be part of the picture. Conscious accessible fantasies of hostile domination and abject submission are often a feature of this disorder and are typically associated with sadomasochistic personality traits/disorder characterized by sadomasochistic interpersonal relationships notable for abusiveness to an unwilling victim or to one who is a willing participant and even provocative partner. Societies of like-minded sadomasochists have been—and maybe are continuing to be formed—such as the FFA, or Fist F——ers of America, created in order to reduce guilt, however minimal; express maximal pride; and enhance or create further opportunity.

In the "what was I thinking?" category, I once agreed to a weekend on a New Jersey lake with handsome Brad, who my friends introduced me to, saying, "Once you get there watch what you smoke." I did, only I didn't watch what I ate, and he slipped a paranoid-inducing drug into my food. Enhancing my consequent paranoid reaction was his attack dog who growled at me whenever I stopped petting him; a trip across the hills in his off-road vehicle—driving in crazy fashion, almost turning over several times; and a foray out onto the early spring ice still brittle and thin enough to be ready to give way under my feet, followed by a drive back on the turnpike with what I suspect were drugs in the car posing a possible threat to my personal freedom/medical license if the police stopped us for a traffic violation. I know I escaped with my life because later I heard that this man is no longer active as a charter member of the FFA. For he is the one who was jailed for killing his partner by setting him on fire.

Group II Paraphilias

Group II paraphilias do not reflect/duplicate aspects of normal foreplay.

Pedophilia

Pedophiles show a preference for the young—boys, even children—as sexual partners. Though many observers link pedophilia with homosexuality (partly because calling gays "child molesters" and child molesters "gay" is the most hurtful/damaging thing they can think of to call anybody at all), pedophiles, unlike homosexuals, choose their sexual object in great measure not on the basis of gender but on the basis of age.

Pedophiles, unlike some other paraphiliacs (e.g., transvestic fetishists), are never simply nuisances requiring mere tolerant indifference. They are always inherently destructive to their victims and ultimately even to themselves.

As individuals, pedophiles may be either shy and passive or outgoing and aggressive. They may be distressed by or entirely comfortable with and even proud of their paraphilia. Many are members of a self-aggrandizing social club formed to recruit new members and find a steady stream of sex objects. A considerable number advocate and proselytize for their pedophilia, trying to convince others, as they have convinced themselves, that it is a good thing since they are a stabilizing, guiding influence on the child and so are "not selfish predators" but "altruistic mentors."

Dynamically speaking, pedophiles often choose children as sexual objects because they feel most comfortable with passive helpless victims, that is, with others incapable of controlling or rejecting them; because, seeking a vicarious mothering experience, they identify with their victims; because they are looking for a substitute for the child they always wanted not only to be but also to have; and because they wish to reenact their own previous traumatic emotional/physical seduction(s)/rape(s) at the hands of someone older, perhaps either their own mothers or fathers, in order to somehow master the experience. (However, that we can understand aspects of pedophilia doesn't mean that we should thereby condone/excuse it.)

The negative impact that pedophiles have on their victims and the justifiably bad reputation they get in society is not merely a random side effect of the pedophiliac process. Rather, it is also an integral part of (inherent in/causal of) the problem—a manifestation of the sadistic social defiance that in the first place motivates aspects of the pedophiliac behavior and as a consequence subsequently imparts an overall antisocial quality to the final disorder—as reflected in our responses of perturbation and disgust so that courting social disapproval and punishment is not merely a fallout from but also an actual primary goal of the behavior.

Transvestic Fetishism

The term "transvestic fetishism" refers to the practice of cross-dressing (wearing drag). The diagnosis doesn't apply when straight men dress up occasionally, as a straight man once did for Halloween wearing a frilly gown with a necklace made out of a carrot on a piece of string. Such men are just doing what not a few men do: wearing women's clothes occasionally while retaining their primary (masculine) identification throughout—merely using drag recreationally, often playfully, in order to, as Kris might say, "regress in the service of the ego."[4] The diagnosis is more applicable to those who have significant aspects of a primary feminine identity yet whose identity is not so fully chaotic that they wear drag predominantly to express outwardly and resolve inwardly severe identity conflicts that they feel inside. Most true drag queens rarely experience an actual split in their personalities (and see their mirror reflection not as a reflection of who they are but as a different person entirely). Generally, they are looking only to find a new, more desirable, enhanced version of favored aspects of a self they already avow, to clarify these, and, as such, to firm up who they already happen to be. Even when the drag queen's inner psychology changes with changes in external appearance so that a male transvestite feels more passive when in drag and more assertive when out of it and even when changing clothes not only changes how they feel about themselves but also alters how they act toward others, changing clothes rarely, as it does with transsexuals, expresses and in turn prompts the development of a full new identity. Few drag queens intend to look like and to even pass as real, ordinary women. Most intend to be mainly theatrical—to impress their audience by looking fabulously different—or to shock their audience by ridiculing social standards and goofing on the hoi polloi, going along with an exhibitionistic need to garner attention, accompanied by a masochistic need to bring ridicule down on themselves in the form of the stares—often of disbelief—that they hope/arrange to garner.

Classically, some drag queens masturbate while dressing up and looking at themselves in the mirror. Theoretically at least, they are having sex with their idealized self. Most, however, in my experience and in contradistinction to what much of the formal literature says, do not routinely couple the wearing of drag with sexual arousal. For them, dressing up is separate from their sexuality, or they dress up as a woman to actually squelch their (forbidden) sexual (manly) feelings.

Most of the drag queens I knew personally and have treated professionally functioned on a high level much of the time, using drag only occasionally and only at special times. A few, however, were isolated schizoid individuals or drag-obsessive-compulsives in the sense of being hoarders of such things as lipstick and hairnets. Some were serious substance abusers who prostituted themselves in order to feed a drug habit. In the latter group, there were individuals who made a successful career out of prostitution and others who failed at that and at most everything else to the point that drag, all they had left, became their entire life, as they fell in love with their wardrobe but nothing and no one else until mostly what remained for them consisted of their outfits and makeup kits. Sadly, in this group, suicide was not uncommon—the premature end of the line: of what was fated to be their very short trip through life.

Our specific reaction to transvestic fetishists can help diagnose any underlying emotional disorder that may be present. Thus, a schizoid drag queen fails to engage us personally; a schizotypal drag queen imparts an otherworldly feeling in us; a hypomanic or histrionic drag queen snaps us to attention and provokes amusement; a depressive drag queen calls forth our pity along the lines of "laugh, clown, laugh"; and a sadomasochistic drag queen not only figuratively but sometimes also literally forces us to duck to avoid that swinging purse. While many drag queens are without significant pathology, for some the wearing of drag itself is a direct manifestation of a larger syndrome, as when cross-dressing is a schizotypal mannerism, part of hypomanic euphoria, stands for a hysterical display, constitutes a depressive begging for affection, and/or consists of a sadistic need to shock. In such cases, dynamically speaking, the transvestic fetishism is defensive, as it reduces anxiety and enhances self-esteem by making the individual feel more like an important somebody and at least a little less like a big nobody.

A friend wrote,

> An image stays with me from a recent trip. On a barstool with his bag/life next to him was a man in his 70s I will guess, with long bright orange hair (down to his shoulders and neatly coiffed), light orange lipstick, eczema all over his skin, a man's dinner jacket but flowered, and a necktie. When he saw me he held his hand out to shake mine (I later had to find soap as I didn't know what the rash was) and he was very soft spoken. I don't wonder anymore how someone gets to that point in life. He was a caricature of loneliness in all of his creativity.

RECOMMENDATIONS

You should consider seeking treatment for paraphilia because of the following:

- You want the treatment, for whatever reason, including because your paraphilia has become so preoccupying and exclusive that you have become unable to control yourself when you want to or on reasonable command from others to do so or because you have reached the point that you experience subjective feelings of distress, are getting hurt or hurting others, or are feeling depressed about your life because you believe that an invasive paraphilia has for any reason disrupted your personal relationships and/or professional activities.

- Your paraphilia threatens to get you into—or has actually gotten you into—trouble with the law.
- You are an active pedophile and therefore need to stop making excuses for yourself and your paraphilia, turn yourself in, and seek help immediately.

Unfortunately, paraphilias are difficult to treat and so have a guarded prognosis for several reasons. Many paraphiliacs do not want to be treated. If they seek therapy, it is because they are forced to go, and if they stick with treatment, they do so only reluctantly. They find paraphiliac sex to be irresistible because it is powerfully desirable and pleasurable—so much so that they are less motivated to change than they might be if they suffered from a bothersome emotional problem, such as an incapacitating phobia. So, not desiring to change, they tell the therapist what they think he or she wants to hear in order that they can be left alone to continue to get sex as usual or, when applicable, so that they can receive a lighter sentence or get out of jail sooner, the latter, not unexpectedly, in large measure so that they can be once again free to seek new sexual contacts.

Productive therapeutic discussion is difficult even for those paraphiliacs who want therapy in order to change, for few have access to the fantasies that underlie the disorder. They either repress them out of shame and guilt or act them out instead of thinking about them/thinking them through. And even when insight appears to be good and psychodynamically oriented therapy seems to be working, it rarely effects actual change. Thus, a gay masochist who could best reach orgasm when he was wearing handcuffs learned through insight-oriented therapy that the handcuffs kept his hostility in check, allowing him to yield to, without hurting, others; that being cuffed helped him atone for his past misdeeds; and that being held down permitted the free expression of his sexual desires because, tied down, he was able to convince himself that he was expressing them involuntarily "since the situation is now entirely out of my hands." And a pedophile learned that he liked thin and hairless bodies because they were too "unmanly" to be threatening and came to understand that having identified with the children he raped, he was succoring them precisely the way he wished to be cared for himself. However, neither man was able to use this insight to change in any significant respect. Each could remain abstinent for short periods of time by an act of will, but in each case their insight, even though genuine, had no significant effect on their underlying sexual urges so that their disorder persisted and did so essentially unchanged.

Cognitive-behavioral methods are unfortunately often less successful here than in the treatment of other disorders, such as social phobia. This too is in large measure because the therapist is asking the patient to think through and relinquish not an unwelcome symptom, such as a phobia, but a cherished behavior.

Approaches reliant on peer pressure from other paraphiliacs whose disorder has improved or is in remission might be tried as offering some hope. Pharmacotherapy, if at all effective, owes its (usually superficial) effect mostly to its general sedative qualities. In the severest cases, some clinicians and politicians still put chemical or physical castration forward as a therapeutic option.

PARAPHILIA NOT OTHERWISE SPECIFIED: THE GROUP OF GENDER IDENTITY DISORDERS

Gender Identity Disorder

Gender identity disorder (GID), as defined in the *DSM-IV*, is "a broad . . . designation *inclusive* [emphasis added] of transsexualism [as well as of] gender identity disorder of childhood, and gender identity disorder of adolescence or adulthood, non-transsexual type."[5]

GID often starts in childhood. It can persist in its original form into "late adolescence or adulthood,"[6] thus representing "the onset of a lifelong condition,"[7] or it can represent either "a phase of homosexual development"[8] or a phase of development into becoming transgendered and perhaps desiring and seeking sex reassignment surgery (SRS).

Boys/men suffering from a GID are uncomfortable with their assigned (anatomic) sex. Historically, there may have been a strong preference for playing with girls, a tendency to avoid competitive and contact sports, and at times a degree or a high degree of effeminacy. Some sufferers believe that it is not as if but rather an actual fact that they have been "born [into] the wrong sex" and so do not live in the right body, have the "typical feelings and reactions of the other sex," "desire to live and be treated as the other sex," and frequently actually attempt to "pass . . . as the other sex."[9] There may be "a preoccupation with getting rid of primary and secondary sex characteristics," including possible "request[s] for hormones, surgery or other procedures to physically alter"[10] their masculine sexual characteristics. And, (rarely) finding their "penis or testes . . . disgusting,"[11] they "want to remove them [perhaps because they] wish to have . . . a vagina,"[12] with genital self-mutilation a possible result.

Some but not all sufferers from GID that persists into adulthood are as adults interpersonally well related. Others are, however, mostly withdrawn and even antagonistic to strangers, friends, and family. The latter pattern is particularly prominent when depression coexists and enhances a susceptibility to substance abuse and addiction as well as to suicidality, all of which are common—especially in those cases where parents and society disapprove of, marginalize, and even ostracize the individual.

Causatively speaking, GID can be a biological condition, the result of "prenatal hormonal or genetic influences," or a psychological condition, the result of "postnatal psychosocial conditions."[13] In the latter case, the etiology may be the male transsexual's failure to "separate from the mother" along with having an "absent, distant, or even rejecting father"[14] that makes (masculine) identification unlikely because the individual believes it to be undesirable.

Transsexualism

Transsexualism is generally considered to be an especially severe form/outcome of GID. There are two types of transsexualism:

- *Primary*, or ego-syntonic, transsexualism, that is, transsexualism that doesn't conflict with one's belief system and therefore does not provoke anxiety. This often develops "directly from GID of childhood" and therefore has "an early age of onset (age 5 to 6)" and additionally is associated with a "low [level of] sexual activity, lack of sexual arousal when crossdressing, and generally a genetic-same-sex sexual orientation."[15]

- *Secondary*, or ego-dystonic, transsexualism, that is, transsexualism that is not ego-syntonic and therefore does conflict with one's belief system. This process starts when "individuals are older. [They] may have had sexual relationship and marriages with members of the opposite biological sex, and [they often] report at lease a phase during which crossdressing was sexually arousing."[16] Also, "sexual preference has more variability than in the primary group."[17] Typically, the secondary type is characterized by attempts to suppress cross-gender feelings and wishes, doing so by using a variety of defenses such as denial, isolation, dissociation, and acting out as well as substance abuse employed both to "suppress the cross-gender feelings and wishes [and to assist in adopting] appropriate gender roles [through inducing the loss of earlier memories]."[18] But the suppressed cross-gender feelings commonly reemerge, generally initially involving *transvestic fetishism* character-ized by cross-gender behavior that reduces anxiety and induces a state of calm. Next the individual begins to seek electrolysis to "remove body hair and begin[s] female nail care [e.g., uses nail polish], 'and disappears for short or long periods of time to be able to' fully cross-dress."[19] Some try genital self-mutilation, which often involves qualities of a compul-sion growing out of the tormenting obsession that they "have been born as the wrong sex."

The many possible interwoven (conjunctive or disjunctive/additive or conflicting) relationships among sexual orientation (straight, gay, or bi), gender identity (male/female), and gender role (man/woman) make the designations homosexual, heterosexual, and bisexual difficult to apply to these individuals. Thus, a homosexual male might want SRS in order to either be able to adequately function as a heterosexual woman or have a lesbian relationship with a female partner. Therefore, to avoid (pejorative) labeling, it is best to subtype transgenderism according to the individual's attraction to males, females, both, or neither—for example, "this MTF transsexual is attracted to males." Most transsexual individuals though "sexually attracted to their own genetic sex" (commonly a MTF transsex-ual is attracted to men) "wish to be desired as, and thus validated as belonging to, a gender they now externally possess."[20] Thus, typically the MTF wishes or demands to be known as a female. Resonating with "partners [who mostly] view physical and psychological gender as one,"[21] MTF transsexual individuals who are attracted to men soon reach the conclusion that they are not homosexuals but heterosexuals. To quote one such secondary MTF transsexual, "I am all woman." She had four daughters when she was married. Now she views herself as a straight woman and additionally as a "single mother."

It can be difficult to determine if a given transsexual is delusional. Some may be in the sense that they develop and retain the belief that they *are* a member of the other gender. Others are less delusional in the sense that they retain better reality testing, for they speak mainly "as if"; thus, it is "merely" "as if" they are a woman inside, and it is that woman inside that needs to come out.

Partial expressions of transsexualism exist, consisting of interim phases somewhere on a continuum from gender dysphoria to full transsexualism. In turn, these may or may not be transitional in the sense of going on to develop into full transsexualism. These include the following:

- Gynemimesis: where a male "presents to society as a female, may take hormones, and may sexually prefer other males but does not seek SRS."[22]
- She-male: when "a biologic male . . . maintains a hermaphroditic presentation for erotic purposes and may have received vaginoplasty without penectomy and/or orchiectomy."[23]
- Autogynephilia: where the individual is "erotically aroused by the fantasy of having a female body or by obtaining female secondary sex characteristics"[24] without any real desire to change sex. A man in our town known familiarly as "Mr. Tits" and "Mr. Boobs" says that "I don't want to be a woman; all I want is a nice set of breasts."

Associated Issues

Sometimes—but hardly always—"marked feminine mannerisms and speech patterns[25] are associated with GID." Psychopathological somatic states can occur involving an intense focus on and discomfort with selected body parts (other than breasts and genitalia) that the individual views as defective and deformed, and a susceptibility to/actual substance abuse and addiction due to inner conflict and external criticism/approbation can exist. Many transsexuals get depressed when they are ridiculed by insensitive people around them. To illustrate, when a transsexual in our area walks into the town's coffee shop, she finds herself greeted with sotto voce hoots commenting on how "she is over six feet tall, has large masculine hands, and has feet that are too big to be squeezed into those little unconvincingly feminine high-heeled shoes."

Too many of the transsexuals with whom I have had personal and professional contact are struggling in life. Unable to pay their bills because they have difficulty finding employment out of the sex trade or in the (always-difficult-to-find-a-job-in) entertainment industry, they are continually threatened by financial problems (e.g., worried about having their electricity turned off or about being evicted from their apartments). As a result, without being innately psychopathic, they may nevertheless turn to individual psychopathic acts just in order to survive.

In the realm of object relations, transsexuals relate to others in a variable fashion. Some settle down into a committed relationship. Others instead rely on pickups in bars for their social contacts as they attempt to seduce a parade of different men in bars whom they convince to buy them drinks/have sex with them. (Sometimes these men want to have sex purely out of curiosity, but at other times they find transsexuals attractive in their own very special, unique way.) Too frequently, such "companions" use them and then leave them, never to be heard from again. After a while, the transsexual then begins to withdraw, starts to show some interpersonal antagonisms, and can even become suicidal out of desperate loneliness.

Prognosis

For males, an "attraction to females and a more masculine body appearance"[26] predict a poor outcome.

Treatment

Suggested treatments range from psychotherapy to reverse the process before undergoing SRS to SRS itself. Electrolysis and breast augmentation without SRS is a limited goal for some men. "Hormonal sex reassignment should precede surgical reassignment," partly because it is at least thought that hormones regularly "produce greater stability."[27]

Contraindications to treatment include discomfort in the therapist "in recommending reassignment," active major psychiatric illness, "active drug or alcohol abuse, history of mutilation or multiple suicide attempts, ambivalence and confusion regarding subjective gender on the part of the patient, and incomplete or unsuccessful legal and social integration as the new gender."[28] Psychotherapy can help those who will not or cannot change over "achieve compromises and alternate routes of gender expression."[29] It can also help strengthen defenses against stresses that can subsequently intensify gender dysphoria.[30] Psychosocial services can help the transsexual deal with "homelessness, prostitution, drug and alcohol addiction, poverty and AIDS"[31] as well as with reduced family and social support.

The medical profession is divided on whether SRS is a viable form of treatment. Some consider it mutilating, others lifesaving. Does SRS make for better or worse social adjustment? A wise conclusion is that "the most direct indication that SRS is a successful treatment would be the absence of gender dysphoria after surgery, and that apparently is the usual outcome."[32]

There are support groups for gender-dysphoric people, such as the Harry Benjamin International Gender Dysphoria Association, founded to develop standards of care to guide both patient and caregiver regarding the steps along the road of transition.

SIX

Identity/Disorders of Identity

IDENTITY

Gay or straight, everyone has three identities: sexual identity, gender identity, and nonsexual identity. The term "sexual identity" defines one's preferred self-concept and behavior as heterosexual, homosexual, bisexual, or asexual. The term "gender identity" refers to one's inner sense of oneself as being male, female, or androgynous. I treated a male-to-female transsexual who had three children when she lived as a married man. Now divorced and completely disavowing her former status as "that married guy," she currently views herself as "a single mother." The term "nonsexual identity" concerns one's sense of self as it relates to nongender-oriented, nonerotic ideals, actions, and pursuits; for example, "It may not surprise you to learn that as a gay man, I am politically on the left, not on the right, not an establishment conservative but, as you might expect, a full-blooded liberal, and, at the gym, when it comes to my music, I am resolutely an avowed lover of seventies disco."

Complex, often paradoxical interrelationships exist between the three (sexual, gender, and nonsexual) identities. The male-to-female transsexual who believes that she is "all woman" (gender identity) may be sexually attracted either to women ("I am a lesbian") or to men ("I am a heterosexual"), thus establishing her sexual identity. (My patient was attracted to men.) Though seeing herself as all woman (gender identity), my patient prided herself on having a stereotypical "masculine interest in sports," not a "feminine interest in designing clothes" (her own distinction); pursued "masculine physical activities requiring brute force," not "feminine intellectual activities requiring little to no brute strength" (my patient injured her arm "acting butch by playing softball"); and displayed stereotypical so-called gender-related masculine personality traits, such as "masculine aggressivity," as well as stereotypical so-called gender-related feminine personality traits, such as "feminine passivity." (My patient, "compromising," presented with a little of both, displaying, as she herself suggested," feminine ways" but ones, again as she herself said, that served a "masculine, assertive, purpose.")

Any of the three identities may be *primary* (basic) or *secondary* (defensive/reactive). A *primary* identity consists of who and what you fundamentally believe yourself to be and relates to what you truly want for yourself in and out of life; for example, "I am comfortable as a homosexual man, and most of all in life, I want to meet a suitable husband and be a wonderful mate to him." A *secondary* identity is one that is defensive like a protective shield (and at times like an assaultive sword), as when a feminine identity defends against being successful, something a man may need to do because he views being successful as unacceptable and forbidden since he believes that it equates to being aggressive, and to him being aggressive means becoming like his frighteningly hostile, hurtfully devaluing father. One leather queen's outfit narrated his *primary* entrenched, masculine identity, while another leather queen's outfit, although almost exactly the same on superficial inspection, instead narrated his (imperfect) *secondary* attempt to suppress anything he thought to be feminine about him, for he saw the slightest degree of femininity as being entirely unacceptable and so became a leather "queen" to actuate what he really wanted to be: a leather "king."

IDENTITY CONFLICT/CRISES/DISORDER

Few gay men feel sufficiently comfortable in their skins to achieve a consistent gay identity: always and fully accepting their being gay and routinely approving of and consequently enjoying everything they are and do over their entire life span. Rather, mildly uneven and shifting identities are very common if not the rule. Sometimes these reflect changing preferences, while at other times they reflect the presence of identity conflict. For example, in college, I avoided the gym because I perceived gymnastics to be an activity that was too straight for my taste, and I accomplished my end by exaggerating the symptoms of an actual—although in fact minor—medical illness. Today, in a complete turnaround, I lift weights to avoid being too femme for my taste (while simultaneously hoping to forestall the development of symptoms of a major medical illness). Identities do—and even should—morph over time with new experiences and personal growth. They should also keep pace with generational shifts as to what is "in" and what is "out." Thus, effeminate flamboyance has virtually disappeared from the gay scene, at least as I know it, and these days nobody, like they used to, thinks it's clever, apt, or acceptable to call someone a "ribbon queen."

However, gay men can have *severe* identity conflicts and go on to experience *identity crises*. These gay men suffer from episodic anxiety about who and what they are and who and what they want to and should be. They go through one or more phases where they have serious difficulty accepting being gay and despair about their sexuality's implications for their present and future lives. At such times, gay guilt and shame can prevail and worry take over, as it did in one of my patients who went through periods of crisis where he feared that as a gay man he would always live with uncaring, hostile people in an oppressive straight world, making it difficult to impossible for him to truly gratify any of his deep personal needs. Identity crises can be seriously disabling if gay men either don't know what they want or, knowing it, lose the power to get it—then, unable to make important life decisions on their own and for themselves, yield too much to pressure from peers and those they love pushing them to become something they are not. Too often that happens when they fall under the spell of a man with a pretty face and a favored sexual endowment and let him into their lives to the point that he becomes more than a crush yet no less than a guru.

A patient with identity crises had difficulty building a fully organized, hard-edged, perfectly stable resolutely firm lifelong image of what constituted his true authentic self. He went through life not only wishing he weren't gay but also constantly regretting all recent sexual escapades, most nights thinking, "Sexual freedom is right for me and promiscuity is my anthem," but in the new light of the dawn changing his mind and thinking, "Quietude is right for me, and promiscuity is my anathema." Not only was he unable to achieve a full permanent immutable identity with complete comfort and clarity and become fully authentic without intrusive serious self-doubts, self-questioning, painful self criticism, and hypocrisy in his actions, but at times he even seemed to prefer *remaining in conflict about his sexual identity. As he said to me, it was as if shifting identities catalyzed an inner sense of comfort and motivated him toward self-realization and true accomplishment because they gave him the opening to try fresh starts in life—where he was constantly and creatively able to reinvent himself.*

A patient looking back over his life recognized that he had philosophical (existential) conflicts throughout. Remaining uncomfortable about being gay well until middle age and beyond, he alternated between being proud and ashamed of himself for who and what he was, wanting to tell the world versus wanting to keep secrets about his true self, even for the many years after he first came out, and, especially when life wasn't going entirely well for him, flirting once again if not with going straight ("LOL!") then, at least, if only momentarily, with going back—into the closet. At times, he even convinced himself that his conflicted selves actually constituted a favored, admirable, healthy *identity because having them made him unique and even contributed to his being more effective personally and empathic professionally as a practicing psychologist than he could otherwise ever be.*

Identity disorder results when identity crises (marked by ambivalence) become fixed and chronic. Fixed chronic *sexual identity* ambivalence may take the form of bisexuality, while fixed chronic *gender identity* ambivalence can result in gender identity disorder (that can, as described in Chapter 5, develop into transvestic fetishism or transsexualism). Fixed chronic *nonsexual identity* ambivalence is common in gay men where it takes the form of work-related problems, as when a gay man, happily embracing the comfort of limits, willingly remains in a low-level position on the job because he anticipates that on-the-job discrimination will be his comeuppance and his punishment just for being gay.

RECOMMENDATIONS

Decide who and what you want to be independent of external pressures to please others whom you deem to be more knowledgeable and important than you are because of your having equated their being in authority over you with their being smarter than you. As you stick with who you are, look for people who accept you pretty much as is. Make your own decisions about what you want to be, for no one knows you better than you know yourself and because people who pressure you to be this or that way may very well not have your best interests at heart. Some are envious people who want to see you fail, while others are narcissistic people who advise you to be what they would want for themselves—just so that they can live their lives vicariously through you.

Never think, speak, or act in a self-demeaning way to please sadists who demand your masochistic submission or to satisfy competitive individuals who enjoy seeing you fail. Don't morph into someone else each time you are criticized, acting differently to satisfy and appease every one of your critics. Don't act masculine just to disavow your feminine side simply because someone called you effeminate or a fag, e.g., for throwing base-balls underhanded and carrying books against your chest like a girl, not under your arm like a man. And certainly don't morph into someone else each time you are rejected because you hope that if you change your per-sona, they will change their minds, and that if you accept their mindless abuse, they will accept you in a heartfelt way.

This said, do try to listen to people who have a point when they say they would like you to be someone and something you basically are not. Don't dismiss them out of hand if they make any sense at all to you. Instead, remaining flexible, change when indicated. Avoid being an automaton who buys in to other's advice unthinkingly, but do let trusted friends and sensible, reliable supporters who have your best interests at heart have input into your identity search as guides in and out of possible identity struggles.

Several times a week, our high school class piled into a bus and went to the soccer field. I promptly sneaked away, piled into a city bus, and went home away from the ball field to my newest classical music recordings. I saw myself both as a loner and, agreeing with my coach, as a sports sissy. But a kindly music professor took me in, put things in perspective, and gave me courage by suggesting that there was life beyond soccer in my music. On the army physical, I didn't tell the psychiatrist I was gay, but, figuring it out anyway, he asked me if that were so. Then I told him the truth, and he excused me from service. I was at first ashamed of myself for being unmanly and unpatriotic— until a kindly clerk said to me on my way out, "You are a lucky boy, rejoice, for the army can't take you."

Allow yourself to experience a lot of life before you completely close off all of life's intriguing possibilities. To do this, give all of your warring personal, philosophical, and religious selves a fair hearing before you deny any or all of them. The common advice to "be you" makes sense only if there is but one you inside. However, most of us have a number of selves to recognize, affirm, and contend with. So the best idea is to postpone life-determining personal and professional choices for as long as you can so that you, having time to think, don't regret today tomorrow as you come to wonder, "What was I thinking about yesterday?" Balance the undoubted downsides of temporary or even prolonged uncertainty and inauthenticity with the equally negative downsides of prematurely settling down before you are all set so that you consider blossoming late, if only to avoid fading early.

Of course, evaluate, critique, and, if need be, suppress any of your less-than-admirable sides (part identities) should these threaten to take over and seriously diminish your personal power. Especially avoid yielding to a conscience-driven rigid morality that dictates who and what you *should*, ignoring who you want to, be, and tells you what you must do, ignoring what you truly desire to accomplish.

Those of you who in spite of yourself remain seriously conflicted about being gay should avoid making that matter worse by becoming highly troubled about that. Just accept being in conflict and build that into your identity and never act out by doing something not in your best interests/something dangerous just to illuminate who you are: elucidating your authentic self but at the great expense of putting a blot on your permanent record. Particularly to be avoided is developing group identities that are indiscrete: satisfying now but almost predictably likely to come back to haunt you later—a kind of reverse Dorian Gray phenomenon where you change positively but the world's unflattering picture of you stays exactly the same.

SEVEN

Midlife and Beyond: Aging and Ageism

Too many gay men waste far too much of their youth fearing getting older. They view their lives as analogous to a long weekend that goes right from the transcendent hope of Friday night to the shattered illusions of Monday morning, leaving them bereft emotionally, decrepit physically, isolated personally, and needy financially. And to an extent this pessimistic view is not entirely unjustified. For, though with plenty of exceptions, aspects of the gay subculture *are* youth oriented, to the point that many older gay men complain that once they have reached a certain age, younger gay men exclude them from their lives, as by the time they hit 30, 20-year-olds call them "sir" and, when introduced, smile perfunctorily, turn tail, and, showing them their rear, quickly recoil, going into full retreat without even making excuses for taking their leave.

This said, to a great extent, ageism in gay men and the midlife crises that ageism typically spawns exist in the eye of the beholder. Often it is hypersensitivity on the gay man's part that leads him to see ageism that doesn't exist and to overact catastrophically to modest ageism that is actually there. And this sensitivity is in turn the product of cumulative real-life stigmatization and rejection that lead him to anticipate more of the same as he ages, only now around the inescapable fact that he is getting older.

A gay patient suffering from "an acute midlife crisis" that was really a long-in-the-making posttraumatic stress disorder experienced

*chronic anxiety; startle reactions to being surprised—even pleas-
antly; frequent and troublesome bad dreams of rejection and abandonment; and, when he was awake, recurrent flashbacks that
consisted of a rush of memories of past rejections and abandonments
he found impossible to erase from his mind. Additionally, he actively
re-created new traumatic rejections and abandonments by going
after young boys, hoping to trade his money and "invaluable lifetime
experience that can only come out of maturity" for sex—only to have
the boys, wanting someone younger and more physically attractive,
reject him out of hand, further reviving old experiences with parallel
tragic outcomes, leaving him depressed, and feeling "I am too old to
still be gay." He then sought a sympathetic ear from friends, only to
have them further traumatize him by avoiding him to get away from
an "old man's wall-of-woe litanies" they didn't want to hear, as they
either withdrew their social support entirely and retreated from him
or stood by him but trivialized his problem by offering flippant solutions to what he perceived to be serious difficulties. For example,
when once he desperately sought help from a buddy, in response to
his plea for succor his friend turned on a videotape of the old movie*
The Women *and told him that if he watched it, all his troubles would
vanish, "quoting Judy, like lemon drops." So, instead of aging gracefully, he changed his mind altogether about being gay and gray,
decided it wasn't for old men, and (the last time I spoke with him)
planned to enter the priesthood and stay there for the rest of his life.*

Depressed gay men are among the likeliest to suffer from midlife crises
because they are most highly sensitive to what other people think about
and do to them because of their having self-acceptance difficulties. They
project self-acceptance difficulties already in place onto others whom they
now come to view as being more highly critical of them than they actually
are. By this means, in this, their new reality, they turn "I abandon myself"
into "and everyone is an ageist, abandoning me."

*A patient, perceiving himself to be "over the hill" and so no longer a
worthy contender, pulled back and retreated from gay life because he
felt "too old" to participate actively in gay society. His pullback progressively began to feed on itself by intensifying his self-criticism
because others, thinking that* he *rejected* them, *avoided* him, *so as a
result he came to devalue himself even more.*

*As he was later to say to me, "Hi. I went to Argentina for a week, I
am back again. There has been nothing going on in my life. I've been*

through the worst time in all my existence, and I still can't put things together and deal with this sadness and depression, plus financially I am broke and literally hungry. My sister got me a ticket to go and spend some time with her in Argentina, but I could just take one week from my job, which was nice for me. But all my interest was in going to see my old lover, Matt, who seems to be way too happy to have been deported back home. Unfortunately, I didn't find the same man who I love with all my heart. There has been a lot of gossip around me, and some people don't even want to say hello to me, especially the young ones, who think that I am too old for them and that Matt was right to get rid of me because who wants to grow old with a man even older? Which is why I did stop calling everyone. I honestly can't take more rejection, for I am sad enough and feel that I can't take any more grief. I still love a few guys who have always been at my side, but I don't know if they heard all the crap about me, and I'm so scared of more rejection. I'm just waiting and hoping to feel strong enough to deal with this, now trust me I have not the energy for it, I am too old."

Though the term "midlife crisis" implies an undesirable condition, a "midlife crisis" can in fact be a positive event should it culminate in an epiphany and so become a time not of involution but of evolution, where new solutions to old problems develop; where ways of coping not formerly realized, acknowledged, or incorporated into a life plan newly evolve; and where as old pleasures vanish, new satisfactions take their place, leading to midlife *competence* enhanced, say, by the successful resolution of earlier crises, such as those associated with coming out and being rejected. There are also inherent in the aging process itself special reasons to feel blessed. Some gay men become joyful in the recognition that they are finally able to put sex in its place and allow other interests and pursuits to take a parallel or even a central role in their lives. As one gay man put it, "In midlife, I was finally able to make that all-important shift—from below, to above, my waist."

GETTING OLD

Many gay men fear that they will go directly from a midlife crisis into the doldrums of old age. But they fear getting old unduly because they overlook the possibility, first, that they have the capacity to age gracefully and with equanimity and aplomb and, second, that for so many gay men, being gay and gray actually has many advantages. Most gay men in fact handle getting older very well, some because they have become used to spending time alone, especially more so than the family man who at an advanced age has just lost his wife of a lifetime and now doesn't know what to do next. Many, having withstood years of prejudice and discrimination, have on that account become survivors. They have peers of their own age to socialize with, live not alone but with a partner/have supportive friends and family, and are comfortable with themselves having put disclosure issues behind them, become self-affirming in the face of stigmatization and marginalization, and developed their interpersonal skills on domestic and occupational fronts and, no longer being so affected by social norms equating sexual and personal desirability with youthfulness,[1] as a result have subdued ideas that being personally valid means being under 30 years old.

This said, there are gay men for whom getting older can, unfortunately, constitute a grim reality. Some, desperate for companionship, prey on young boys or, desperate for sex, cruise the highway rest stops for a hit. A diminishing few fit the stereotype of the seedy old aunty darkening the corners of the local "wrinkle room," resorting to extreme but generally ineffective self-improvement measures that can lead only to their becoming a satire on themselves, as they deaffirm themselves and defeat their own attempts at self-improvement with excessive makeup, too-dark black hair dye, obvious comb-overs, and heavy perfume, all to hopefully mask underlying issues that should be not veiled but accepted or, when possible, corrected. For artifices like these actually diminish their attractiveness by the making of too-obvious repairs that can become only embarrassingly ineffective because they scream, "I am ashamed of who and what I am." Too many who try to rejoin old or join new groups find themselves excluded and as a result turn to hoarding objects or animals or to overeating, leading to obesity, which creates a series of potentially preventable medical difficulties—as it did for the older gay man who got so big that he could no longer leave his house without assistance, eventually, before suffering a fatal stroke, becoming entirely homebound and dependent on visiting nurses not only for his medical care but also for what companionship he had left in life.

The ones among my patients who felt that aging weighed especially heavily on their lives were those men who had serious problems with losing their all-important physical attractiveness, their support groups, and their involvement in their gay community. They were severely down because they were without a partner and with little to no chance of finding one. They lacked a large, accepting family and devoted children. Poor finances and bad health, often due to lack of sufficient access to doctors, not infrequently plagued them. Some couldn't maintain their intellectual interests because they lived in a sterile environment and could no longer go elsewhere without the car they could now not drive.

But even here, a difficult reality was not the only reason why they had serious problems with getting older. Being gay and gray had become a problem less because they faced inevitable physical or mental decline and more because they suffered from ongoing personality problems that lead to ennui and thence to social incapacitation, then on to their giving up entirely on life because they felt that it was impossible for them to become generative in new, creative ways. So often it was perfectionism that kept them from effectively coping and adjusting to the inevitable physical and mental changes as well as changing circumstances associated with aging. They discounted the many things available to them because they found them all less-than-fully satisfactory and were unable to compromise by embracing what they could get, even though it wasn't exactly what they wanted.

RECOMMENDATIONS

Because family members, friends, and lovers generally overlook your age to the extent that they like you, being likable, starting early in life, helps you make good friends in the beginning and keep them as you get older. A good part of being likable involves acting your current age, as most people, sensing the falsity involved, prefer that over your trying to act younger than you actually are.

As an aging gay man, I developed a relationship with a man in his twenties who worked at The Saint, *a once hot nightclub in New York City. My younger friend would get me in free. I would hang around all night waiting for him to get off work, then we would dance for a few hours listening to the disco music; then, the disco music fading into grunge, we would, early in the morning, at last, lie down upstairs for a few hours in the balcony—which was, depending on how you handled it, either a place of rest and repose or a spot for mega-orgiastic fulfillment. Then after a few hours, we would get up and go home to bed. I, not surprisingly, was tired for a few days afterward because my sleeping schedule was off because, having slept all day Sunday, I was unable to sleep much Sunday night and so was shot on Monday. Not surprisingly, too, the people my young friend worked with were less than impressed by me and my performance. They were, in fact, making fun of us both: me for robbing the cradle and him for snatching my body from the grave. I should have accepted that my behavior was out of sync with my age and that it was time to try becoming more impressive to other gay men, both younger and older, by acting like a youngish mature man rather than like an aging youth. As it turned out, when I finally made the changeover to a new mode and man, I was just what Michael wanted, he being a "country boy" at heart, looking for farm more than fun, and I, just in time, having decided to become less the prodigal son, had become the more established, better settled Country Squire.*

Of course, getting married and staying that way, remaining with your partner throughout life, aging together so that as you get older you always have a loving home to go to and an inbuilt social life you can rely on, is the best idea. For, now your reaction to people shying away from you because of your age will be, "Who cares?" So consider—if possible and if it's what you basically want—making your mark on the world by making it not on the whole world but on one special person in it, helping both him and you go to heaven. Throughout, I stress the importance of a long-term monogamous relationship to fill your life with the joys of getting and giving, as a substitute for just about everything else you may or may not be lacking, and as a replacement for what you may be missing. Additionally, as it did in my case, a lasting partnership can serve as your means of giving back for some or all the questionable things you no doubt did when you were young: loving just one man a lot now to make up for not being loving enough to mankind then—in my case, because as a younger man I just thought of sex, damn the torpedoes. Now I give to Michael all I can partly as my way to say, "I am sorry for what I did to everyone else when I was young, and immature, and inconsiderate, when I thought that just about everybody who crossed my path had in some way planned to cross or had actually crossed me."

It also helps if you lower your expectations of others—expecting less in order to actually get more. Restructuring your self-expectations is also a good idea. Self-acceptance of what can't be changed increases your chances of becoming self-satisfied. In particular, try to remember that most "birds," gay or straight, flock with those of a feather—their contemporaries, so to better accept the undoubted limitations of aging, you should avoid hopeless searches for unattainable youth—yours and others, and make it a general practice to favor people of your own age to be the central core of those you hang with.

Simultaneously—and perhaps most important—stop viewing yourself as damaged goods and start promoting yourself and your advanced age as something that makes you, although different, uniquely valuable. Work through any specific guilty fantasies that lead you to devalue your aging self. And never use your advanced age as an excuse for developing and retaining a sense of low self-esteem that, though you blame it on your age, actually comes from elsewhere in your makeup.

A patient who gave up on himself because he was variously "too old to live" and "disgustingly aged" was really paralyzed not by his age but by survivor guilt. Many of his friends and his partner had died young, and he felt ashamed of being the one to survive and wished that he could have been the person to have been taken. So when he was looking for a mate, whenever he found someone satis-factory, he quickly demurred and introduced him to a younger friend who "deserved him more and ought to be the one who got him." Most of his friends said, "Poor Chuckie, you are too old to find a husband for yourself." But one of them got it right: "Lucky Chuckie, you can find all the men you want, but at the last minute you give them away because you feel everyone deserves them more than you do."

Many of the most impressive and successful older gay men I know and treated were those who substituted a quiet generativity and substantial cre-ativity for their progressively ever more and more elusive youthfulness. And to make that substitution, they altered an identity strictly dependent on being fully unregulated and instead developed self-discipline, heading in a more suppressive direction to help them win a struggle with excessive self-permissiveness that led them astray by leading them into acting out.

To realize their full potential, gay men should consider mentoring, garnering further occupational successes, and participating in gay-related social causes, but with one important caveat: joining dedicated groups and becoming active in age-appropriate community endeavors is most helpful when one faithfully adheres to another caveat, namely, it's possible to carry altruism too far and become depressed through giving too much of oneself to others, to the point that you become depleted, feel deprived, and run so on empty that you become unable to give anything to anyone any longer, including—or especially—to yourself.

Getting over the posttraumatic stress elements of aging involves inte-grating past traumas into your present life. That starts with not blaming yourself "shoulda, coulda, if-only" style for traumas you think you did (but actually didn't) bring down on yourself. It continues with relinquish-ing an overinvolvement with the need to constantly revive toxic memories in order to disinter them so as to relive them by hopefully purging and burying them once and for all. It also involves accepting new traumas with equanimity, that is, without responding catastrophically to minor annoyances or even to major setbacks, especially becoming able to accept (the inevitable) being dumped and doing so without becoming depressed because "here we go again" and "now, certainly, all is lost."

Young or (especially) old, you should always avoid listening to those who would push you beyond *your own* comfortable limitations. Marriage is right but not for everyone. For example, serious avoidants may do best by accepting themselves just as they are—even as lonely—without making a herculean but futile attempt to partner down.

You can compensate for diminishing sexual performance within a long-time ongoing partnership by avoiding relational negativity, the most powerful of all sexual antagonists, and accentuating relational positivity, the most powerful of all sexual stimulants. Treat your partnered relationship as nothing less than a treasure that cannot be replaced. Don't start thinking that you can live without him or find another one just as good as the one you have now. Instead, have a "this-is-it" mindset and engineer the necessary adjustments to make certain that that will be the case—self-abdicating when necessary to keep your relationship going even at the cost of the sacrifice of some personal freedom and independence. As you do everything you can to avoid his rejecting/dumping you, rarely if ever contemplate being the one to do the dumping—being always disenchanted by what you already have and mainly—or only—attracted to what you might still get. If necessary to keep the peace, abandon your treasured personal philosophy enough to adapt to his, as you relinquish some of your unique personal needs to gratify him, even if that means acceding to some of his irrational demands that aren't gratifying you.

This said, it isn't always easy to know exactly how to handle a difficult partner and avoid a split or divorce. At least not a partner like Don:

Yesterday was tough. Don called, after being gone for three days, and said he really missed me and what did he do "wrong." He couldn't believe our marriage fell apart so fast. I tried to tell him at first that nothing went wrong, that two people spend time together to see if they are a fit, and that it is no one's fault if who they are just isn't a match.

But he dug for specifics, so I commented about his inappropriate grabbing of me and other people, making fun of what I do and who I am, and also making fun of others for who they are and what they do. He told me I can't be serious about criticizing his teasing behavior, for his father always teased his mother, and she laughed her head off. I said that then maybe I'm too sensitive because it hurts and I didn't feel safe with him in a sense—physically or emotionally.

He got snotty and mused about my not being able to take the good with the bad. Why couldn't I accept the little boy in him?

Well, I said, if I recall back when I was a little boy, there was the little boy who called me jolly green dwarf because I was too short, thus losing me completely, and the other little boy who picked up a pencil when I dropped it and won a place in my heart. He felt like the first one.

He replied, "Can't you just roll your eyes and let it go when I do that?"

I said, "Well, maybe, I don't know, though. We can start over as friends if you want to see if it works."

"Forget it Lew," he says. "This marriage is dead, sorry."

And he hung up.

Theoretically, I know I can't have everything in one person. He had some good traits that I will miss, and it was nice having a husband. I am wondering if I was being too sensitive/picky and if instead of drawing the line I should blur it for the sake of accepting those inevitable human shortcomings in everyone. NOT.

As an aging gay man, you can compensate for what you never had or newly lost without going on the prowl. If you are not handsome, you can balance your compromised looks in many ways, especially through being professionally successful. Or, depending on individual preference, you might consider seeking partners among men who are less youth oriented than some. Perhaps you want to settle for nothing more than a sympathy screw or, just forgetting about loving relationships, instead seek to gratify your sexual needs anonymously and separately from your need for companionship. The wealthier among you can pay for sex, for as the joke goes, "when I was young I was selling it, when I was middle-aged I was giving it away, and now that I am older I am buying it all back." Or, like not a few older gay men, you can just decide to become happily celibate: focusing away from sex and instead onto nonsexual pleasures, such as group activities like cooking classes in preparation for pleasurable rotating dinner parties strictly with best friends.

Most important, older gay men who are depressed should consider therapy from competent gay-aware therapists and not avoid seeking help because they feel unworthy of assistance or fear further stigmatization and marginalization because they are both gay and aging.

EIGHT

You and Your Parents

DID YOUR PARENTS MAKE YOU GAY?

Some gay men who ask me if their parents made them gay are looking to blame someone for something that they disavow in themselves. Others (and possibly most) gay men are healthily curious about what, if anything, has happened to lead to their becoming homosexual. The two commonest questions men in the second group ask me are, in essence:

- Did I get to be gay because I had a strong binding relationship with my mother and a weak or absent father, so that as a result I became homosexual because my mother was my primary identification figure, since she had an attractive personality that proved more appealing to me than my emotionally removed, dolt of a father?

- Did I get to be gay because I had an actively disdainful mother who put my masculinity down either directly or indirectly, the latter by not responding with congratulations even when they were in order. (One gay man, for example, finished playing some beautiful musical compositions of his own devising only to have his mother, withholding the kudos he believed deserved, routinely say not, "That was beautiful," but, "Did you get that out of your system?") (A fuller discussion of the theories to explain the origin of homosexuality is offered in the Appendix.)

While problematic parental relationships like this are by themselves, in my opinion, not enough to *create* the homosexual boy, parent-son interactions certainly do *influence* some aspects of a boy's homosexuality—once he has become gay for whatever reason. In some of my patients, parental input seemed to tip an already bisexual gay son over to becoming more thoroughly homosexual. In other of my patients, parental overcontrol seemed to encourage contrary rebelliousness so that the boy became a *reprobate* homosexual—one who came out both sooner and more abrasively than he otherwise might have—primarily to counterattack his parents for what he believed they did to him, and in preparation for detaching himself from them as quickly and efficiently as possible. Parental input almost always helps shape the kind of gay person a boy becomes through influencing the development of his personality—for example, by facilitating obsessional guilt about being gay, or enhancing isolative schizoid personality trends characterized by remoteness and shyness not only in his gay, but also in his straight, interpersonal relationships.

YOUR PARENTS AND COMING OUT

Many of my patients ask me, "How can I best come out to my parents?" The answer lies in coming out with full empathy. Empathy involves treating your parents as individuals in their own right, as people who have feelings and problems just like you do, which both need to be taken into consideration and your help in resolving. That means that you should always come out to your parents with respect, ever avoiding being abrasive, aggressive, or hostile through using the coming out process as a sword: to get back at them for some imagined slight or actual deprivation, or to punish them in turn for a punishment you believe they meted out to you.

When coming out, give your parents time to talk with you about what you just told them—meaning that after you come out to them give them the opportunity to come back out at you. Never come out then figuratively walk away. Instead let them vent—to ask you for further explanation, express any worries and concerns they might have, and reveal any negative emotions and beliefs, even though narrow-minded, that they might feel/harbor, such as disappointment that you are not heterosexual. In the ideal world, your parents will respond to your coming out supportively by saying, "That's wonderful, no problem; tell me what you need and I will give it to you." In the real world, parents generally feel negatively about their son's being gay then hide what they are really feeling and believing—yet it comes through. Ultimately, what you intuit, if not hear, from most parents is something along the lines of "being gay is more of a liability than an asset [although it is neither, it just is]; harder than being straight; and probably going to be responsible for some real present and future personal and interfamily problems." So if you hear, "How wonderful, it's the best thing that could have happened to you and me," or "I support you no matter what, and give you permission to do anything you please," don't be glad, be suspicious. If you hear, "You are a bad son, how could you do this to me?" don't be angry, be relieved. For here is an opening for you to let your parents bring their concerns to light, so that together you can resolve these concerns (which are generally mutual) in a loving way. You probably won't be able to resolve all the significant issues, and to do so once and for all. But you can at least start forming an alliance that presages a better, more honest working relationship in the future. Resolving festering negativity now, when possible, can keep it from hardening later into a full and permanent rift.

One gay man's mother said that she was not disgusted that her son was gay; she just couldn't believe that he was actually having anal sex. While she could accept his being gay, that is, she could accept his being a gay man, she found his doing that exact gay thing abhorrent. At first he was tempted to ask her for an apology, but instead he told her that he understood where she was coming from. Then he said, "But while I respect you, including the thoughts you have about my sexual practices actually being abhorrent and revolting, I hope that you will ultimately come around and be more fully positive to and supportive of me, and in this as well as in every respect." She did not actually do that, but at least she never said another word along similar lines. And, going forward, she and her son got along fairly well—but unfortunately, not perfectly, for the truth about what she really felt about him (and all gay men) would regularly sneak out. Thus he complained, in spite of his protests, that she would continue to do embarrassing and ultimately negative things to him, like give him pink Poinsettias at Christmastime, then explain, with some seriousness, that that was "because you deserve nothing less—than the right color for a queen."

Avoid allowing projection to color/determine your impression of your parents' attitude about you and your homosexuality. Many gay men, already at some odds with who and what they are, deal with their personal shame and guilt by projecting these to become the belief that others are criticizing and ashamed of them. So, "I don't like myself" becomes "you dislike me." Then they allow that mindset to shape what happens next, including, and sometimes especially, between them and mom and dad.

What if your parents outed you when they suspected that you were gay and trying to hide it? Perhaps they felt entirely justified in setting a trap for you because they supposed you were homosexual and not being forthright about it, and, as my parents said, "We just had to know." With that excuse, my parents, hoping to catch me in flagrante, arranged to come home unannounced after they acted like they were going away on a trip. Other parents install a hidden camera to spy on their sons. Whatever the method, parents who do such things (like anyone else who does them) will, guaranteed, learn the hard way that their cloak and dagger plans ultimately cause them to lose their son's full trust and love, and perhaps forever. (As a recent case of outing illustrates, that may not be all they lose: they could also lose their son to suicide.) I personally never forgot what my parents did to out me and the way that they did it. The best I could do from then on was to keep my negative response sufficiently limited to rescue and retain the barebones of a relationship. I didn't run away from home and stop seeing them altogether. I didn't attempt suicide. Instead I tried to chalk their actions up to sectorial poor judgment, then give them a second chance. But that was me. Not everyone would do the same thing, and so not every outcome would be so sanguine. And what made things worse was that they never apologized or recanted. As a result, although I am not proud of it, each time psychologically I needed something to resent them for, I dredged this incident up, doing so just so that I had something I could use against them.

YOUR PARENTS' RELATIONSHIP WITH YOUR FRIENDS

Some gay men want their parents completely out of their private lives. Others hope that their parents will accept their friends and partners—only to disappointedly discover that they never do—and, here too, with tragic consequences.

A patient's mother was unable to accept both her son's being gay and his current lover. Because she didn't want the family to know she had a gay son, she insisted that he attend family functions and holiday dinners alone, or with a girlfriend. Resentment of his being gay also led her to refuse to treat him as equal to her other, straight, kids. All things taken together alienated him completely both from her and from the rest of the family. The final blow came when after her husband, his dad, died she remade her will, and left him less than she left her other children. And she told him about it. As she put it,

*disingenuously, "Because the others have children of their own, and
there is only one of you, they need more, and you need a lot less."*

*She totally missed the opportunity to give her fragile boy emotional
and financial support and help him better manage the difficulties he
was to personally encounter in his gay life. He tolerated his mother,
but he always missed having a mom he could fully appreciate, and
truly love.*

Difficult parents like her require their gay sons to make difficult
choices. Should you leave a partner behind on special occasions (like the
holidays) because your family won't accept him, or should you rather
leave your family behind on special occasions (like the holidays) because
they won't accept your partner? I personally believe in putting marital
relationship first, favoring your partner's needs and wishes over those of
your family. So, I make sure that, whether or not they want me and my
partner around as a couple, we go everywhere together. Depending
on your personality, special circumstances, and individual needs, my
philosophy may or may not be right for you. But I strongly believe that
it is the only choice that can ultimately make you fully comfortable, leave
you feeling truly proud of yourself, and make your partner truly proud
of you.

The luckiest gay men I know have parents who join in their gay lives as
if nothing earth-shattering at all is happening. They accept their son's
friends and partners almost without a second thought. Of course, though
they generally feel blessed, they still can—and perhaps should—remain
secretly or openly dismayed about any *bad* companions that their sons
might take on and bring home. And not infrequently, they have a point
here. Do accede them this should they reject your partner not because they
are rejecting you for being a gay man (and would reject any of your partners outright) but because they have good, gay-neutral taste and just don't
like a particular person. I wasn't being entirely fair to my parents when I
expected them to accept friends of mine who were not entirely appealing,
even to me; welcome them into their homes; and even serve them dinner. I
am not sure I would have returned the favor if my mother had brought
someone home to me—like some of the boyfriends I brought home to
mother.

As a son, you should always try to avoid putting your parents into can't-
win binds by subjecting them to nonnegotiable demands. Equally problematic are making conflicting demands on them so that if they respect
your privacy, they are being disinterested in you as a person, yet if they
involve themselves in your life overly much (as you see it), they are being

intrusive; and if they are being permissive, they are being unprotective, yet if they try to keep you out of trouble, they are being controlling and judgmental. Perhaps, again as you see it, whatever they do *always* has a hidden negative agenda. But maybe, as they (properly) see it, much of what you do leaves them wondering—making it impossible for them to know how to respond to you in a way that allows them to both discharge their responsibility to you and keep the peace with you.

Many problems between parents and gay sons can be resolved by getting beyond pettiness on both sides so that all concerned can work with each other through having an open discussion: expressing needs, wishes, and fears; and then clearing up misunderstandings and resolving differences while (when indicated) agreeing to disagree without letting that or anything else seriously come between you. Always remember that your parents may have other sons and daughters. But you will never have another mom and dad.

RECOMMENDATIONS FOR PARENTS

When you find your son to be in potential danger, you have the difficult task of respecting his individuality and freedom while exercising your responsibility—to do what you can to keep him safe and happy. My rule for parents faced with such a dilemma is to err on the side of being protective: setting limits on him for his own good while for now ignoring his protests, doing so in the recognition that any fallout from these protests will be more short lived than any possible consequences of all the truly bad mistakes he can make when he is still new at things.

In one case, a mother preached financial responsibility when her son bounced checks. When he had unsafe sex, she reminded him that a life she valued was in danger. And when he drank too much, she strongly recommended that he attend Alcoholics Anonymous to become sober, then followed up to make certain that he was staying with the program and remaining alcohol free. At first, he complained that she was telling him that it was not okay to be himself. Eventually, he understood that there were many, equally authentic selves inside of him, and he needed to be true not to "himself" but to his "ideal self"—which was a composite born of more than unfettered id impulses and superego retaliative responses but also of a rationality that could come out of only the observant, judging part of himself— a compromise attitude, as Freudians might say, created not solely from the impulse-driven id or the retaliative conscience (superego) but also from the peacemaking, integrating, mediating, negotiating psychic structure called "the ego."

In conclusion, with your son, as with everyone else, always be prepared—through philosophizing, reading, and consultation with others in the know, including (but not exclusively) therapists—for what comes next so that you don't make mistakes because of having to think on your feet. Focus away from your emotions about the situation and onto the facts of the situation. But always avoid being remote and uninvolved with your son. When indicated, be prepared to set necessary limits on him (and for his setting necessary limits on you). Where you see danger looming from your having gone too far too fast, pull back. When you see criticism coming for your having said or done something he thinks you shouldn't have, accept it, even though your immediate response may be to feel pain and hurt as if "we don't deserve this; look at all we did for you." He might dub you "too parental" and "overly interfering." But when you dispassionately adjudge yourself to be right, remain fast and firm though supportive and never shaming. Then if, as is likely, you do have a few shortcomings, attempt to find out what these might be from him—so that you can make timely changes and, hopefully if it's not too late and should they be indicated, necessary amends.

PART II

Overcoming Emotional Problems

NINE

Emotional Disorder in Gay Men

Too many observers overlook that what laypersons believe to be "typical gay behavior" is in fact "atypical, unusual, neurotic behavior in gay men." As a result, they mislabel manifestations of emotional disorder in gay men as "characteristically homosexual," thus stigmatizing all gay men as "queer" in the sense of being "different and strange." But to illustrate, "typical gay bitchiness" is likely not to be as "typically gay" as generally believed but instead to be a characteristic symptom of histrionic personality disorder in gay men when the gay man is anxiously attempting to deal with his own low self-esteem by becoming castrative, that is, putting others down to prop himself up. Similarly, overpossessiveness and jealousy between partners, routinely dismissed as typical of gay relationships, is often a symptom of paranoia; the relational fickleness to which gays are considered prone is often symptomatic of a fear of commitment that is part of avoidant personality disorder; and "gender and sexual identity confusion," so often thought to be inherent in all gay men, is often a symptom of gender identity disorder, affecting only a few.

Not surprisingly, overall gay men suffer from essentially the same emotional disorders as straight men. For gays and straights alike have similar developmental problems, psychological conflicts, and life stresses. However, there are at least two exceptions to this rule. First, psychopathology in gay men, while fundamentally much like psychopathology in straight men, is almost always superficially altered by the gay context in which it occurs. Thus, gay men who get paranoid often do so about something other than conspiracies out there. Generally, they think not "They are out to get me" but rather "He is cheating on me." Or gay men who get depressed commonly bury their down mood in acting up so that what we observe is not a classic mood disorder characterized by sadness and withdrawal but an impulse disorder characterized by frantic driven promiscuity. Second, homophobia puts some gay men under a higher degree of stress than we generally find in straight men, creating more and more severe *reactive* disorders. (On the other hand, in some ways, many gays have *less* stress than straights because they don't sweat bringing up children, feel confined to sanctioned "legal" marriage, or, being DINKS, do have higher incomes than many straight married couples who have only one salary coming in.)

Following are some common so-called typical gay problematic behaviors that are generally symptomatic of specific emotional disorder in men who are gay.

EROTOPHOBIA

With the exception of erotophobia, the following are disorders outlined in the American Psychiatric Association's *Diagnostic and Statistical Manual of Mental Disorders* (4th ed.) So-called typical coming-out difficulties marked by painful guilty self-denigrating conflict over disclosing being gay are often the specific product of erotophobia (fearful phobic avoidance of sexuality and sex). So-called typical gay sexual identity problems are also often the product of erotophobic guilt-driven hostility to the self originating within and taken out on the self, here directed specifically to one's homosexuality.

PARANOIA

So-called typical gay disclosure conflicts are often due to a fearful paranoid hesitancy to be honest about oneself, leading to extreme reattribution defenses where gay men project their self-dislike onto others and then become excessively fearfully shy and withdrawn because they see danger— often dangerous homophobic threats to their persons—everywhere.

Gay promiscuity within a supposedly committed relationship may be not "typical gay infidelity" but rather the product of a failure of basic trust originating in paranoid hypersensitivity and suspiciousness due to the projection of one's own desire to cheat onto a partner, leading to unwarranted assumptions/false perceptions about partner infidelity. In one not uncommon scenario, a patient, based not on external evidence but on a pure projection of his own forbidden desires onto his partner, incorrectly came to believe that his partner was saying negative things about him behind his back and cheating on him. So-called typical gay bitchiness can also be the product of projection when gay men in true paranoid fashion savage others to disavow their own disfavored traits along the lines of "you, not I, are the defective one." So-called typical gay geographical wandering can be the product not of gay instability but of paranoid-like externalization of one's problems onto place, typically the place where one lives ("nobody can find a lover in unwelcoming Detroit"), resulting in moving about that is based not so much in a true desire to leave a given spot as in trying to leave one's imagined persecutors behind.

Recently, I received the following letter:

I met Arnie through the Internet, he was one of the few in almost 2 years on the Net that seemed truly interesting and caring. He just came out, he claims he didn't know until he was 28 (he is now 30) although "all the signs were there."

He was a series of contradictions—we met for the first time after many long letters—at an Italian restaurant in a very Italian section of Queens, and we kissed in my vehicle. Probably not a good idea on the first date, but both he and I wanted to do more kissing. I said, "Are you sure?" He said he didn't care. Only later when I wanted more affection, he referred to "I told you several times in e-mails that I am not a publicly affectionate person." (?)

Later, we went to get an AIDS test, although I was almost certain he would be negative, and even though I had been celibate for at least 10 years, I still wanted to be sure. Turns out we were both negative. While at the gay community center, after our test appointment I wanted to introduce him to Sean, the owner of a gay business, who is sort of an older confidante. Arnie said, "I'm not going to be your show pony." Later when we discussed this, he also claimed that I said something in the hallway behind his back at the community center. I'm like "WHAT?" You're two feet from me and I am going to "say something about you?"

Perhaps I needed the experience after finally coming out of the closet myself, and Arnie had his good qualities, but he was basically unpleasant. Even now, he probably thinks he "Tried everything" and "I just challenged everything he said." (He did speak a lot in generalities and it is hard to let it all go unchallenged.) Another couple of things that were amazing with him: he e-mailed me twice about "never talking about his work." The first time I thought he was joking, the second time, I rattled off about three long paragraphs of all the things we talked about regarding his work. And when we finally spoke, he still insisted we shouldn't talk about his work!!!! Finally, grudgingly, we spoke "a little" about it, but not as much about his as about mine.

Then the issue of his parents came up. He told me his mother is ill, and his father alcoholic. We spoke about that almost weekly. One time, after a short phone conversation, he complained about "not speaking enough about his parents." I said we speak often about your parents, but you know I care very much about you: just let me know you want to speak more! You are a big boy! Only then I get a "I don't think we should see each other anymore" letter: coupled with "I wouldn't mind seeing you at a restaurant to talk if you want" and "my daughter Laura still asks about you frequently." I have an idea what those two phrases are about, but not how they jibe.

This wouldn't bother me so much if I could meet someone else, but just about Easter time, a man came to an historic site, we exchanged phone numbers ostensibly to discuss joint efforts to restore the place. Then he came on Easter Sunday, sat next to me in the vestibule for at least 30 minutes at my invitation, ALL SMILES and laughs . . . seemed very interested, but no response to a telephone invitation to go out to eat. Then I called him about cleaning the Church. He finally answered his cell phone, said he was at his niece's baptism, would call back, and didn't. That was a month ago.

And on and on it goes, over and over and over. I went to a therapist, who didn't see anything major; one good friend said maybe I'm a bit too intense at first, but that is about it.

So go figure. Are these guys having problems themselves, and blaming me for them instead of resolving them on their own?

A gay man wrote to me,

I answered an ad by saying "you seem to have an interesting life; nice to meet you, Ron."

He responded: "Instead of 'nice to meet you,' which sounds final, I wish you would have written 'why don't we get to know each other?'"

I replied, "Yes, why don't we? Tell me about yourself, what you like to do in your free time, what your work is like, etc."

He replied: "You seem to want to know way too much for the first encounter. Good luck to you in finding a kindred spirit."

OBSESSIVE-COMPULSIVE DISORDER

So-called typical gay conflicts about coming out are often the product of obsessive-compulsive disorder in gay men. Typically, we see a troubled conscience fraught with sexual guilt manifest as scrupulosity taking the form of self-homophobia prompting self-apologies that block self-acceptance and self-expression. Bisexuality too can be the product of gay guilt so that the gay man who just came out goes back in again trying but failing to become heterosexual, perhaps convincing himself that that is for strictly rational reasons—in order for him to be able to get married and have children.

So-called typical gay alternating approach-avoidant behaviors characterized by proclamations of love followed by distancing and proclamations of fidelity followed by fickleness and cheating are often the product of the painful indecisiveness associated with obsessive-compulsive disorder. Men like this often at first accept the closeness of love and sex, only to then quickly pull back as "I am looking for love" becomes "Yes, but, I also need my space."

Compulsive sexuality, often a prominent manifestation of obsessive-compulsive disorder, is discussed in Chapter 4.

AFFECTIVE DISORDER—DEPRESSION

Gay men are often believed as a group to typically manifest low self-esteem along with feelings of personal unworthiness characteristically pervading their self-view and hence identity, leading to the diminished functionality generally associated with excessive self-criticism and imaginings of inequality due to extreme hypersensitivity about being treated shabbily lived out in self-defeating behaviors, such as picking the wrong partner, entering into and sticking with a profession that doesn't fit the person, and suicidal ruminations/behavior. But these symptoms, though commonly found in gay men, are not characteristic of what is so often viewed as "typical gay existential moodiness." Instead, they are more likely to be intrinsic, characteristic symptoms of an affective disorder—depressed type as it appears in gay men. Internalized and internal homophobia is often the cause, as gay men both buy into others' homophobia and bully or stigmatize themselves, on their own, in a self-homophobic fashion.

AFFECTIVE DISORDER—HYPOMANIA

Typical "wild-and-crazy" gay behaviors are generally the product of hypomania in gay men:

Dear M:

Too bad I am wasting my money and time on Mitch and now I have to keep my Internet profile down so as to not have him see I am in the market again.

When I saw him Tuesday before "breaking up" we went for a walk along the beach. I drove, to make things easier for him, since he drives to Boston and back every day. So when I get to the parking lot and am trying to decide which space to pull into, he becomes red in the face and then ducks down, saying that I am aggravating the person who is behind me waiting for me to decide, and that I am an embarrassment to him. So then I pull in, and he gets out of the car, comes around and says "watch this, I'm going to freak everyone out," and proceeds to yell in my face at the top of his lungs and wave his fists in the air as if admonishing me for not knowing how to park. People around us begin to look, only then he laughs and hugs me and tells everyone he is joking. Then we proceed to walk, and now he calls every black person walking by us with a white person a "twinkie." I never even heard that expression used that way, but I was sure it was rude and would probably get us killed. So I told him to please stop it, and he did, until the next bigoted or generally off color comment he couldn't resist making.

Once I asked him how his trip to the casino with the boys went. Instead of telling me about the exhibition he saw there, he told me how much fun they had farting in the car and smelling it up. Hardly a romantic image when you are dating someone.

Had I not spent time with him I would not have known these things about him. My sister, who has met him a couple of times, offered to call him and talk to him about the things that he might be able to change so that we could give our relationship another chance. But I am not his therapist and have no need to see if a person can really change what is in his heart, especially long held behavior patterns. I know why the 24 other men he said he dated before me ran the other way. It would be so easy to give him pointers so as to avoid his endless search for love, but unfortunately, I can't as I don't want this asinine adolescent as MY love. Yes. He does have a problem. And maybe the antidepressants that he is on are tipping him in the other direction. But that doesn't mean that I have a problem as well. I guess it's back to being lonely for awhile, and of course that sucks, too.

Commonly so-called typical gay *flamboyance* is a hypomanic protestation that "See, I am not depressed but having lots of fun." There is often associated promiscuity where the goal of having as much sex as possible is at least partially a nonsexual one: undoing feeling hated, reviled, and despised through the kind of self-affirmation achieved via multiple conquests along the lines of "If lots of bodies want me, then I myself must be somebody good."

HISTRIONIC PERSONALITY DISORDER

So-called typical gay *effeminacy* may be innate when due primarily to genetic and/or hormonal influences. Or it may be a symptom of histrionic personality disorder, as when it is a theatrical statement meant to impress oneself and others through attention-seeking flamboyant emoting and clowning.

PSYCHOPATHIC PERSONALITY DISORDER

Opportunistic behaviors such as hustling, swindling, running up bills and not paying them, and narcissistic sexuality where "my orgasm comes first and who cares about yours," often attributed to the so-called unreliability/irresponsibility of gay men ("always on the make and thinking only of themselves"), are in fact not common/typical aspects of being gay but are common/typical symptoms of psychopathy in gay men. This was the case for a gay man who got sex by telling lies about himself (passing himself off as a titan of industry to impress younger gay men into bed), for a gay man who synthesized poppers in his apartment kitchen and sold them to a constant parade of gay men looking for sexual stimulants, and for a gay man who, although he knew he had AIDS, continued to have unprotected anal sex as a top with a procession of young boys as bottoms, saying that he didn't care if he infected them—he just refused to deprive himself of any pleasure to which he felt entitled.

BORDERLINE PERSONALITY DISORDER

Gay men are often looked down on as having intense engulfing relationships that they follow with rapid interpersonal removal and withdrawal, followed in turn by new, intense, engulfing relationships and an endless repetition of that cycle. As a result, they remind one of Freud's porcupines, which, needing warmth, huddle together, only to prick each other with their quills, and move apart, only to feel cold once again. But this so-called characteristic relational shifting of gay men is in fact likely to be symptomatic of a borderline personality disorder in the gay man. This disorder is notable in whomever it affects, gay and straight, for its cyclic relational merging and emerging—where the abject dependency associated with the merging alternates with a fear of closeness expressed via the emerging.

The so-called typical Holly Golightly floaty feyness of gay men can also be a classical borderline symptom. Such was the case for a borderline gay man who stormed out of a town council complaining that "those in power aren't doing enough; what they should be doing is promoting ultimate, transcendental harmony between humans and animals."

IMPULSE DISORDER

Though many real-world gays are simply solid, trustworthy, and dependable citizens, the belief persists in hard-core homophobic circles that gays are characteristically impulsive, unreliable, and mercurial. Impulsive, unreliable gays certainly exist, but they are generally troubled individuals. Developmentally speaking, they might be prolonged adolescents still having difficulty leading adult lives, and it shows—both in their personal relationships and in the form of career difficulties.

SADOMASOCHISTIC PERSONALITY DISORDER

So-called typical gay impulsiveness characterized by mercurial relationships notable for difficulty forming and maintaining contacts with others in turn characterized by a succession of rapid, loving incursions followed by as just-as-rapid hateful dumpings, when not the product of borderline personality disorder or impulse disorder, can be symptomatic of sadomasochistic personality disorder in gay men. A difference between borderline personality disorder/impulse disorder and sadomasochistic personality disorder lies in the quality of the actual separations. In borderlines

and impulsives, the reasons for the separations are often somewhat difficult to comprehend, for it is as if they come out of nowhere, being seemingly unjustified and with little deep personal meaning. In contrast, in
sadomasochists, the separations characteristically follow fights with
meaningful content where there is emotional and often even physical
abuse. Also, borderlines and impulsives characteristically attach to and
detach themselves from "innocent" victims, whereas sadists tend to attach
to and detach themselves from "masochistic participants" who seek out
and even provoke the sadists—in a way that fulfills the masochist's own
needs and complements his own problems.

> *A gay patient asked his partner to accompany him to his country
> home for the Fourth of July holiday. The partner didn't want to go
> because back in New York he was planning on sneaking in a new boy-
> friend to help celebrate the holiday. So, in response, the partner, to
> avoid laying out his own plans as closure, instead, asked, over and
> over again, "You want me to go?" "You want me to go?" without
> ever actually saying what he wanted to do or would actually do. After
> an hour of this, my patient, ultimately losing patience and control,
> slugged him. His partner then called a protective society to intervene
> and save him from further physical abuse. Then he left him for good.
> (Then he came back because he couldn't "stand living at the 'Y.'")*

Generally overlooked is that gay men who act self-destructively and
seemingly without concern for consequences often do so not because they
are gay but because they are masochists. Masochistic gay men calculatedly select a negative outcome—if not through picking obliging sadists
to partner with them, then through becoming alcoholic or addicted to
drugs on their own or by having unsafe sex—deliberately, if unconsciously, to self-punitively put their well-being and even their lives at risk.

A gay man wrote to me,

> Hi I have some questions about a person I have been with we have
> been on and off for a while but he has been seeing me again for a
> month he asked me if I wanted to be his boyfriend again I said yes but
> the problem is that on his answering machine I heard another guy and
> he calls everyday what should I think I confronted him about it and all
> of a sudden he was different. The other thing is that I always clean his
> house for him and do his laundry and other stuff. My question is: do
> you think this guy is using me he tells me he likes my companionship

and tells me he likes to party with me but he does not like clingy guys. I already know that the guy that calls him all the time I think would be clingy but who knows, I really care about this person but don't know if he cares about me do you have any suggestions I could email him, I need advice so that I can get back in his good graces, well thank you for listening to me.

AVOIDANT PERSONALITY DISORDER

In the mythology surrounding gays, typically every gay man is looking for a relationship, only no gay man is finding one. Researchers and laymen alike often ascribe this state of affairs to characteristic gay fickleness associated with promiscuity associated with typical and fundamental nonchalant gay personal remoteness. But such behavior, should it occur in a gay man, is generally symptomatic of avoidant personality disorder occurring in a homosexual. So-called typical gay bitchiness can also be a symptom of avoidant personality disorder. Here gays are bitchy less to put others down than to put others off: to ensure that they themselves can continue to avoid the closeness and commitment that they fear even more than they are likely to miss.

NARCISSISTIC PERSONALITY DISORDER

Some professionals say the equivalent of "By rights, all gay men would have to be in love with themselves, for all of them are by definition personally and sexually attracted to a self-object, that is, to themselves." Along even more pejorative lines, many homonegative laypersons view all gays as superficial queens who allow issues of style and status to trump matters of substance. According to this homo-hating way of thinking, while not all gays might have two perfectly coiffed French poodles, one black and the other white, they all find ways to parade themselves around in the hope of being admired—and not for what they are but for what they have; all mince and swish effeminately to parade their feminine queenly personal and sexual proclivities; and all are grandiose and inordinately proud of and excessively stuck on themselves and think too much about how they look and too little about how they act, especially toward others.

A homophobic patient of mine, himself gay, stereotyping all gay men as "a bunch of narcissists," complained that you have ongoing interpersonal problems with "all queens because they are all the superficial pretentious people you hear about and actually run across virtually on a daily basis." As he went on to say, "Every time I ask someone in the performing arts how he is doing, he answers, 'I have been named to the Meet the Composer Panel' when 'fine' or 'I had the flu recently' would have been called for and sufficient. And they are all selfish people, like Stu, who nominated me for president of our club—just so he could run against: me. Too they are all bitchy people with temper tantrums who pout and hold grudges, like one of my colleagues who would not talk to me again because I could not attend a party he gave—even though he knew I had a good excuse for not going: I had just met my partner of a lifetime and did not feel comfortable taking him to a gay bash so early in the relationship. Moreover, all my friends turn out to be petty and selfish. They just drop me when they get a new lover because they are afraid, I'll admit not without reason, that I might try to grab him away from them."

Last weekend consisted of my cooking for a friend's fortieth birthday party (I was the only one who brought food), spending too much money for his gift (he actually asked me for a gold watch), and getting snubbed by his gazillion bipolar/schizo friends. I tried to be the bigger one by introducing myself, so I say to his partner, "You must be Nick," to which he responds, "That is NICHOLAS to you." Ya gotta love that bunch. They also had pictures taken with their immediate family but left me out. I had to hang at the edge of the mob and got totally ignored. Next time I will have my brother come with me so that I at least have someone to talk to!

Though these attitudes/behaviors are familiarly/too blithely associated with being "typically gay," when they do occur in gay men, they are in fact generally not stigmata of being gay but rather symptomatic of being gay *and* suffering from a narcissistic personality disorder. However, this said, to some extent, there *is* an association between being gay and narcissism, but it is generally secondary more than primary, and is due to gays feeling forced to install excessive self-approval to counter equally intense bigoted disapproval coming from others along the lines of "I have to love myself because otherwise nobody else will." Such narcissism, less a basic trait than a defensive facade, is in turn generally too brittle to be sustained. So, it readily reverts to depression, where the gay man, now no longer primarily narcissistic, instead becomes depressed because of being overly self-alienated and, no longer excessively selfish, becomes overly altruistic and self-sacrificial—because of having gone from being a serious narcissist to having become a serious/committed masochist.

PASSIVE-DEPENDENT PERSONALITY DISORDER

Gays who get a reputation for being typically passive, dependant, and lacking in autonomy "in a feminine way" may in fact be suffering from passive-dependent personality disorder. This was the case for a troubled gay patient who "emphasized his feminine side" in order to *act* desperate and helpless primarily as his way to get others to take care of him "just as if I were a needy little girl."

POSTTRAUMATIC STRESS DISORDER

Many so-called typical gay problems, such as relational difficulties characterized by overt promiscuity (that often covers relational fears/a need to distance), are in fact typical symptoms of posttraumatic stress disorder in gay men.

Traumatized by the World

In this scenario, gay men are traumatized by the world's constant incoming social stigmatization related to their being gay. Their individual sensitivity then makes that social stigmatization intolerable. Next, the gay man, never having become fully inured to the ravages of bigotry, cannot live his life at all happily and successfully. Instead, he crumbles under the cumulative negative weight of the hurtful sadistic people all around him and becomes a heartbroken individual full of fear and dread. In turn, he defensively meets the world head on in defiant hypomania. Or he goes into depressive "funky" withdrawal that accompanies, becomes intensified by, and then spins off further traumatic flashbacks when he is awake as well as recurrent trauma-oriented nightmares when he is asleep—all together bringing him back, over and over again, to situations where he was once seriously abused emotionally and never got over it and perhaps was beaten physically without ever having fully healed.

For one gay man, ongoing trauma came from the locals who harassed him verbally and beat him up physically, knowing that they would not have to pay for their actions because small-town injustice denied that anything out of the ordinary actually happened or, admitting it, refused to call obvious acts of antigay bias criminal along the lines of "it may be hate, but if it is, what's wrong with hating gays anyway, the First Amendment protects that?" For a gay couple, it was the owner of the bar downstairs from where he lived who in

*one run-on sentence called him a "f——ing faggot" three times in a
row. For another gay man, a younger fellow from a harshly repressive family, the traumatic shock came from his classmates bullying
him around the time that he first recognized and then admitted that
he was homosexual. For some, coming out provides them with a
degree of relief. For him, his classmates' maltreatment in response
to his disclosure provided him with yet another reason for despair.*

Traumatized by One's Parents

So often, serious traumatization occurs at the hands of parents who
respond negatively when first learning of their son's homosexuality. Some
parents help and guide their gay sons through the difficult early stages of
self-awareness and learning, effectively medivacking them out of the
"front lines" of the internal and external battles that can especially charac-
terize the initial stages of coming out. But other parents seize this moment
to further traumatize their gay sons—setting up in them a foxhole mental-
ity that stays with them for the rest of their lives—and ultimately becomes
associated with a kind of battle fatigue accompanied by acute flashbacks
to the original traumata that occurred around disclosure time. This all
intensifies should the parents fail to support but instead continue to abuse
their gay son throughout his life, month after month, year after year. They
might side with competing siblings in the family, disfavoring the gay son
while making favorites out of his brothers and sisters simply because they
are the ones who will give them grandchildren. Mother and father make
their continuing love and financial support contingent on their son's going
straight and even threaten to disown him outright if he continues in his
homosexual ways while trying to force him to choose between them and
his lover in little things, as when, in a typical him-or-us gesture, they
invite their son but not his partner over for family events, banish his partner from the house completely, or, as happened with me and Michael
once, try to break up a budding affair by sending their son off to medical
school "for the opportunity of your lifetime."

*A patient complained that although his family treated him miserably
and rejected him constantly, they nevertheless expected him to treat
them with respect because, as they saw it, all parents "are entitled
to love because we brought you into this world." They provoked
him to attack them personally by way of coming out by their needling
him to come out to them before he was fully ready, effectively forcing*

him out much too precipitously—only to then complain (not surpris-
ingly) that he behaved "inconsiderately to us."

He said to me, crying, that after he came out to them, they were
horrified and expressed that horror by citing biblical references to
prove that being gay was a sin. They also kept him away from his rel-
atives so that the relatives would not find out that he was gay (and
that they themselves had produced a gay son), hid the fact that he
was living with another man from everyone they knew so that he
would not embarrass them, and refused to allow his lover into their
home saying, "We don't care if you stay away from us completely,
but that boyfriend of yours is never going to set foot through our front
door again." Then they went on a campaign to discourage and invali-
date his healthy partnered relationship by harping on what they
believed to be the professional downsides of living with another
man, strongly suggesting that either he get married heterosexually
or, for propriety's (and their own) sake, he resign himself to always
living alone.

Traumatized by the Dark Sides of Gay Life

Gay men just getting started are sometimes traumatized by the surpris-
ing and even potentially shocking news that gay life, no different from
any other life, can have a dark side. Especially during beginnings, traumatization can occur when newly out gay men are still exploring the subculture but not yet ready to settle down and put some of its less palatable
aspects behind them. They are now faced with—and have to integrate into
their lives—the sometime drug usage; the occasional long, late hours; and
the frequent rejections they experience when they involve themselves in
dating through the bar scene or on the Internet. Some can't take it in stride
and as a result retreat into themselves completely or harbor the main hope
that they can use the bars and the Internet as places to meet a lifetime partner—so that they never have to go back to such places again.

Traumatized by Gay Society/Gay Relationships

At times, gay society traumatizes some gay men by facilitating the tran-
sitory nature of gay relationships through generally being overly tolerant
of or actually encouraging relational motility. Too many gay men give
big knowing derisive laughs when told about gays wanting to be monogamous, joking (LOL!) that a gay golden wedding anniversary takes place
after 50 days and speak humorously—and with too little regret—of how

gay men should set aside time on the first date to call the trucking company and move in so that they can get established before they or their partner develop the seven-hour itch and move out.

Many gay men are traumatized when they actually go forth into the gay world trying to find a lifetime partner. One such gay man wrote to me as follows:

> I hate how trying to find a lover exposes me to other gay men's medical and psychological problems. There are just too many weirdoes and flakes out there. Once I spent hours and a small fortune wooing a potential lover only to be disqualified because after I took a sip of wine that nut rejected me for "being an alcoholic just like his father." Combing through the ads is a low yield activity too, because many ad-placers lie, particularly about their height, age, finances and desire for a relationship as distinct from quick sex. Blind dates are a horrific chore as well. One of my blind dates, someone I had just met through the Internet, in the elegant straight French restaurant I took him to (at a big cost to me) openly French-kissed me before we sat down to dinner. Then he spent most of dinner loudly serenading me with campfire songs about miners in the shaft and sailors at sea, and reciting tongue twisters, both embarrassing me and annoying the patrons at nearby tables who had not bargained on the floor show. Once I went on a date that was really awful—so stupid because he said things like, "I really like macaronis with pestos," and "my mother killed my father by all the salts she put in her foods." Then I went on a lunch date with someone who works as supervisor of the mail room at the company where I work, but we found each other on my dating site. His profile seemed really intelligent, laced with elegant French words (he lived and worked in France for three years) and ripe with philosophy quotes (he was a philosophy major as an undergrad). However, on the phone tonight he was just a bit creepy with no sense of humor, a flat affect, and told me that he looked me up already and studied my website by just using my first name because after all finding people to deliver their packages is what he does best. I just hope he doesn't stuff me in a laboratory wall somewhere. We will have lunch tomorrow, and later on I am also giving a laughing hyena I just met one more chance by meeting him for pizza. (He is the one last from Saturday who after fifteen minutes felt the need to shove his tongue in my mouth for some reason. Is that how you kiss on a first date?)

Many gay men complain that relationships are as hard to maintain as they are to first locate. On the one hand, without legal ties, it's easy to wander. On the other hand, when relationships become too intense to the point of becoming a merger, they exclude friends and family who are potentially in a position to keep things from overheating or completely collapsing—then are no longer there for you when the relationship, as can happen, doesn't work out.

Some gay men, because of moral and practical considerations, find the promiscuity that can be part of the singles life (gay or straight) deeply exhausting and potentially distasteful to the point that they even begin to refer to all gay men, themselves included, as "whores" and "sluts." The situation can even become dire should their gay friends, treating them badly, put them in a double bind/lose interest in them/dump them outright both because they aren't sexual enough and because they are "too sexual." Thus, one of my closest friends, acting shocked, actually dropped me because I had sex with our bartender, who was supposedly a happily married family man—this even though the "happily married family man" was the one who seduced me.

Aging gay men often find relational loneliness particularly traumatizing. A patient said to me,

> I worry that I will be lonely forevermore due to being humiliated by younger gays who make fun of me, take my money and run, or ignore me completely. And just recently, all my friends moved away or died. No longer, figuratively speaking, everyone's desired son, I have instead become everyone's burdensome grandparent. Being childless, I fear I will become more and more isolated as the years go by and especially around the holidays. When I am old, other gay men will stop paying my way and caring for me emotionally, until I begin to wonder, "Who is going to take care of me when I become even older and more fragile? Will I have to enter an assisted-living facility or a nursing home where I will be ignored as invisible, or be, all too visibly, mistreated and physically abused?"

Traumatized by One's Professional Problems

Some gay men find the seemingly irreconcilable pull between the pressure for sex good and plenty and the desire to succeed professionally wearying. They find it difficult to make choices between sexual pleasure and nonsexual productivity after considering the negative professional consequences of being openly gay in a chosen profession where heterosexuality or asexuality can be required to build a career. I know of at least one gay hairdresser who dates women and takes them out to where colleagues will see him because he doesn't want it to be known that he is gay, which, as he believes, might kill his career! Certainly as a doctor, a gay man has to choose his medical subspecialty carefully, for example, after considering the possibility that, because of the anonymity involved, anesthesiology may be more accommodating than surgery.

A physician-patient sacrificing medical productivity to gay sexuality gave up a thriving private practice in Chicago to move to Los Angeles in pursuit of a handsome lover. He moved back to Chicago again when the relationship soured, then went to Utah to pursue another love affair, only to return to Chicago when that did not work out. As a result, he never got the proper training or established the professional contacts he needed to build the large private practice that he really wanted. At first, for him, being gay all the way was the most important thing in life, more so even than being professionally successful. But later he suffered from regrets, spending the rest of his life ruing his past actions, bemoaning their negative professional consequences, and fighting off a posttraumatic stress condition with prominent depressive symptoms that began when he realized, he believed too late, that he had not lived up entirely to his professional ideals just so that he could have a "gay booty-shaking life."

Gays under considerable stress because of homophobia at work often manifest symptoms of work-related stress disorder, including insomnia; Monday morning blues; frequent absences, especially just before or after the weekend; drinking and smoking to excess; what looks like on-the-job laziness that actually involves anxious inattentiveness to and disinterest in one's work; and a compulsive desire to quit a perfectly good job and move on, not infrequently to one of lesser value and status, just to avoid the stigmatization of being out there and exposed in one's current workplace. Some manifest an inability or a refusal to take orders from the boss due to burnout in turn due to a boss's rejection and stigmatization, which may or may not be more feared than actual. For even these days, too many homophobic bosses are particularly hard on gays while denying it. They assign them the worst jobs and treat them like second-class citizens by not taking them seriously because they are gay. They push them around; criticize, humiliate, and ridicule them; and, believing that no gays can ever be the best of workers, downsize them first and promote them last.

Once I asked for a raise. My boss replied, "Not for you because you are making the same thing as a (straight) colleague." Only the straight colleague's training and experience didn't come anywhere close to mine. (My straight boss was simultaneously having an affair with at least one of his patients, but it would seem that just because the liaison was heterosexual, though everybody noticed, no one mentioned it.) Colleagues can be problematic too when they needle gays like children needle peers who wear glasses or old people who walk slowly. A doctor at a Veterans Administration clinic where I worked continuously repeated the negative things a paranoid patient said about me, to me, because "he thought it was funny." I was virtually ostracized from my work with students because I started an affair with one of the doctors at a nursing home adjacent to the hospital where I worked, and, because of the proximity and my lover's lack of discretion, everyone knew about it (another example of how stressful it can be when your personal life becomes everybody's business and grist for their critical, homophobic mill). At times, underlings are the problem, as when they refuse to be supervised by, supervise, or even work with gays on any level at all. To add to the stress, those concerned about losing out in the competition that is part of all life can view the *talented* gay man as a double threat, traumatizing him by double binding him, leaving him in a can't-win situation where others hate him the most: both when he does badly—for being a failure—and when he does well— for being the winner who takes all, having as such become too much the competition.

TEN

Substance Abuse

Substance abuse (alcohol and/or drugs used either separately or, as is often the case, together) falls into four categories according to the different causes for the abuse, with each implying a different remedial focus.

TYPE 1 SUBSTANCE ABUSE

Type 1 substance abusers abuse substances because of being isolated individuals—gay men with few or no friends and little or no romance in their lives. For some, their cats and their television sets are their only and best friends. In a vicious cycle, they abuse substances because they are lonely, and they become lonelier because others abandon them because they abuse substances, causing them to abuse substances even more.

Many substance abusers are isolated because of suffering from an avoidant personality disorder. They want and try to connect, but anxiety, paranoid hypersensitivity to criticism, and fear of rejection make it difficult to impossible for them to get close and be intimate. So they gravitate to the anonymity/promise of bars, only to find that the bar scene leaves them feeling lonelier, worsening their drinking and/or drug usage. Fortunately, because their heaviest abuse tends to be on weekends, they can—and often do—work without serious occupational impairment although not always as effectively as they otherwise might be able to do.

Other substance abusers are isolated because of pathological perfectionism, often part of obsessive-compulsive disorder.

A patient was severely isolated because he was unable to relinquish a too-resolute perfectionism that resulted in his inability to meet and marry a Mr. Right who was less than Mr. Perfectly Right, just as is. Because he set his standards way too high, no one could possibly match up to them and be what he wanted exactly. In therapy, he learned that the more stringent his desires, the fewer his possibilities and so the worse his chances. Eventually, he formed a relationship with someone good enough, even though to do so he had to soften/ abandon some of his principles and compromise some of his desires, becoming less insistent on what he wanted so that he could become more accepting of what he could actually get.

Still others are isolated mainly because of their circumstances:

There was a time in my own life when I drank heavily because I was lonely. I was going straight through a psychoanalysis whose unin-tended consequence was to leave me as gay as ever but now also— and newly—alcoholic, with drinking my (problematic) way to handle my being celibate as I followed the psychoanalytic "rule of absti-nence." My loneliness became even worse when, after five years, I gave up all notion of becoming heterosexual through therapy and reemerged into the gay life, coming out of the closet again, only this time to an empty house—as might be anticipated after five years of social withdrawal that had, predictably, decimated all my gay rela-tionships. Now I drank even more, mainly in bars, to feel connected and become reconnected. Only instead I wound up feeling even more isolated. For I didn't, at first, meet too many people who wanted to leave the bar and join me in a happy home life away from the night-life. Instead, many of the people I met in bars were there for one rea-son only: they were just where they wanted to be and hoping to stay put, happily and forever, right where they were.

A survey of gay men in the town where I currently live, which has a large gay population, indicates that, comparatively speaking, here sub-stance abuse is not a serious problem, probably because many of the gay men who now live here came here already coupled and to live the classic suburban-type life with a partner. To me, that suggests that substance abuse is less a function of being gay and more the outcome of being alone.

Therapeutically, lonely substance abusers need help solving the under-lying problem, emotional or real, causing their isolation so that they can emerge from their isolation to form and keep healthy, sustaining relationships. Many of my patients stopped their drinking/drug abuse on their own when they met someone compatible and become part of a stable couple—with a relationship that worked and a love that lasted.

TYPE II SUBSTANCE ABUSE

Type II substance abusers abuse substances because of being involved in a difficult relationship. There are five common scenarios, as follows.

In the first scenario, two partners have a sadomasochistic relationship where each is effectively driving the other to drink. Such sadomasochistic interactions tend to be between one partner who is angry and hostile and the other who is easily hurt yet masochistically provoking and putting up with at least some of the abuse he gets and then getting stoned to get through it and what comes next.

I remember suspecting that a relationship was in trouble when I saw one member of a couple, hesitating to go home, standing below the window of the apartment he shared with his partner. His cell phone rang—and it was his partner calling. But instead of taking the call, he monitored it and, seeing who was calling, deliberately didn't answer the phone, leaving his partner to wonder "where is he?" and "is he back yet from walking the dogs?" Then—and with a flourish— he turned the phone off and hid it in his pocket so that he couldn't hear it ring. I was not surprised to learn that a few months later, the man making the call had started drinking heavily because the man receiving the call, his partner, was now threatening to "hang up on him permanently" by walking out on him and for good.

In the second scenario, one partner is a paranoid individual who feels mightily provoked even in neutral or positive situations, then abuses substances, and then uses the perceived provocation to unfairly and unrealistically blame everyone but himself for the substance abuse, doing that in order to avoid looking within and resolving his own difficulties.

In the third scenario, one partner's substance abuse occurs in response to the other's being a cool and distant avoidant, fearfully withholding or being by nature incapable of giving affection and love.

In the fourth scenario, one partner drinks and/or takes drugs because his partner is a competitive histrionic man provoking him to do so. One partner provokes the other because of being a rivalrous individual whose goal is to make the other man into a loser who, by being less of a rival, thereby becomes less of a threat.

In the fifth scenario, one man's dependency is the culprit because as a dependent individual, he encourages his partner to stay stoned, hoping that he will remain ineffectual so that he will have to stick close to home— whereabouts always predictable, location always known.

In some of these cases, only one partner needs treatment. At other times, both should go.

Once when I was in a difficult unsupportive relationship, I was drinking because I knew my partner was cuckolding me. Although he came close to it, he never actually abandoned me for another man. I believe that a main reason he went with others was to let me in on what was going on "accidentally on purpose" just to get my goat. For example, once—knowing that I was most vulnerable at the start of a vacation when I was really tired, needed to get away, and was looking forward to the change—he picked the night before we left to disappear with a boyfriend and not return until early morning, leaving me wondering if we would miss the boat and have to cancel the trip. Another time, he said he was staying with his brother in Boston, although I doubted that. I traveled to Boston to meet up with him to join him as planned for the weekend. Only when I arrived, he was nowhere to be found. His excuse? Drunk, he slept through my phone calls. The reality (as I was later to discover)? He was out with someone and spending the night in his place. Ultimately, using his bad behavior as my excuse, I too started getting drunk on a regular basis in order to anesthetize myself so that I could feel less emotional (close to physical) pain. Eventually, of course, my drinking started affecting the relationship, making things not better but far worse. Realizing that, I stopped drinking. Only now, he, unable to satisfy some deep-seated ongoing need to keep me upset, in response starting drinking even more heavily himself.

Ultimately, I entered therapy. Fortunately, I picked a therapist who cut me off when I started complaining about my partner and instead focused on how I contributed to the problem by providing a sadistic partner with a willingly masochistic subject, so willingly masochistic that it was hard for him to resist beating up on me. When I did, finally, cease my whining and started putting my foot down, essentially setting limits on his abusiveness, the fights and arguments, going nowhere, stopped, allowing me to become far more supportive and

loving to him. His accusations and my counterallegations first dimin-
ished and then virtually ceased. The buildup to blowups stopped; his—
and so my—temper tantrums subsided; my binge drinking ceased;
and I no longer sought divorce to seek a new guy because my old
Mr. Wrong had now changed around enough to approximate being a
new Mr. Right. Finally, the vicious cycles had broken—a slow process,
with setbacks on the way, but one that worked through effecting one of
the basic principles I advocate throughout this book—that in the sado-
masochistic interactions of life, the good graces of one can generally
repair the bad karma between two.

TYPE III SUBSTANCE ABUSE

Type III gays abuse substances to medicate themselves for an affective disorder. For them, grief and depression, especially when these follow losses, are special times of vulnerability. Instead of healing in a healthy way on their own or through treatment, they abuse substances seeking not slow recovery but instant, on-the-spot anesthesia. Treatment is that of the underlying disorder with psychotherapy/pharmacotherapy.

TYPE IV SUBSTANCE ABUSE

Many gays abuse substances actively because they are involved with and have fallen under the spell of a social group advocating doing just that and applying peer pressure to egg them on and join in. Such social groups are often made up of serious social contrarians—typically, individuals who equate being wild, unfettered, and even frankly antisocial with being good, for to them good means being "free" and great means being "me." Bar owners foster the formation and continuance of such groups and the subculture of substance abuse by forging and fostering links between bar going/barhopping, drinking/taking drugs and being exquisitely happy and fulfilled. To accomplish their ends, they promote such things as bus tours to the gay bars in town and contribute money to creating alluring bar-themed floats in gay pride parades—insidiously enabling alcoholism/drug usage by stressing, often strictly for business reasons disguised as pleasurable enticements, the appealing social aspects of the bar culture, even though they know that the heavy substance abuse that goes on there generally not only doesn't sustain but can ultimately replace healthy sociability.

RECOMMENDATION

In all cases, gay men who are abusing substances first need to sober up. Then they need to find out why they are drinking heavily/taking drugs. Then they need to do something about that, which involves treating both the symptom (the substance abuse) and its underlying cause by the following means:

- Enhancing their own happiness through self-help and formal therapy where they work on resolving their own internal emotional problems, especially the problematic relational components of any underlying emotional disorder. That often starts by not totally blaming everyone but themselves for causing their own difficulties.
- Being positive to basically helpful friends, family, and partners, anticipating that they will respond by returning the favor.
- If they don't respond favorably, minimizing contact with or entirely dispatching them, especially those who are recidivistic enablers, and finding a new, more loving fictive family; a more supportive health-inducing partner; and a brand-new circle of very best friends.

ELEVEN

Shame, Guilt, and Low Self-Esteem

All gay men experience some stigmatization and a degree of banishment during their lifetimes. The ones who suffer the most are those who accept these incursions as deserved, then respond accordingly by buying into their victimization extensively and failing to live their lives contentedly. Most seriously affected are those gay men who haven't worked through feeling guilty about being gay but have instead developed moralistic negative self-destructive self-attitudes that have in turn spun off pejorative self-evaluations leading to a self-punitive mindset and consequent lack of self-confidence. The result is a self-damaging outlook spewing hurtful feelings and behavior characterized by gay men becoming prisoners of their own low self-esteem and feelings of insignificance, then acting as if they deserve their incarceration because they are somehow deficient and possibly even criminals—who should be not through disclosure set free from constraints but through closure fully constrained behind bars, now and forever.

While low self-esteem in gay men is often irrational, that is not always the case. *Appropriate and rational* low self-esteem can exist as a response to real personal imperfections that lead to appropriate criticism from self and others that is, unfortunately, all too well deserved. In such circumstances, guilt about being gay makes some sense but only as an understandable reaction to being gay *badly*. If this is your mindset, full gay pride has to come not from changing the way you think about yourself but from changing the way you behave toward others—as you stop making excuses for yourself, cease normalizing questionable actions as acceptable simply because they occur in someone who is gay, and stop allowing blanket self-affirmation to cover your shortcomings because, as you see it, being gay trumps all by excusing everything.

Most times, however, low self-esteem in gay men is thoroughly inappropriate because it is *irrational*. Irrational low self-esteem is associated with and leads to even more unnecessary and inappropriate guilt and shame, creating unrealistic, spreading self-dislike. If this is your mindset, enhanced pride has to come not from changing your behavior but from changing your mind, altering your self-view so that you treat yourself better, as a more worthy object of your own affections, then maintain that improved self-view, almost no matter what others think of you and regardless of what they say about or do to you.

Clinically, the guilty gay man with low self-esteem experiences excoriating self-criticism associated with excessive "don't-make-trouble" submissiveness that goes along with a high degree of collaboration with his abusers due to feeling personally, globally, valueless, and vulnerable—sheepish and ashamed, shattered by thoughts that he is "stupid," and even convinced that just by being gay, he is doing something seriously wrong. If this is you, you hide out in nondisclosure, which you rationalize as personally and practically appropriate, however much your staying in the closet involves unnecessary painful isolation associated with moody withdrawal from others. Erotophobia and sexual masochism are your continual prompts and constant companions as you push yourself to become abstinent or even try to go straight or, reluctantly remaining homosexual, do that but while remaining unable to fully experience physical and mental sexual joy as if, because it is wrong and shameful to have a body, you should instead erect crippling inner barriers and prohibitions to threaten your smooth eroticism and effective sexual functioning. Thus, one gay man I urged to mine the personals on the Internet dismissively replied to me, "You have to have special self-confidence for that, which I definitely do not have and don't have time to develop right now." You then rationalize your abstinence/trying to go straight as you misidentify what are in fact misguided attempts to disavow who and what you are as sensible and proper, a way to please and satisfy your parents and the parental figures in your life, such as the boss or society at large. Anxiety leading to a fear of success associated with a serious need for failure implemented through passivity accompanied by spreading temerity also occur, often taking the form of a personal narrative of self-compromise accompanied by specious philosophizing that goes something like this: "Because I am a homosexual, I am necessarily second rate compared to heterosexuals, for my homosexuality is not a different or an alternative but an inferior life form, so that I should just get used to being subpar and not on the same level as straights and calmly, willingly, and graciously take my proper place in line as the second-class citizen that, however unfortunately may be the case, I nevertheless, in reality and immutably, just happen to be."

Ultimately, such gay men often come to sink into becoming overtly depressed. They believe that they don't deserve much, belittle what they have, and fear that they will never get what they want, convinced that they will instead go through life missing out on all of its joys and perks. Simultaneously, they eat themselves up with envy for people whom they believe have what they think is missing from their own lives—as did the patient who, selling short his happy, quiet life with his partner, could do no better than brood about not having children like his friends and (he was now only 36) like them a big family to care for him in his old age. Looking on themselves with the same jaundiced eye that they believe others to be ogling them with, they turn on themselves and, if out, go back in again. Constant anger with others and at their own fate spins off not only poor interpersonal but also compromised professional skills as an overwhelming fear of retribution leads them to hesitate to extend themselves professionally and to instead stay put on a job that even they believe is beneath them. They shun the limelight not because they don't want to advance but because they fear that getting ahead will cause them trouble—simply by putting them out there, where they will, predictably, get shot down.

Alternatively, gays suffering from guilt, shame, and low self-esteem can become hypomanic to the point that they do not appear to be undergoing and seriously affected by guilty shameful ruminations. Going into denial, they embark on a life of surface glitter that, however, covers a depressive undercoating. In such cases, we often see uncontrolled impulsivity without concern for consequences, hypersexuality manifest as promiscuity, and abuse of substances, especially an addiction to alcohol and methamphetamine combined. Such gays are lysing low self-esteem by acting "as if," that is, "as if" all is well and "as if" they are unquestionably and fully deserving (i.e., narcissistically entitled to everything), with no need to accept self-deprivation of any sort because they are entitled to nothing less than having it all.

CAUSES

Homophobia

External Homophobia

External homophobia remains an important and generally recognized source of guilt and shame for today's gay man. However, while it might seem as if these days there is a greater, more widespread tolerance and acceptance of gays, to some extent that is an artifact for at least two reasons: currently being and acknowledging that one is homophobic is politically incorrect; and being openly bigoted and gay bashing is mostly a criminal offense. True, there has been a reduction (but hardly a disappearance) of physical assaults on gay men—with less in the way of throwing eggs at their houses, denting their cars, and physically attacking their person. But simultaneously, there has been an increase in emotional bashings, though generally these have been of a passive-aggressive nature. These days, fewer homophobes devalue and stigmatize gays openly by the likes of calling them "faggot" from the windows of moving cars. But homophobes still put gays down; only now, they do that subtly, using their intellect to attack. Thus, instead of calling them "faggots," they "just" call them some less impolite equivalent, like a "sexually preoccupied hedonist who suffers from compromised judgment that turns them into perpetual adolescents who cannot be expected to take on adult responsibility and so will never satisfactorily be capable of doing a man's work—or any work at all." Also, hiding their true intent, homophobes displace their homo-hating onto purportedly sociologically and morally neutral issues like dancing and music ("disco sucks") or, alternatively, replace gay bashing with "mere" shunning, often done subtly, so that instead of cursing at gays, they murmur about them literally and figuratively under their breaths. A decade ago, some teenagers in the New Jersey town where we used to live threatened to set Michael, my partner, on fire. Today, these teenagers have become adults who "just" push gay men out of the same town by being unwelcoming to them and for supposedly rational reasons—such as "so that my children won't be forced to endure and be contaminated by the gay subculture." Today, a relative of mine (who once also merely asked me, "Why don't you wear a yarmulke like all the other Jews") still refuses to bring her child to my hometown because it has a gay presence. Apparently, she believes that being gay is somehow catching and that her daughter, should she step into these environs, might become contaminated, adversely affecting her overall well-being, personal growth, healthy development, academic score, and even perhaps her reproductive capacity. Homophobic commentators on television never actually come out and say something openly antigay. They "only" regularly take the gay-unfavorable side in one gay-themed legitimate controversy after another—classically, those relating to gays serving in the armed services and when the issue of gay marriage comes up.

Unfortunately, this less overt homophobia is more pervasive and widespread and thus overall more damaging to its victims and society than the formerly seen, openly, and so known violent enemy. It is more toxic just by nature of its invisibility constituting as it does the kind of assault that gay men most readily buy into and take to heart, then use to treat themselves just as shabbily as the homophobes in their lives treat them. At least, when it hurt or killed them, they could dismiss violence that was overt as "not me but them." Covert violence, when thusly done "well," tends to come across as deserved and so taken to heart and incorporated into one's self-image.

Commonly, homophobia goes down with no one even mentioning the word "gay."

One of my doctors, no matter how many times I asked him to call me Dr. Kantor, kept calling me Mr. Kantor to the point that I began to wonder if he were making a mistake or sending me a message.

A gay patient became extremely upset after reading the following evaluation by a homophobic student who I know, for personal reasons, that though she never came out and said so, disliked him because she thought he might be gay: "What a pathetic excuse for an adviser, teacher, or person in general. Alzheimer's definitely has kicked in; he'll screw you over big time. People like Fred should know when to call it quits when it comes to academics. ... He does not have a clue as to what is going on in life. ... Don't take his classes. It will be the worst decision of your life ... oh, and good luck if he's your adviser, any info he gives you is wrong. ... Found him wanting ... seems stuck in the 50s ... boring and most of all self-centered and talks with an annoying lisp (!!!)."

Cognitively, today's homophobia, though less overt, still employs the same old warped reasoning as yesterday's and for the same purpose: creating and validating pseudological homophobic conclusions so that in spite of their homophobia, homophobes can both remain guilt free and suffer fewer personal consequences. What we hear are selective abstractions of reality carefully crafted to *seem* to proceed *to inevitable* when they in fact *actually* proceed *from prior fixed* conclusions. For example, homophobes having already decided that all gays are wanting, go back to select those *few* gays who illustrate their point, then go forward to deem *all* gays to be religiously, civilly, traditionally, and morally just like their "chosen sinful few."

Motivationally, homophobes are often opportunists who push gays out so that they can move in, for example, into a certain neighborhood. In addition, they are strivers who leap ahead using the bloody bodies of gay "opponents" as stepping-stones, puffing themselves up by putting gays down in order to ensure that since only heterosexuals belong, they will be the ones who win and the winners who will take all—for if gays get less, they get more.

Structurally, homophobes are often paranoid individuals who unconsciously project their own forbidden gay wishes onto others, condemning in them what their conscience decries in themselves, resolving their personal guilt by loudly proclaiming, "It's not me who unreasonably thinks bad thoughts about you; it's you who inspires them because of the bad things you are and do."

Internal Homophobia (Self-Homophobia)

Stressing how gay guilt is a response to the homophobia of others can downplay how much of gay guilt originates within oneself in self-homophobia. Too many gays are themselves erotophobics who quash their own sexual feelings and stifle any and all pleasurable sexual experiences for some entirely theoretical or completely imagined greater, characteristically moral good. Too many gays are masochistic men who need to experience pain over pleasure. Low self-esteem, predictably part of this picture, results in and is characterized by self-disgust due to perceiving one's being gay as constituting a shattering narcissistic injury so that the individual, somewhat or entirely independent of external input, views gay love not as an erotic gain but as a sexual loss.

The manifestations of self-homophobia in gay men are at times heartbreaking. They range through the behavior of the negative bitchy queen who, angry and miserable himself, is all too eager and willing to put other gay men down to the sadistic behavior of the therapist who, though gay himself, intervenes in harmful ways based on that self-homophobic hatred much too common in the healing professions. Gay men who are highly self-homophobic go on to be extremely vulnerable to, as they seriously buy into, the heterosexism and homophobia of others. They even try to go straight in the belief that heterosexuality is the gold standard and that success and happiness in life are definable according to the model of the ideal heterosexual lifestyle: marriage with children and a house in the suburbs. At the very least, when they hear, "No straight marine would want to be in a foxhole with a gay man," silently agreeing, they do not counter, true or not, with, "And no gay marine would want to be in a foxhole with a straight one." They sometimes develop cultural hierarchies within their own ranks so that they see exclusive homosexuals as a cut above those who are bisexual and promiscuous gay men as ideologically somehow holier than those in a committed monogamous relationship. Thus, not a few gay columnists tried to humiliate me by calling me an Auntie Tom in reply to my professional advice that *some* gay men (such as those who are hypomanic) ought to cool it, calm down, take stock of themselves and their lives, and change course in favor of a life less genitally and instead more generatively oriented.

Rejection

Gay men's guilt and shame and consequent low self-esteem are generally intensified when others reject their advances. When love is unrequited and relationships in progress go wrong, gay men often erroneously assume, "If he doesn't want me, it must mean that I am undesirable, which means that there is something wrong with me, and that means that I am doing things all wrong and all the wrong things," for "if I had been smarter, richer, and better looking and done more with myself and my life, all those nice men on the dating sites would have contacted me/called me back, and things would have worked out, while none of them would have blown me away so that by now I certainly would be partnered and probably happily married now and forever."

Cognitive Distortions

Specific cognitive distortions leading to a guilty conscience marked by shame accompanied by low self-esteem include the following:

- Viewing merely a few of your negative past actions/less-than-stellar present performances as constituting the entire, inadequate, valueless, or evil self; feeling thoroughly bad if even one person reacts negatively to you; and seeing any sign at all that you are not fully accepted as evidence that you have been completely rejected, totally unloved, and forever abandoned
- Thinking catastrophically as you overreact to your own peccadilloes and others' responses, perceived or actual, to you as if you had just committed a major faux pas or a significant sin
- Judging your own behavior in terms of similar = the same thing, along the lines of assertion = aggression = murderous intent = homicidal action so that simply thinking bad thoughts = having done bad things
- Thinking projectively, that is, in the paranoid mode, leading you to exaggerate the importance/magnitude of even a few minor negative bigoted

remarks made to or about you so that even a good joke at your expense becomes an official, major, off-putting, pride-shattering homophobic slight due to your having projected your own guilty self-recriminations onto others in newly creating a concocted world now become full of malevolent people, malignantly inclined toward you

REDUCING GUILT AND SHAME AND CONQUERING LOW SELF-ESTEEM

Don't be concerned if at first you cannot reduce your guilt along suggested lines. Guilt reduction takes time and requires work.

As a gay man, you have to take responsibility for living as guilt free a life as possible regardless of how other people look on/treat you. What matters most is not that as a gay man you will be victimized (stigmatized or marginalized) throughout life but rather how you respond to the inevitable victimization that *will* occur along the way. Along these lines, never join in with "them" to victimize yourself further because you feel you got what you deserve. Never compromise your life to please or coddle others or to fulfill the expectations of those who want you to be and to act compromised. I spent a good deal of my life thinking I deserved the personal and professional abuse I got because I was gay. Instead of protesting/fighting back, I tried to make myself over to please my detractors, hoping that they would love me more and so abuse me less. The reverse, predictably, occurred along the lines of "people demean people who kiss up to them for being butt kissers."

Decide if coming out will make you more comfortable and enhance your self-esteem and, if so, come out boldly, effectively, and creatively, seeking to attain true pride not only about being gay but also about as many other aspects of yourself as possible. Always keep in mind that disclosure can *intensify* shame by inflaming your critics, and that is not a good thing when, should they respond negatively to you, you care too much about what they think.

And what happens next counts too. As Henry Pinsker said in a 2010 personal communication, "We hear about the pain of concealment and the relief of coming out but the problems associated with *being* out are infrequently mentioned, sometimes dealt with in movies, but even then as a comic question." That's why I often refer not to "coming" but to "being" out, with coming out only a first step in an ongoing process and one that needs maintenance: finding a way not only to be free but also to remain joyful—self-tolerant and authentic to yourself all lifelong in the face of the predictable and inevitable negative fallout from others who often as not respond to your revelations by feeling annoyed, shocked, or disgusted by what you just told them.

So, try to refuse to let any antigay bigotry that occurs in reply to your disclosure drag down your self-image and lower your self-esteem. You have come out, not confessed to a sin or an abnormality. You have simply announced your sexuality and that you have accepted it. You have at last abandoned at least some of the unreasonable, rigid, all-pervasive, crushing hypermorality that plagues you, and you hope—if you don't actually expect—that others will do that same thing in return.

Don't blame yourself for relational difficulties simply because you cannot fully control all your relational anxiety at all times. Try to avoid making as many relational mistakes as you can, but if you do make some, recognize that that doesn't make you a relational failure. Also, keep in mind that there are bright sides to relational anxiety. Many people like shy people. They find them charming, and sometimes other people are much less threatened by you than they would be if you were boldly superconfident.

Consider countering guilt with defensive *denial*—short of becoming shameless. Denial figuratively puts a vapor barrier between you and the unjustified negativity that comes from others around you, leading to depression. Another valuable defense is *suppression*, where you engage and talk back to your guilty, critical, punitive conscience directly and demand that it go away or at least be less critical of and more positive toward you. Forcefully affirm your overall humanity—to yourself at least but to others too—doing so in spite of any minor imperfections you may have, being especially willing to accept your life/lifestyle and sexuality as it is, even though in some respects it falls short of what you think it should be.

Seek peer support to help you steel yourself against the internal and external gay bashings that lead you to stigmatize yourself or cause you to allow others to stigmatize and peripheralize you as immoral or disgusting. But because friends can be as unsupportive as enemies, pick your peers as carefully as you pick your partners. Don't wind up with a fictive family that is as dysfunctional as your family of origin. Don't hang out with others who instead of giving you what you need and compensating you for losses just substitute exactly for troublesome people you should be rid of. The best peers/other associates for you are those who tell you, "In my eyes, you a worthy person." The worst are false friends—those who are supportive to your face but stab you in your back.

Never make your self-esteem *entirely* dependent on external sources of approval from any collective, including collectives within the gay community. For no matter what you say or do, someone will disagree with you or find you offensive and say as much. Decreasing your need for impression management, stop grading yourself based on what others might be thinking about and how they are responding to you and instead develop internal strong, independent, unvarying, honest, personalized self-standards, creating a stable positive self-image. Always view yourself as a basically viable individual, asking yourself not, "Do I have what he or she expects of me?" but, "Do I think well of myself?" Simply refuse to calculate your self-worth entirely by what you assume your reputation with others to be. Instead, start finding strength and self-approval where it counts—from within. Never let the need for approval/congratulations from others trump your own self-congratulations. And never lower your self-standards just to appeal to other people first, though that requires appealing to yourself second.

Meanwhile, counter distortive empathy where you simply assume that others are judging you negatively because you conclude, without good evidence, that they are measuring you using the very same rigid, unfair, and excessively self-punitive yardsticks you use to measure yourself. In fact, always distinguish perception from reality by distinguishing projecting from perceiving and so imagining from determining.

Recognize the truly cruel people in this world and dismiss them as having problems of their own. In this regard, it helps to remain ever aware that people who criticize you are mostly talking only about themselves. Especially avoid those who are actually *trying* to make you feel guilty. Identify friends who deliberately induce guilt in you and certainly don't go back to them for more or to change their minds, hoping that they will relent and like you better. Indeed, consider at least temporarily protecting/enhancing your self-esteem by minimizing some—even considerable—aspects of your social interactions. Although protective withdrawal is generally a flawed and self-defeating attempt to manage/improve your self-image, there are times when it makes sense to avoid at least some aspects of gay life so that you can, for now anyway, steer clear of running into hateful others and finding out what they think of you. Sometimes, it is even a good idea to give up gain to avoid pain as you decrease your functionality here to enhance your functionality there.

A patient said to me,

At the risk of sounding like a depressed isolated loser, I have started to eliminate friends and family who don't treat me well. Essentially, that leaves few. I decided to do that after a nightmare I had the other night. I was in a classroom teaching about a nonsense syllable psychological experiment and one student said, "This IS nonsense, and I don't feel like learning it," to which the others chimed in and I blurted out (in this dream), "Well I don't feel like teaching it either and especially to a witch like you." Then, aghast, I realized what had slipped out, but it was too late, for the witch was on her broomstick on her way to complain about me. When I saw her heading in the direction of the dean's office, I frantically scanned the corridor for someone I could talk to about this, but the only people I saw were the ones who I don't see anymore because of what they did to me. In my dream, for instance, all I saw was:

—K, who used to be my friend/coworker but decided I was spending too much time with my family and not enough with him and then wrote me a "Dear John" letter, saying, "You don't seem to have enough time for our friendship."
—Z, my friend who stopped coming to see me because my house had bad vibes in it due to my partner's sudden death, and then to boot stood me up several times when we made plans to meet outside.
—D, the "leader" of my "widowers" group, now a therapist in training, who stood me up three times and then blabbed to everyone else in the widowers group the stuff we had talked about privately in the context of our "friendship."

So then, in this nightmare, I went home to look for my dead partner because he always had such a compassionate ear and would regularly offer comfort and insight—and, of course, I could not find him in my dream.

Then, yesterday, in actuality, I took my dog for a walk around Boston, only I started to sob because the budding spring made me think of my dead husband and how we would walk around those parts and how he loved the first spring flowers.

For a while, I felt like retreating into a cave. Now I have, and, guess what, I feel much better inside that enclosed space.

Deal with homophobia by choosing people who prefer gays to straights. Sometimes, you can do that where you live, but if where you live is a place where homophobes rule and roving antigay gangs menace, consider using the geographical solution and moving to someplace more simpatico. In making your decision to move, keep in mind that because the character of a given place invariably changes with the passage of time, sociologically speaking you might wind up worse off than before.

Here is a typical pattern of evolutional change I and Michael lived through but survived, if only by chance:

I and my partner Michael moved to the West Village in New York City and stayed there for 25 years watching it change from a gay/Bohemian outpost to a heterosexual backwater. We did what gays classically do: we moved into a run-down area and helped fix it up. Then the straights moved in and had conventional families. The first wave of straights was gay neutral or actually homophilic: they preferred to live with gay over straight men partly because they wanted to bring up their children in a place where the kids could experience and become acclimated to diversity. We were very happy there. But the next wave was of straights who wanted to live only with other straights and had no affection for or actually wanted us out so that we wouldn't contaminate their children. Sadly, our gay bookstore, where I used to see some of my books in the window, even turned over to become a place called "Belly Dancing," where all I now see in the windows are maternity outfits on pregnant mannequins. Some of our neighbors, ignoring the antidiscrimination laws, even became personally antagonistic or physically aggressive to us—a few verbally but most nonverbally. Among the latter group were women using their baby carriages as a battering ram to push us out of the way as they cut their straight swath through what they seemed to treat as a kind of gay tangled underbrush—less because they were in a hurry to get somewhere and more because they wanted to send us a powerful "get-out" message—and those who would "merely" refuse to say hello while giving us the fish eye/silent treatment. Paradoxically, these were the very people who moved in in the first place because they admired what aspects of the gay life were left and wanted to vicariously share in it, only to later decide to expunge it through gentrification, suburbanizing the area while still trying to rescue some of what they considered to be favorable aspects of the gay life that, unfortunately and largely through their own efforts, were by now irretrievably lost.

Further gentrification occurred when the property values began to rise, almost forcing us and the few other remaining gays out. For, many of us, being artists and performer types, had only a modest income. And all of us were very unhappy.

But, fortunately, and unlike many other gentrification stories, this one has a happy ending. For instead of selling, we rented out our apartment, and now times have changed, and the suburbanized neighborhood is actually attracting back a different subculture of gays: those with permanent partners and children of their own. So, finally, in a way we could never have anticipated, the neighborhood has become integrated once again and has once more turned into a simpatico place, safe to go back and a joy to return to.

Permit yourself to be successful. Allow yourself to be competitive without undue guilt over causing others' misfortune—especially survivor guilt due to believing that the world is a zero-sum place where because there is a finite quantity of "X"—anything you get by definition you got by taking it away from someone else. Instead of experiencing guilt over doing well because you believe others are doing poorly in comparison, start viewing yourself as a distinct entity entitled to fulfill your own destiny, regardless of whether others fulfill theirs.

Do less of what makes you feel guilty. Harness the power of positivity to all even—or especially—when and where that seems difficult to do. Treat everyone you can kindly and with respect, anticipating that if your love goes around, it will come around, secure in the knowledge that being a nonbully generally minimizes the possibility that you will be bullied back.

Correct self-sustaining, guilt-inducing/guilt-enhancing vicious cycles based on looping cognitions such as "I can't do this because I am deficient, and I am deficient because I can't do that" or "I can't socialize effectively because I don't feel worthy enough to attend social events, and I don't feel worthy enough to attend social events because I can't socialize effectively." Interrupting such vicious cycles allows you to experience satisfying small successes that ultimately break the impasse through incremental achievement, leading to less withdrawal and enhanced guilt-free motivation to go forward and get ahead. Avoid vicious cycles starting with inept disclosure where you reveal yourself to certain others, only to find they use what they learn about you to devalue you, ultimately leading not to more but to less pride. If I had never proudly told my old boss that I was writing this book, he never would have asked me, "What does an old guy like you have to offer the young gay men you hope to be in your audience?"

Understand how your past experiences mold your present, negative self-view—and that generally in an unfortunate way. Parental deprivation of love and physical abuse meted out long ago (and at the time presented as if deserved) often lead gay men later in life to become overly attracted to similarly negative-thinking parental substitutes who predictably perform as feared. I would often compulsively engage others who were not in fact at all interested in engaging me—just to reverse their negativity so that I could somehow be made whole again. Of course, their devaluation of me continued anyway, and naturally I viewed their continuing disdain as a further reason for self-disapproval because, as I concluded, it's not that I had picked people who for reasons of their own can't love me or who can't and don't love anyone at all; rather, it's that nobody can love me, and that is because of who and what I am—which is clearly "completely unlovable."

As one gay man put it, insightfully explaining the origins of his guilt and low self-esteem,

Everyone I meet now reminds me of my parents who kept the mood negative in my growing-up years. All I got was deconstructive criticism, said in the most negative of spirits, telling me I was embarrassing, dirty, had a birdbrain, a big nose, was ugly, and was a tramp (that last name was for when an altar boy walked me home from church one Sunday in eighth grade and my parents accused us of having sex). Good thing at the time I thought a tramp was someone who had no home, so luckily I wasn't offended—until years later. You can see why my grandparents were my only refuge.

Here is a potentially helpful exercise. Make a two-column list where you identify your positive features in column A and inscribe these beside the negative features you go on to document in column B—then do the math to see if overall you are "okay as is" and, if not, determine what you can do to develop a more balanced, more positive attitude; better behavior; and hence an improved self-view, one now newly created and maintained by you, independent of what others seem to or actually do think about you.

Develop firm, meaningful, generative goals and remain thusly goal directed by avoiding impulsive behaviors that divert you from where you ultimately want and ought to be. Never let compulsively self-destructive behaviors become equally self-destructive substitute goals. Shopping and hoarding, even if that involves only decorating and redecorating your apartment to loving perfection, must not divert you from more significant life achievements, especially having loving relationships with others and with one special person. It's highly misguided to do what one of my patients did: move to another state because there the bars stayed open later.

Never attempt to reverse the ravages wrought by low self-esteem through methods that fail to work or that are actually even more guilt enhancing, like the following (some of which have been discussed previously here):

- Attempting to make up for your presumed flaws by devaluing other people
- Being flamboyant not because that is you but rather to proudly display yourself to make up for feeling ashamed of who you are—fanning your feathers to feel less like a crestfallen peacock, acting like a princess to feel less like a peon
- Becoming codependent in a way that involves hiding out with one to feel safe from all others because you believe the world to be a dangerous place for you, although the danger exists only in your own fiery imagination
- Behaving "holier than thou," for example, overindulging in morally superior abstinence
- Trying to go straight to placate and satisfy someone or something else, such as your parents or your church
- Seeking value for yourself by collecting trophy men, only to ultimately have unsatisfactory/failed relationships because all you get is "living dolls"
- Notching your gun with sexual conquests
- Being promiscuous where you seek sex as accomplishment and triumph, especially in a futile attempt to relieve a depression (When I was an intern, I was very depressed because, though I had gotten the internship I wanted, I was lonely and feeling stuck in Chicago with no family or, at least in the beginning, no friends. So I dealt with my perceived predicament by becoming extremely promiscuous. Every free night, which was usually one out of two, I would pile into my little car, an import that was almost literally, not just figuratively, a tin can and very unsafe, especially for a driver who had partied too much. Driving on dangerous streets in a snowy city, I did the bars until very late in the morning. Those days, I could pick up men without difficulty, and that's exactly what I did: one after the other and so many that I was exhausted all the time to the point that that affected my work. I wouldn't listen to the constructive talking to I was getting from others who were trying to help and stop me before I killed myself. Fortunately, nothing untoward occurred: a testimony to good luck and the resiliency of my youth. But I could have made some medical mistakes and spent the rest of my career with a lifetime of regrets doing penitence for momentary pleasures that had a very short half-life.)

- Refusing to set limits on being you so that you can "be me all the way" even when being you entails a being "yourself" that you ought to stop fully admiring and start at least partially disavowing

And when all else fails, try saying over and over again to yourself the two magic words of guilt reduction: "So what." Mean that, and add that all is not completely lost, just because for the moment all is not entirely well.

TWELVE

Suicide

For most gay men, suicide is a permanent solution to a temporary problem. Never the wise choice, it is always the wrong one and for at least two reasons. First, if the suicidal individual survives, he almost always wakes up realizing in hindsight, "What was I thinking? Why would I even attempt to do that to myself? Wasn't there another way?" Second, suicide never resolves anything, especially since, in a final irony, the gay man who successfully suicides is not around to appreciate the benefits of what he has just "accomplished."

Still, suicidal thoughts and behavior are very common in gay men and threaten not only their happiness but also their very existence. Some gay men, both those just starting out and those who are older veterans of the life, become suicidal without having significant emotional problems. This is commonly due to their having been *brutalized* by homo-hating bullies, such as those who out them gratuitously, criticize them unduly, and/or attack them physically. Other gay men become suicidal because they have emotional difficulties, and these lead them to feel as if they have lost control of their destiny and so to see themselves as being helpless in the face of the coming difficult life they convince themselves that that they will assuredly live and never survive. Often, suicidality is a symptom of post-traumatic stress disorder (PTSD), where it is an immediate or delayed response to discrete *trauma*, particularly the trauma of having been rejected, especially when the rejection actually consisted of having been dumped. Common too is suicidality due to depression or bipolar disorder. In addition, some gay men become suicidal because of being antisocial personalities who use suicide psychopathically to manipulate others into doing their bidding, as they make suicidal threats or attempts as the best or only way they know how to get others to pay attention to them, mind them, and, doing their bidding, bend to their will.

THE PRODUCT OF BRUTALIZATION

To some extent, everybody's self-esteem depends on what people say about and do to them. And gay men are certainly no exception to this rule. But not a few gay men become especially vulnerable to others' ill will and negativity when being gay goes along with their being ashamed of themselves, and that easily translates into readily feeling humiliation, as when disclosure meant to enhance gay pride instead intensifies gay shame. Particularly thus affected are the gay men who are victimized by a homo-hating family, friends, classmates, and teachers and then, buying into the bullying, introject all the hatred and go on to hate and bully themselves, most unfortunately by attempting/committing suicide, using methods that range among cutting their arms to hanging themselves to jumping off a bridge. In effect, by attempting/committing suicide, they are agreeing with all the negativity on the part of others saying to them, by their words and deeds, "If you were dead, then the world *would* be a better place."

THE PRODUCT OF LONELINESS

Some gay men recognize that they are lonely. Others, though extremely lonely, fail to recognize how lonely they actually feel and how much that bothers them. This may be because they feed themselves interpersonal methadone in the form of alcohol, drugs, or compulsive television/pornography watching. Or it may be because they deny their loneliness through defensive hypomania—as did the teenager who repeatedly and gloriously hummed the lyrics of a song that said that his was the greatest love he had ever known—although no lover was anywhere on his horizon.

Some gay men are in fact lonely and have every reason to feel that way. But others, even the youngest among them, feel lonelier than needs be. Often, this happens when cognitive errors about minor loneliness creep in, take over, and catastrophize the situation, turning it into major feelings of alienation as the gay man comes to believe that "because I am lonely now, I will be lonely forever," "a little loneliness is a reason for a lot of despair," "all gay men are fated to be lonely lifelong, as I am," and/or "being alone means being helpless or close to death."

Such gay men experience a crushing aching feeling that "I would rather be dead than spend the rest of my life this way." Now, impatient to find someone to love and to love them, they panic as an hour without love becomes a lifetime of lovelessness. Becoming impulsive, they act out of desperation, frantically cruising to deal with their emptiness and forming self-destructive liaisons to fight back tears, only, failing to succor themselves, to become thoroughly pessimistic and depressed as they sink into a state of hopelessness and give up completely, having come to truly believe that everyone is most definitely gone out of their lives now and certainly lost forever.

A traumatic past almost always tends to intensify present problems with loneliness. A patient said,

Each time a potential partner rejected me, I flashed back to childhood times when my parents left me alone in our apartment without a baby sitter, and I was terrified that something would happen to me and no one would be around to help. I still felt that way well into my adult life, even though I was living in the Big City where help, unneeded anyway, was readily available. Also, each time a potential/actual partner rejected me, that reminded me of the time my mother got pregnant when I was an adolescent, by which time I had become used to being the only child. She and my father would sneak off to the obstetrician, but instead of telling me where they were going and had just been, they would leave and return with a shamed look on their faces, making what were clearly phony excuses for their absence. I began to think that something was seriously physically wrong with my mother—that she was sick, going to a doctor for cancer, and was never going to get well. And so I became convinced that at a very early age I was fated to become the one thing that I, like most children, dreaded being the most: that proverbial "motherless child."

THE OUTCOME OF EMOTIONAL PROBLEMS

Gay men who become seriously suicidal as a result of emotional problems require timely diagnosis and proper treatment. But too often, all concerned—gay men and those who love them—view suicidality as a given thing in gay men and as such completely apart from emotional problems in this population. Commonly, that's what they do when they dismiss personal paranoia as the cautiousness appropriate to being gay or overlook the symptoms of depression, grief, and PTSD as just part of the hard life that all gay men are, simply because they are gay, fated to live.

Paranoia

The following case vignette illustrates how paranoia can affect relationships and spin off suicidality. (It also illustrates today's often fatal tendency on the part of too many diagnosticians to misdiagnosis paranoia as affective disorder and prescribe antidepressants even though these can make suicidality worse.)

I read your book, *Paranoia*, and it solved the puzzle of my gay brother who had been diagnosed 25 years ago as bipolar. He's my older brother, and I realized something wasn't right. For 17 years he was on lithium. Throughout that time he had few interpersonal relationships with the family, was generally antagonistic towards family members, and became unable to work. His psychiatrist tried to put him on one of the newer mood stabilizers because his lithium levels had become toxic. But all seemed to have horrible side effects. For the last six years he found a partner but had paranoid delusions about him ending in separation and a serious suicide attempt. Then he started going in and out of hospitals. He is currently in the hospital, and I now believe that the antidepressants put him there. The antidepressants made things worse, but antipsychotics made things better. The antipsychotics really contained the psychotic delusions almost making him seem normal. But he is very anxious about staying in the hospital—especially when he does group. He fits your description of a paranoid schizophrenic. How do I know? I have listened to his psychotic delusions and tried to understand them as horrifying as they were! I think my grandfather was paranoid, my father is too, but he is older now, so the symptoms have subsided, but he still does the weird things that you mention in the book. I need to find a doctor who can help him with psychotherapy once he gets out of the hospital and especially one who can keep him from attempting suicide once again. We need help! He is very intelligent and an artist, but he has become suicidal all over again. One problem is that he doesn't think he has a problem anymore. Another is that his doctors continually call him "bipolar." So it is complicated. Can you help us?
Leah.

I discuss paranoia in gay men further in Chapter 3.

Depression and Grief

Gay men who are suffering from a *unipolar disorder* feel blue and despair much or most of the time. Gay men who are suffering from *bipolar disorder* feel blue and despair—until they become euphoric when hypomania supervenes to cover their depression with a "life-is-wonderful" denial defense.

While paranoid gay men feel blue because they imagine that others, antagonistic to them, are mistreating them, even though they have done nothing to deserve it, *depressed* gay men feel blue because they imagine that they themselves are unworthy, and, while others are mistreating them, they are doing so appropriately—because they are responding to the supposed unworthiness in however a negative, still an eminently sensible and realistic fashion.

Younger gay men often get especially depressed because they feel hopeless, something they feel because they pessimistically project their present hard times onto their future so that "all is lost now" comes to mean "and also all my tomorrows will be a complete loss."

The symptoms of *grief* overlap with those of depression. There is a continuum between grief, pathological (complicated) grief, and depression. Depending on your theoretical perspective, these either represent different degrees of seriousness of the same problem/disorder or indicate the presence of different problems/disorders entirely.

Gay men often grieve because of suffering two kinds of losses. The first is *concrete* losses, such as those involving being rejected/dumped or losing a friend or partner to physical illness, formerly commonly (but fortunately now far less so) to HIV/AIDS. The second is *abstract* (*symbolic*) losses resulting in a compromised self-image, perhaps tarnished by the passing of their youth or due to failing to realize their gender ideal, as in "I am not now and never will be the real man I want to be" or "because I was born in a man's body, I will never be the woman of my heart's desire."

When grief is mild, the grieving may have been attenuated because what was lost was predominantly a negative force in the man's life so that "good" lessens the impact of "riddance." Paradoxically, grief can also be mild under the opposite circumstance—when the relationship with the person lost was so predominantly positive that enough good memories remain and prevail to sustain the griever through the process (but see below). A grief reaction can *seem* (but not actually be) mild when preceded by *anticipatory* grief. Here, because the loss is expected/predictable, the mourning process occurs in advance as a way to prepare for what is clearly to be, so that by the time the actual event occurs, the grieving process is well under way or just about over.

Mild grief is merely somewhat distracting. It interferes only minimally with day-to-day functionality. Though it can last even for months or years, it usually ultimately resolves spontaneously or in response to therapy. Should therapy be necessary, all that may be required is a brief supportive tiding over in anticipation that the tincture of time will do most or all of the healing.

In *serious* (complicated) grief (as with depression), the sufferer may feel blue and cry or feel blank and be unable to weep. Severe demoralization can occur if a loss comes to feel incalculable, overwhelming, and irreversible. Those feelings often swell when a gay man whose partner has dumped him stops thinking, "He will return, he always does," and "anyway, I can live without him," and starts realizing, "He isn't coming back, and now I understand that I can't live without him, or at all."

Often, in serious (complicated) grief, there is a degree of withdrawal. One gay man felt, "My life goes on, but around me, like I am a stone in the river, lying there inert as the water just flows by." Somatic sensations like pressure in the chest or an empty gnawing feeling in the pit of the stomach commonly occur, and in severe cases somatic preoccupations, like an HIV-negative gay man's irrational fear that he has developed HIV/AIDS, can be present. Such somatic preoccupations often express secret wish fulfillments, such as "I actually hope a fatal illness will take me so that I can join my partner in the next life."

Grief often becomes severe in gay men, even in those not otherwise at heightened risk for emotional disorder, when the individual is inexperienced and so has had little familiarity with losses and therefore has not yet developed adequate philosophical, spiritual, psychological, and practical coping mechanisms/defenses to fall back on. It can also become severe in *experienced*, generally older gay men, with few or no supportive friends and family to help make any losses that occur more bearable, without the mindset or wherewithal needed to find someone new, and with little time left in life to make up not only for the personal problems associated with being alone but also for the financial problems that result should they be left strapped because of no longer having a second income. Particularly at risk are gay men in a truly loving dependent merger that excludes others for years, only to then dissolve, leaving the surviving partner truly at sea and thoroughly floundering.

A serious complication of all grief in gay men involves the partial or total loss of *self*-support, whereupon the gay man feels guilty, self-blames, and misperceives himself as bad because of unacceptable fantasies, such as "I am selfish and hate myself for even thinking, 'I welcome losing him, for his loss is my gain, and I will be better off without him.'" Though completely understandable, somehow particularly shattering is the discovery that one's grief is more narcissistic than altruistic, more for oneself than for one's partner—so that what one is really grieving for is one's own loss: of personal status or of the social life a couple had together when both partners were still alive.

One grieving man felt guilty for not being able to do any better than complain, "Now that I have lost my partner, other couples are not going to invite me to their country house. As a single man, I will pre-dictably threaten all the married men in my group, who will fear that I am about to steal their husbands." He was particularly ashamed to find himself "foolishly" preoccupied with and bemoaning minor changes to his routine, such as, "Now, who am I going to go to the theatre with?" We also heard, "What kind of person am I to have bought him such a cheap casket just so that I could save some money and use it for new clothes and electronic equipment?" He felt guilty because he felt just as devastated about such "silly things" as by the actual loss of his partner.

Of course, the loss of self-support is most serious when (although not so in the case just mentioned) guilt and self-blame are partially or wholly warranted, as in "I am bad for not taking him to a doctor earlier, having that affair, being nasty to him all these years, encouraging him to go back into our burning house to save our cat, and not even being there at his bed-side at the exact moment that he died."

An almost routine component of the loss of self-support after a death is anger over having been abandoned, accompanied by the feeling that it is wrong to get angry with someone who did, after all, die. Emergent anger is particularly prevalent when the lost relationship was in the first place significantly marred by that familiar love–hate admixture we call "ambiv-alence." After death, the (previously kept-in-check) anger aspect of the ambivalence fully emerges—first, because it no longer needs to be con-tained as formerly, and, second, because the target of the anger is no longer around to do a reality check of runaway angry fantasies, say, by countering unfair accusations through rational explanation or by making amends. Also, now the flourishing anger, having no external target to affix itself to, has no solid place to go, so it can be expressed only through being turned around on the self. This can but lead to intensified self-hatred, and along with the *self*-hatred comes overvaluation of the lost *object*, a posi-tive distortion of the other's image, which makes a new saint even out of a partner who might very well have been an old sinner.

Rolf grieved long and hard for Mario. When someone reminded him that "Mario was a whore" and suggested that he "give up the grief, he wasn't worth it, and I have the evidence to prove it," Rolf replied, "I don't care; no matter what he did to me, he was perfect, and I loved him, even in spite of it all. Yes, there were things he did wrong, but the wrong things were not so bad, after all. I know he cheated on me, but that was acceptable because he was just a man, and all men seek variety. And I know he dumped me, but I suspect I provoked it. For I was a bad person because of all the things I said about and did to him when he was around and remiss for not fully realizing how good he was at the time. And, anyway, what difference does it make? I loved—and still love—him so much that I would then tolerate almost everything and would now continue to do so if only he could be with me still. After all, the only thing that currently matters is that he is gone, and I have lost a wonderful, wonderful, person, the only true love of my life. We laughed before we went to bed, and we laughed when we got up in the morning. Now there is laughter no more—only tears, tears, and more tears."

Ultimately, the hardest-hit grievers I know of are those who deal with their low self-esteem by going into denial, as in "I am better off without him, for now I can have all my old friends back—both the ones who didn't get along with him and the ones he didn't get along with. Anyway, there are many nice things about being alone and going solo, such as being able to keep my bedroom at the temperature I want and having all the sex/sexual variety I need." Such denial thinking often becomes hypomanic behavior as the individual rushes about trying to find someone new to make life whole again. He intensely and often futilely attempts to reestablish relationships with old lost friends, family, and in-laws, many of whom by now have closed ranks and extruded him from their lives—no matter what promises they previously made to stand by and take care of him in any moment of possible need. Unfortunately, the hypomanic denial doesn't really lessen the true impact of the loss, for that involves deep-down hurt, including missing the substantial and gratifying pleasures of being partnered/married, such as always having someone around to make plans with for the holidays. So underneath, the griever continues to feel sick at heart and ultimately crashes. And a special danger of this particular sickness and the crash afterward is that it has distinct physical effects that are not quite as easy to deny. For example, grief can seriously compromise the immune system at the same time that it compromises judgment—and the griever badly needs both now should he be becoming sexually more active. For this is the very time that his body requires maximum protection both from the sexually transmitted diseases that he can encounter and from the emotional battering that he will likely experience. For predictably, he will attempt to form new relationships, only to get rejected, or actually form them, only to experience precipitous, further heartbreaking losses.

Usually, gay men recover relatively quickly and essentially completely from their grief. Bereavement tends to be a self-limited process partly because such an intense response is unsustainable for long and partly because time tends to heal this wound too. In other cases, however, the mourning process is prolonged to the point of becoming chronic. This often happens because of the difficulties involved in disentangling and resolving, after the fact, the complex mixture of love and hate that exists even in the best relationships and because grievers hesitate to do the work that mourning requires, for, finding grief pleasurable in a masochistic way, they resist abandoning even an undesirable lost object: wanting to forget yet reluctant to forgo remembering.

Unfortunately, grief can lead to suicide. Here, the suicide can represent the ultimate form of self-blame and self-abuse as well as an additional element of desperation. Or the suicide can be a kind of orgasmic culmination, a Wagnerian love–death scenario where putting an end to one's life is considered to be not an act of despair but one of affirmation of joy: in a sense, the ultimate of orgasms.

PTSD

Gay men with PTSD suffer from flashbacks to and the need to compulsively repeat old childhood traumata, in the latter case trying to this time make things come out right (the "repetition compulsion"). Those who suffer from flashbacks tend to withdraw from old relationships and avoid forming new ones to the point that they become isolated and depressed. Those who suffer from a repetition compulsion attempt to form and maintain relationships precisely with new people who are cynical, critical, cantankerous, caustic, childish, and churlish just like the old ones they had trouble with, doing so to test themselves to see if they can survive anew and this time get things right. They hope that, for once, things will go better and come out okay. But not surprisingly, mostly the results continue to be just as before. Should the negative outcomes become cumulatively devastating, the gay man begins to wonder, "Is there any longer much— or any—reason for me to hope and go on living?"

Many such gay men, going into denial, attempt to deal with their flashbacks or repeat difficulties with unloving others through camping and promiscuity—their (unhealthy) way to "just get over things" as they clear their minds by repressing their problems. If this works at all, it is generally only incompletely because mostly this suppressive mechanism falls far short of full forgetting, and therefore satisfactory healing never occurs.

PTSD can be *mild* when gay men have solid coping mechanisms to deal with its manifestations—including a (overly) tolerant masochistic personality where they actually enjoy their troubling flashbacks and a macho gender identity where they so treasure their masculine image that they will go to any lengths necessary to "avoid acting like a whiner." PTSD can also be mild when a fortuitous environment helps muffle the response—as when a gay man has a sympathetic uncritical family to cushion the blows by being there for him, helping see him through.

Unfortunately, PTSD can be *severe* under less favorable circumstances: when coping mechanisms are ineffective, one's personality is unaccommodating, one's preferred identity does not include resolute stoicism, and one has to suffer virtually alone. Now, everything seems to remind the gay man of earlier traumatic occurrences. Something about his present invariably reminds him of something frightening that happened to him in the past. He tends to have recurrent nightmares even in the midst of a loving relationship as he continues to suffer from recurrent dreams of being abandoned. Such nightmares are both the product of an underlying depression and the cause of further depressive response. When he is awake, his flashbacks combine with the remembered nightmares to make the entire experience so onerous that he contemplates or attempts suicide "just to make it all go away."

Psychopathy (Manipulative Suicide)

Manipulative suicide involves suicidality as a power play meant to exert influence on—really to exact tribute from—a significant other, to gain some (deserved or undeserved) specific, often immediate advantage.

Once I asked a companion to leave because he had received a love letter from someone he had just met—sent to where we recently moved in together—by certified mail. In response, he took an overdose of valium. That got me to back off, change my mind, and allow him to stay. Only I then found myself enmeshed in several more years of painful infidelities culminating in his *leaving me. I learned two lessons*

from this experience: send people away who aren't more careful and
be careful (more than I was) about how you send people away.

PREVENTION AND TREATMENT FOR SUICIDALITY

Suicide prevention and treatment involves determining the cause of the
suicidality and intervening accordingly and empathically.

Prevention and Handling of Being Bullied

Bullying, including cyberbullying, is responsible for much in the way of
personal inhibition and loss of power. It also leads to destruction of some
of the finest, most creative, highest-functioning members of the gay community based simply on their sexual orientation.

There are three categories of actions you can take to prevent, cope with,
and deal with interpersonal and cyberbullying. A caveat is to always consider that each person and situation is different, so the ultimate course of
action that you take is highly dependent on your age, personality, intellectual and physical capabilities, stylistic preferences, and special, often very
personal circumstances, including the nature of the bullier and his or her
bullying.

You can deal with bullying *intrapsychically*: by understanding the
bully's illogic and so appreciating his or her irrationality as you view bullying as the product of mental illness that it usually is (commonly
attention-deficit/hyperactivity disorder, adjustment disorder of adolescence, paranoia, or substance abuse) and as such not to be taken at face
value. You can set up internal firewalls to help you become inured to bullying as you just let it roll off your back, developing personal pride independent of what others say about and do to you while living well as the
best revenge. And you can get educated and stay informed about the reality involved in the bullying so that you can spot misinformation thrown at
you and use the raised intellectual awareness to counter any potential catastrophic responses you may have to your bulliers.

You can deal with bullying *interpersonally*: by developing a support net-
work—informing your parents/others what is going on and (when applicable) talking with them about it while joining groups for support and
counteraction. Whether to just walk away or take a counteraggressive put-
up-with-nothing stance (without exposing yourself to danger) or (in
selected cases, few and far between) to stay and harness the power of positivity in the hope of manipulatively ameliorating the bully's negativity by
bringing him or her around depends on your preferences, your personality

style, your resources, who exactly is doing the bullying, and the attitude of peers, colleagues, and educators/employers both toward you and toward those who are bullying you and to bullying in general. (Many people who should be supportive of you are less so because of problems of their own and/or their own situational needs. Many are sufficiently ambivalent about your being bullied for being gay [and want to themselves bully you for the same thing] to withhold that support or to offer support that is merely luke-warm and not as helpful as it could potentially be.) Froias sums it all up nicely when he puts it this way: "If you are young and have to put up with assholes at school (or home), there are other people in this world who will stand by your side and help you deal with any situation."[1] Also, never bring bullying down on your head by being a bully yourself, for if you mistreat people, they are more than likely to mistreat you back, either by bullying you openly and actively or by doing so subtly and passive-aggressively, especially by ignoring your cries for help.

Finally, you can deal with bullying *socially* by conducting research and being an activist, for example, urging the media to popularize the distor-tive aspects of bullying—say, writing editorials and giving public work-shops on the home front, at social clubs, in churches, and in schools.

Prevention and Remedy for Loneliness

You should identify, not deny, your loneliness and instead, refusing to accept it as the inevitable product of being gay, view it as likely (depending on you and how you handle it) to be a temporary condition that is a manifes-tation of currently negative and unfortunate but probably (happily) transient circumstances. If you are an inexperienced gay man, remind yourself that because you are just starting out, it is too early for you to overreact cata-strophically to interpersonal problems that you have so far encountered in the gay life. In particular, you should not assume that because you are lonely for a moment, all is lost for a lifetime. Refuse to view temporary setbacks as a definite indication of what is to come. Understanding the past, pundits notwithstanding, is not always the best way to cope with, manage, and change the present and prepare for the future.

I didn't follow my own advice when one New Year's Eve I felt abso-lutely desperate just because the person who invited me out didn't show up and I didn't have anything meaningful to do that night. Just imagine: I was all alone for one New Year's Eve! So I got drunk and spent hours having unsafe sex, the more the better, basically attempt-ing to degrade myself as my way to take my anger at the cruel world

*out on myself, meting out to myself my own deserved comeuppance
for being such a complete failure, especially when it came to my relationships. Subsequently, I learned that there are times in every man's
life when we all feel—and even actually are—very much alone, and at
such times self-defeating desperate measures, particularly involving
drinking to excess and promiscuity, are not only unnecessary and
overkill but also counterproductive because, though they provide
temporary balm, they are not a permanent long-run solution, for ultimately the only permanency they create is permanent loneliness—
and even more of that very loneliness that they are attempting to
relieve.*

Telling yourself, "I don't have to be lonely if I don't want to," take specific, constructive, step-by-step action to arrange to become less isolated.
Plan and plot your way out of being alone. Instead of feeling desperate
and freezing, actively act relationally task oriented, working efficiently
on the problem without getting sidetracked, especially into diverting dra-
matics caused by catastrophic imaginings.

Instead of assuming that your loneliness stands for itself, analyze your
loneliness as a symptom that, like any other, has meaning. As noted
above, it is often your personal history that is partly the determinant of
your feeling especially lonely as a traumatic past contributes to your
present isolation by changing its complexion through making it seem
graver and more emergent than it actually is.

Also consider the possibility that you are bringing some of your loneliness down on yourself. Is much of your loneliness the product of anxious
distancing due to shyness that defends against stigmatization—so that you
pass up good opportunities that come your way because you believe that
seeking gain can lead only to pain? Perhaps, too, yours are self-defeating
cognitive errors leading to irrational, excessive, self-destructive actions,
errors like "because *some* is lost, *all* is gone forever" or "my loneliness
is not a reflection of my circumstances but on me." Recognize that early
terrifying experiences do not invariably presage a malignant here and now
or problematic future. Thinking they do leads you to feel helpless, suffer
from panic attacks with flashbacks, and then take desperate action—to
solve a nonexistent problem.

Not surprisingly, the best way to counter loneliness is to develop new
relationships while taking care to select the right people as friends/a partner, not the wrong ones just to have a warm body, any warm body, by your
side. If you choose to start looking for a Mr. Right to assuage your loneliness, do so calmly and purposively without cruising frantically. Seriously

consider networking: meeting your Mr. Right by first developing a circle of buddies and then ultimately, hopefully, meeting your lifetime companion through your new, large, interconnective group, one that consists of simpatico people who can—and want to—introduce you around and may even themselves develop into potential or actual lovers.

When it comes to seeking relationships, as noted throughout, be practical and realistic so that you do not expect too much too soon from relationships generally or from a given relationship specifically.

Don't expect to get all your relational maneuvers completely right the first time around. If you make mistakes, pull back and try again. Always be willing to give up something to get something, particularly the passing pleasures of sex good and plenty for the greater and more permanent benefits of a long-term, solid, perhaps monogamous liaison. In making specific relational choices, be willing to compromise—to settle as much as to select. Consider the possibility that you are being excessively perfectionistic if you always want this and never that, to the point of becoming unable to be satisfied unless certain of your often exceedingly unforgiving standards are met so that you reject everything that is less than 100 percent, leaving you with nothing and nobody at all because you feel that any man less than perfect is not worth bothering or sticking with. Be satisfied by less than the ideal so that instead of demanding Adonis, you happily go for and gladly stick with Don. Don't prematurely reject someone based on excessively high standards that lead you to pre-judge others according to some exclusionary template you create that must be satisfied and satisfied right from the start, leaving no room for how people can change and improve as a relationship progresses. Because relationship problems that loom in the beginning can be worked on and worked out, troubles at the start do not necessarily permanently doom a relationship forever. Many relationship problems should be viewed as not the end of the liaison but as presenting an opportunity to start healing negotiations. In making relational evaluations, think beyond the present, giving your guy a chance to prove himself and change for you along jointly drawn lines. And if things don't blossom immediately, stick with him, trying to imagine what he will be like in time after you and he are together for a while and, should you become a couple, as you stay together long afterward.

Throughout, minimize type fixation, as when "type" = specific physical characteristics and only men of a certain age. On the one hand, the individual who mans the desk at my gym constantly complains that he is lonely. On the other hand, he plays favorites with all the young muscled cuties while mostly ignoring anyone over a certain age who is less than fully armored. This, I infer, eliminates some men that might, if he only used his imagination, be good future possibilities.

Remember that many gay men being trauma averse are as sensitive to rejection as you can be. Therefore, make your romantic encounters as unthreatening to others as possible. Never devalue anyone by being pissy either to their faces or behind their backs. Be both empathic and altruistic as you intuit what a man needs and wants and then give that to him even though it's not exactly what you need and want. Remember that being warm, accepting, and nurturing is one of the quickest ways to many men's hearts. In this regard, always keep in mind that even the (supposedly unavailable) great beauties of gay life, though they seem to be always looking in a mirror, are actually looking for a mother.

Do not attempt to deal with your loneliness by looking and acting desperate. This said, be certain to distinguish being desperate from being ready to go so that you yourself do not reject someone for being desperate when his so-called desperation about finding love actually consists of his serious interest in having you.

Prevention and Treatment of Grief

Most gay men get over grief on their own. At times, however, they need therapy to help alleviate its symptoms and shorten its course. The camaraderie of group therapy can help some gay men who grieve after a significant loss. But when grief is sufficiently severe to come close to being a clinical depression, the griever might need individual psychotherapy and pharmacotherapy instead of or in addition to group.

If you should be a partner, friend, or family member of a griever, I advise you to do what you can to help your loved one deal with his grief/depression. That involves first and foremost taking special care to avoid making things worse by failing to understand and sympathize, as when you tell someone grieving to just "cut it out" along the dismissive lines of "get over it, things aren't so bad after all." In particular, never minimize the significance of abstract as compared to real losses and then criticize another for being a sissy getting depressed over nothing. For, in fact, anyone who gets depressed gets that way over something. Minimizing his pain in this or in any other way sends the message, "You are a weakling who can't cope," leading the griever to feel abandoned and then come to the dangerous conclusion that "I am as deficient as others believe me to be, so I don't deserve to live," enhancing suicidal rumination and possibly even provoking a suicide attempt: often after leaving behind a classic passive-aggressive get-back-at-you suicide note that reads,

"I don't want you to feel guilty, for you are in no way responsible for having caused my death."

My grieving patients complained a lot about the following two specific comments people misguidedly made to them trying to be helpful, in large measure feeling hurt because they felt that such remarks worsened their depression because they felt accused of being unable to do what they were asked because they were too helpless to act when faced with something they should be able to handle; of being too uncooperative and headstrong to yield when others were simply making reasonable requests of them; of being spoiled brats who just wanted their own way; and of being too stupid to understand what others wanted.

The first comment is "Get over it/him, it is a waste of time to brood like that. It/he isn't (wasn't) worth it." Belittling the object of grief generally provokes even more grief in defense of the still-beloved lost object and even sets the griever up to make a suicide attempt to "show how much I care."

A close friend, hoping to convince Manny that in his grief over a lost partner he was wasting his tears, told Manny that Mark wasn't worth grieving over because when he was alive he was making passes at other men. When Manny heard that, he responded with, "I don't believe you" ("and if I did, that would make me feel even worse"). When the friend escalated to say, "I happen to have evidence that he was cheating on you all over the place," Manny's response was, "You can't prove it, and anyway you are making this up to make me feel better as if I am grieving over nothing—but you are instead making me feel worse because now I have even more to grieve about." When the friend asked him, "Why should that SOB be having such a good time while you sit around and mope?" not surprisingly Manny's answer was because "he is a great guy who deserves everything, and I am a no good person who deserves nothing." Ultimately, Manny got even more depressed because "even you, my best friend, don't understand why I feel the way I do."

The second comment is "Go find yourself someone new right now." Here the response will likely be "I can't because I feel too bad to date, there is nobody in the world like him, and all I want is my old friend/partner back."

Better responses include the following:

- "Everybody grieves/gets depressed from time to time."
- "I understand how you feel."

- "It's only human nature to feel the way you do."
- "I have been through this myself; we all have."
- "The pain is time limited, generally to about a year or at most two."
- "You will move on with your life when you are ready, but until then, don't force things and push yourself excessively, for that might make matters worse."
- "If you want to meet another Mr. Right, you will in time, usually within two years. For if you were the sort of person who had a relationship once, you are also the sort of person who can find a relationship again."

Prevention and Remedy for PTSD

Gay men with PTSD should make a special effort to avoid situations involving criticism and rejection, for these predictably relight old and produce new related or unrelated traumata. In addition, they should seek self-understanding to help them distinguish actual external traumata from their own hypersensitive elaborations of unimportant events that they make into decisive occurrences because of thinking catastrophically. They should also try to avoid blaming external events for all their problems as their way to avoid taking at least some responsibility for their own feelings and, perhaps especially, for themselves.

Well-run self-help groups on the positive side offer the comfort of belonging, reduce isolation, and provide the griever with shared useful knowledge about PTSD. But gay men with PTSD should avoid badly run self-help groups that prolong rather than relieve illness by overfocusing on a problem and then making its continuance a condition of belonging to the group. Some do well and others do not do well with therapists/groups that advocate returning to the original site of one's traumata to once and for all achieve mastery, in effect encouraging flashing back to test and retest oneself and progressively enhance one's ability to bravely cope. Generally speaking, it's wise to avoid groups that foster extreme ongoing resentment toward society and all the social injustice supposedly rife in this world. As a mindset, this can temporarily help by fostering a "me-against-them" group solidarity/feeling of belonging/affiliation. But on the downside, too much social protest leads to feeling too much the victim, and that tends to divert the sufferer from a personal resolution that can come only from true, honest, effective problem solving.

PART III

Therapy

THIRTEEN

Getting Professional Help

In this chapter, I discuss psychotherapy for gay men who think they might need professional assistance to overcome emotional problems that they believe are keeping them from having fully creative, effective, self-fulfilling lives. As one of my patients put it, "My goal for therapy is this: after a productive day at the office, I want to be able to leave for home to return to my loving partner, the man of my dreams awaiting me at the door with a kiss, so that, as Voltaire might say, together we can till our acre, and make our garden grow."[1]

But when that's what you want but can't get, you should consider the possibility of seeking treatment to help you discover what went wrong and learn what can be done to make it right. You as a gay man need to seek a form of therapy and a therapist who can ameliorate your symptoms and resolve your functional problems by enhancing adaptive skills through resolving adaptive difficulties that can lead to ineffective functioning. Several types of therapy can do these things for you, but one type, as we shall see, will predictably do no good or actually make things worse.

What follows is a discussion of the indications for seeking help and the kinds of valid help available—specifically, individual therapy (affirmative-eclectic, affirmative, and short-term therapy) and couple and group therapy. (There are overlapping boundaries between the different therapies. For example, the best eclectic therapy is affirmative and vice versa.) I also discuss reparative therapy, which, being invalid, is never recommended. (Some of the professional approaches I outline here can with appropriate modifications be readily adapted for self-help.)

As I emphasize throughout, homosexuality is not an illness, nor is it invariably, as some might suggest, associated with neuroticism, such as histrionic behavior and depressive/masochistic features leading to a high incidence of suicidality. While there may be discernible developmental and dynamic reasons to account for becoming homosexual (I discuss these in the Appendix), that does not mean that homosexuality can and should be made right through understanding what went wrong.

Of course, homosexual men, like everyone else, can and do have emotional problems, and when that is the case, they enter psychotherapy with the same types of emotional difficulties as everyone else. This said, the criteria for diagnosing emotional disorder in the *Diagnostic and Statistical Manual of Mental Disorders* (4th ed.; *DSM-IV*) do not apply to gay men *exactly*.[2] That is because homosexuality often changes the superficial clinical manifestations of *DSM-IV* emotional disorders as a result of the unique, gay subcontext in which the disorders are embedded. To illustrate, paranoid gay men develop persecutory delusions, as do paranoid straight men, but paranoid gay men less often believe that the television set is talking to them than that an in fact innocently faithful boyfriend is cheating on them. Mood-disordered gay men often manifest their mood disorder not as bipolarity but as acting out, often in a frantically promiscuous way. Also, gay men seem, with increased frequency, prone to develop unique reactive symptoms because of the stresses commonly found in the gay world. However, paradoxically, with some gay men (not all), the stress disorders they develop, as compared to the stress disorders straights develop, tend to be milder, more self-limited, and both likelier to be healed by the tincture of time and more highly responsive to therapy. For while some gay men find it hard to be gay, in many respects being gay makes life a lot easier—especially for those who are in an ongoing gay relationship (gays who are DINKS, that is, "double income no kids")—for they are often financially all set, without the anxiety attendant on the stresses associated with bringing up children and free of the binding, often confining ties of straight marriage. Some specific indications for psychotherapy in gay men are given in Table 13.1.

AFFIRMATIVE THERAPY

The term "affirmative therapy" can be used to refer either to a pure or dedicated approach where affirmation mostly or entirely replaces traditional therapeutic methods, doing so based on the belief that these are inherently hurtful and detrimental (e.g., "unaffirmative"), or to an approach involving

Table 13.1   Indications for Psychotherapy

- Suffering from severe gay-themed problems, such as conflicts about coming out, being seriously uncertain about your identity as a gay man, or, certain within yourself about your identity as a gay man, uncertain about your
  acceptability to others as an identified gay individual
- Feeling isolated because of being unable to meet Mr. Right
- Having relationship problems with a partner, such as being frequently
  involved in spousal arguments/domestic violence
- Having relationship problems with friends, including having too few or no
  friends at all, and/or with family, such as never wanting to see Mom and
  Dad again and not actually going to see them at all
- Having emotional problems related to your job, such as undue fear of
  promotion because getting ahead means being exposed, which to you
  means being humiliated or actually getting fired
- Suffering from situational work-related difficulties, ranging from job dis-
  satisfaction to job-related burnout due to on-the-job antigay discrimination
- Suffering from unduly low self-esteem
- Experiencing more-than-transient mild depression, especially when accompanied by suicidal thinking
- Experiencing sexual problems, such as a troublesome, preoccupying
  paraphilia; impotence; or retarded or premature ejaculation
- Having serious problems with alcohol and drug abuse (often part of the bar
  scene)

affirmative *modification* of traditional therapy—what I call not "affirmative"
but "affirmative-eclectic therapy."

Pure, Dedicated Affirmative Therapy

Pure affirmative therapists, or simply "affirmative therapists," as distinct
from affirmative-eclectic therapists who modify their eclecticism with
affirmation, focus on stepping out of the traditional role of passive listener
to offer closeness (if that is what the patient wants but without violating
boundaries) and empathy, which can, as Pinsker says, "do . . . more good
than anything the patient learns."[3] The therapist takes the patient's side
when not too many people are on it, accepts him as such, recognizes the
importance of his achievements, cheers him on to accomplish more, and
tells him, perhaps for the first time in his life, good things about himself,
hoping to inspire him to rise to the occasion and act worthy of his therapist,
now happily someone he can include among his admirers. Of course, the
acceptance has to be sincere, the positive feedback deserved, and the

reassurance knowledgeable, or the therapist will come across as—and might actually be—in denial, accepting bad behavior, offering congratulations that are not in order, and extending reassurances inappropriately. This was the case when a therapist told a patient who was in the process of a tragic divorce from which he was never actually to fully recover emotionally, "Don't worry, I'm sure you are going to get over this and that everything will be all right."

Affirmative therapists sometimes hold the extreme view that all gay men are so conditioned by negative social feedback that they find it difficult to tolerate—or can't tolerate at all—much of the pain associated with the self-exploration that is an integral part of the insight-oriented process of traditional therapy. They view being gay as inducing a state of fragility that renders gay men unsuited (too tender) to embark on a program of self-discovery. Even if an individual is eager and able to learn about himself, they deem him insufficiently emotionally strong to handle the critical impact predictably attendant on attaining self-knowledge. Therefore, their therapy focuses on the role played by passively experienced stress and trauma over the contribution of active personal involvement, that is, on victimization by an unfriendly environment characterized by political shunning and personal devaluation. They thus avoid blaming gay men for causing their own brutalization and marginalization—their way of assisting them in their struggle to cope with social stigmatization and so helping them avoid further self-devaluation and deaffirmation.

In their emphasis upon stress and trauma and reliance on the curative power of the positive therapeutic milieu they offer the patient a corrective emotional experience where the healing aura of a kindly concerned therapist treating compassionately can be enough to bring about symptom relief and existential calm, ameliorating anxiety and encouraging growth simply by providing a nonthreatening relationship that fosters the positive transference, the uplifting effects of which can spread to favor emotional health in a global way. And this approach is especially helpful for gay men who are suffering primarily from *stress*-related symptoms due to being gay, typically the stress that gay men can experience when they live in a small town with small-minded families and neighbors.

But there are also downsides to the purely affirmative approach. For by according the greatest significance to external events, it minimizes the exploration of self-issues, and while that avoids dubbing gay men "people with problems" and thus slapping them with enhanced social stigmatization, it can ultimately harm gay men by depathologizing any true problems they might have through spinning them as normative conflicts between the individual and a society full of homophobia and heterosexism. When too resolute, that approach overlooks the potential benefit to be obtained from causal understanding based on psychodynamic hypotheses, such as the understandings to be obtained from delving into personal infantilism, boundary confusion, oral fixation with pathological introjection and the turning of anger around on the self, excessively harsh superego, and personal masochism—so often clear and present issues for a given gay individual. Thus, the gay man whose so-called healthy sexual freedom is more like harmful sexual disinhibition or whose so-called healthy independence is more like the avoidance of all closeness and intimacy misses the chance to improve through the therapeutic mechanism of understanding where he is coming from.

Additionally, too much interactive therapeutic closeness can *create* anxiety, especially in masochists who hesitate to be affirmed, cynics who don't buy into all the compliments going down, rebels who view the therapist as establishment up to the usual no good, conformists who view the therapist as antiestablishment equally up to no good, and seriously angry gay men who, stubbornly wishing to stay that way, remain hard to soothe no matter how much comforting the therapist offers them. In addition, often excessive positive feedback affirms narcissism ("I'm fine just the way I am") perhaps increasing antiestablishment rebellion that enhances defensive extravagant flamboyance as the product of intensified social combativeness.

AFFIRMATIVE-ECLECTIC THERAPY

I do believe that many gays who come for therapy are not only applying for treatment but also starved for love and running from persecution. So, especially *in the beginning* of treatment, they can benefit from uninterrupted affirmation consisting of having their hands held and do best with a therapist who resembles less a clever dietician than a mother figure who actually serves them a good meal.

But I do not believe in continuing with pure affirmation over the entire course of treatment. Being personally kind may not be enough. Kindness is not a cure-all that always and completely trumps science.

Indeed, many gay men, already knowing perfectly well that they are behaving in some not entirely desirable fashion, actually long for someone to explore with them such matters as why they hurt themselves by what they do, what they can do to stop it, and how they can improve who they are and how they behave. Fortunately, gay men who have been mauled and de facto exiled by a lifetime of homophobic deaffirmation and insult have usually as a result become the strongest of survivors. As such, they are as fully able to obtain and tolerate insight and to easily do so without swooning as anyone else.

So I personally believe that many gay men who need psychotherapy will do best not with affirmative therapy per se but with eclectic psychotherapy with an affirmative tone (affirmative-eclectic therapy). This affirmative modification of traditional therapy involves a *gay-aware* approach, that is, one that is highly attentive to the special needs and unique circumstances of the gay man. A positive, generally nonthreatening framework infuses the whole, softening and padding the invariably generally negative and hence gay-negative aspects that normally creep into traditional therapy, modifying without materially reducing the overall effectiveness of any of that procedure's individual parts. Such a gay-aware therapist offers a positive holding environment for its special effect—directly lessening the impact of the specific losses that many gay men experience while simultaneously undoing the long-standing negative effects of homophobia and heterosexism—what Kort calls that cumulative "covert cultural sexual abuse"[4] that has likely left a gay man so bruised in the past that he is highly sensitive to more of the same in the present. But additionally, affirmative-eclectic therapy offers the gay man something else: a combination of psychodynamic, cognitive-behavioral, and interpersonal techniques to help him learn from his past, correct his errors of thinking; change his misguided/self-destructive fixed, conditioned patterns of reacting; and repair his flawed interpersonal relationships—all in the context of the proffered gay-aware approach.

Kort and others like him, though calling themselves "affirmative therapists," are more like the affirmative-eclectic therapists to whom I refer. More realists when it comes to the patient than apologists when it comes to their cause, while emphasizing support through affirmation, they routinely apply mainstream therapeutic techniques to the unique task at hand: treating a diverse population with the shared problem of early and ongoing cultural victimization. They are not merely a companion on a journey to health; they guide the figurative tour—offering not only corrective positivity to counter lifelong negativity due to cultural sexual oppression but also a scientific revisionistic approach to curing the problem(s) at hand. To this end, they make a differential diagnosis that forms the basis of classical therapeutic intervention—modified (but not obliterated) by the affirmative framework in which they work. They avoid failing to recognize emotional disorder in gay men in the guise of being (counterproductively and overly) humanitarian. They do not believe that making a diagnosis involves stigmatizing gay men as emotionally ill, is incompatible with rooting for the underdog and empathizing with the downtrodden, and uses diagnostic labels as oppressive tools—what Kowszun and Malley call part of the "unthinking attitudes and abusive practices [nurtured by the] medical and psychiatric establishments."[5] To them, taking a history does not mean pursuing their own line of inquiry when they should instead be paying attention to their patients' thoughts and needs and demonstrating trust in their patients' essential wisdom. They do not believe that by telling the gay man that "this is wrong with your way of life," they are necessarily introducing political and social prejudice and discrimination into the therapy hour, thus reinforcing cultural oppression. Recognizing that depression, anxiety, and substance abuse exist in gay men just as they do in any other group, they resist reframing all psychopathology in a gay-friendly way, hoping to normalize everything potentially off center. They don't call depression "existential crisis" or paranoia "homophobia." But they do realize that the classic diagnostic criteria don't always fully apply in this population so that, for example, as Kort specifically points out, what appears to be "oppositional disorders, personality disorders, or sexual addictions"[6] can actually be stage 5 of the coming-out process where gays and lesbians display their gayness almost too proudly and expect—and even pressure—everyone else to go along, no complaints or questions asked.

I dealt with a gay patient's loneliness using an affirmative-eclectic approach that consisted of first offering him reassurances *that it seemed to me eventually things would work out in time. Then I* analyzed *his loneliness' deep developmental roots, particularly how he drove off people because, having identified with his rejecting mother, he was sending friends and lovers off just the way she rejected him;* corrected *such of his* cognitive errors *as the belief that if someone did not love him completely, that meant that that person did not love him at all; and worked on resolving such of his* interpersonal *problems as those due to excessive impatience to score. As I explained to him, "When it comes to your relational difficulties, you haven't been unable to find someone because you are unappealing but because you are not ready, for you are still not over your last breakup and so are not yet fully up to meeting someone new—and, as you know, like anyone else, you will likely get what you want only when you are prepared to receive it," and urged him on through the use of* behavioral *remedies, in his case advocating he use a geographical solution to solve some of his problems by his moving out of the square, repressive town he lived in and instead going to live in a city where it would be easier for him to meet someone to love—for, as a gay man stuck in a stress-making homophobic small town, he was one of the fortunate gay men more likely on relocation to leave his problems behind than to take them along with him. I also used total push behavioral techniques—suggesting that you "get out there and meet people, report back to me what you find in the world outside, and tell me how you handled things." And, occasionally, I gave him actual advice about where to meet people and then, when he did meet them, on how to enjoy safe and to avoid unsafe sex.*

Many affirmative-eclectic therapists willingly give advice to patients, hoping to counter their poor judgment. I will give my patients advice but limit it to making general suggestions, such as "Don't be a victim of your fascination with certain types." But I withhold more specific advice, such as "You should go, not stay, with a particular individual, for you are not compatible with him." I believe that patients should be the ones to make such important personal decisions on their own. So I ask them to do so and then, should it be necessary, offer to intervene by helping them *implement* the decisions that they themselves have made.

Affirmative-eclectic therapists routinely identify and attempt to elevate gay men's low self-esteem. As one of my patients put it, "The world makes me feel like my dog—she sleeps with my partner head up but with her rear end in *my* face." Many gay men suffer from intrinsic and socially induced low self-esteem that is both appropriately and/or inappropriately low. When dealing therapeutically with *appropriately* low self-esteem, I give my patients a kind of absolution, recommend self-forgiveness for actual sins committed, and then advocate self-control and future improvement. When dealing therapeutically with *inappropriate* low self-esteem, I first clarify that the negative self-evaluation is problematic and then help the individual gain insight into why—by exploring the developmental, defensive, cognitive, and interpersonal components of their poor self-image.

Naturally, affirmative-eclectic therapists never view homosexuality as an illness in any respect. In this, they differ from more psychoanalytically oriented therapists who may do just that, citing castration anxiety, negative oedipal resolution, phallic narcissism, regression, conflict, and defense as being at the root of what they conceptualize as a true disorder. But when such psychodynamics apply at all (and they sometimes do to an extent), they are incidental to, not an integral, causative aspect of, homosexuality. And, anyway, since homosexuality is a variety of normalcy, not a form of psychopathology, it follows that when pathological trends like this are present, identifiable, and qualitatively and quantitatively significant, they will by definition be and remain within the range of normal.

Affirmative-eclectic therapists carefully avoid being overly permissive. For example, they help gays see that they do, like everyone else, create some of their own problems actively and then, to avoid taking full responsibility for themselves, unfairly blame externals for everything. For example, they teach gay men that dating problems may be due not to the difficulties inherent in dating in the gay subculture but rather to acting silly and selfish, to toying with being unfaithful because they want to win and doing so because they feel they have to be the ones to die having the most toys, or to procrastinating—failing to strike when the iron is hot because of a fear of closeness and commitment and instead always striking after the iron has cooled down.

In the realm of acting silly and selfish, I recently received the following e-mail:

> I went out with a lawyer from the area, who arrived with a red corduroy hunting cap, jeans and a flannel shirt to a formal restaurant/dance. He holds off on the wine because "Jesus spoke to him" and told him that kings don't drink wine. Then he orders it anyway later on, gets on the dance floor and starts doing splits, then springs into the air, jumps, clicking heels to buttocks and lands back down in a split, knocking over everyone in their suits, as those sitting at tables stare at us with mouths agape and breath held.
>
> Then the bill comes and he tells me exactly what I owe on it (says he is not a financially successful lawyer) then says he needs to run to the bathroom and I could start heading out to the car without him, but could we go out again sometime soon?
>
> How about NO.

In the realm of toying with being unfaithful,

> *One of my patients misguidedly brought old partners back into new relationships, hurting his new partner's feelings, accounting for why his own and his partner's "monogamy" turned out to be "serial." In a similarly unhelpful way when looking at some beefcake in a gay magazine, he told his partner he wouldn't mind spending the night in a place where that guy slept, and then, after openly admitting to a current partner that he thought that many other men were attractive, he took that back, too late, by adding a weak retraction: "But I wouldn't think of actually doing something about it." Then he came to me in tears because his partner had just called it quits, and he didn't know why, except that since all gay men wandered, his partner was just being one of the guys.*

In the realm of procrastination, I received the following letter from a gay man who blamed his loneliness strictly on the lack of suitable marriage candidates where he lived when obviously other factors were in play.

Dear Dr. K,

No divorced men for me. And I am looking for complete relationships, not these neither-here-nor-there ones. I seek a man who is smart, professionally successful, ac[c]ultured, and makes a decent salary. I am on two dating services but so far I am only looking because I haven't yet gotten up my courage to jump in. Really I think it's best for someone else to take the initiative, for then I can be certain that he is interested in doing more than "winking," as they call it in on-line dating lingo. I also believe in playing hard to get because I am convinced that that makes me more desirable to have. I do want a man, but something seems to be holding me back, so that as I find myself answering a letter I hesitate to go through with a date because I am afraid that a man will hurt me physically or scam me. Too my work as an accountant demands a lot of my time and energy, but I have to keep on working all night and day even though I am running out of time to find love. Worse, my mother keeps making fun of me, saying "Why can't you meet someone like your brother did?" And I don't want to give her the satisfaction of seeing me as being desperate, and being right about that.

Am I excusing my fears or am I not fearful, just not yet ready?

SHORT-TERM THERAPY

Short-term therapy is crisis/conflict/problem oriented, depending on whether the main focus(es) is a defined crisis, such as that arising from a job loss or a breakup with a lover; a defined conflict, such as an inability to accept a desirable promotion because of a fear of success associated with an unreasonable, possibly paranoid fear of being found out and exposed as a gay man; or a defined existential problem, such as indecision about whether to come out or to leave a particular partner.

Gay men who are having trouble breaking up or are depressed after a difficult dumping should seriously consider seeking short-term therapy. For at such stressful times, many gay men's good judgment fails them, and temporarily giving this aspect of your life over to a concerned, competent therapist can keep you from making unwise decisions and burning bridges you may later need to cross. You might think, "My pain is real because my problem is my reality, so how could you, as a mere therapist, possibly help me?" But just another person's presence and professional interest can at such times be particularly soothing and healing. So give therapy a try and a chance and stick with it even if you think "it's going nowhere"—for it often has a delayed effect, helping you cope and grow even months or years after it's over.

COUPLE/FAMILY THERAPY

Couple therapy involves your partner in the process. Couple therapy can help minimize one partner's paranoid reactions about what a therapist actually said and did during the other's session. It can help the therapist avoid getting caught up in family fights, as when one partner calls up during the other's individual session to find out whether his partner is actually attending therapy (as he said he would be) or is somewhere else, like out with his latest boyfriend (as he undoubtedly will deny). The inexperienced therapist doing couple therapy can, however, actually find himself caught up in endless family fights and adjudicating battles instead of performing treatment. (Special techniques for working with couples in mixed marriages where one is straight and the other gay are available but beyond the scope of this text.)

In *family* therapy, the therapist sees the patient and significant others who are part of the patient's immediate or extended family or just good friends. An important goal for some gay men involves learning how to understand and deal with intrafamiliar conflicts, such as those that arise when Mom and Dad, learning that their son is gay, find out the "shocking" details about what actually goes on in his sex life.

REPARATIVE THERAPY (TO BE AVOIDED)

Reparative therapists feel that being gay is an illness needing a cure, so they recommend reformation—in the complete absence of malformation. Some honestly, however misguidedly, believe that treating homosexuality as an illness is a theoretically sound approach yielding positive results. Others are actually acting out, sublimating their own sadism into concern and pity in the form of rescue fantasies meant to make them feel bigger and better as individuals and more fervently concerned, charitable, and caring than thou—and who, alone having the word, are the only ones who can help the supposedly sad homosexual get happy. What they overlook is that their message is characterized less by the empathy and altruism that they believe it contains and more by the self-indulgence that they deny motivates it, and how saying that "you ought not to be the way you are, and I am here to fix you up" is innately critical and extremely damning.

Technically, while some *affirmative* therapists speaking out of an over-arching need to be gay friendly and gay affirmative hesitate to make any psychiatric *diagnoses* in their gay patients, some *reparative* therapists do that very same thing, only *they* do it for entirely different, far less sanguine reasons: because they believe that calling homosexuals sick encourages pity and that pitying queers obscures how they are not sick but evil.

Other reparative therapists, going to the opposite extreme, overdiagnose gay men, sadistically figuratively "throwing the book" (the *DSM-IV*) at them, giving them more—and more severe—diagnoses than they warrant. As Isay suggests, "Homosexuals have been said to suffer from a large variety of ego deficits . . . including 'primitive features of the ego' . . . similar to those found in schizophrenia . . . and sociopathy . . . Socarides (1968) wrote that approximately half of the patients who engage in homosexual practices have a 'concomitant schizophrenia, paranoia, are latent or pseudoneurotic schizophrenics or are in the throes of a manic-depressive reaction. The other half, when neurotic, may be of the obsessional or, occasionally, of the phobic type.' . . . Most of the patients he labeled as schizophrenic would probably be classified in his later formulation (1978) as belonging to the class of Preoedipal Type #2, 'Suffering from a transitional condition lying somewhere between the neuroses and psychoses.' "[7] Along similar lines, Krajeski quotes Albert Ellis as expressing the following sentiments: "Although I once believed that exclusive homosexuals are seriously neurotic, considerable experience with treating many of them (and in being friendly [!] with a number of whom I have not seen for psychotherapy) has convinced me that I was wrong; most fixed, homosexuals, I am convinced, are borderline psychotic or outrightly psychotic."[8]

Using diagnostic concepts pejoratively, some reparative therapists employ the term "histrionic" as a critical euphemism for being wildly irrational; the term "borderline" as a critical euphemism for being overly mercurial, by which they mean unreliable, promiscuous, and amoral; and the term "schizotypal" to denigrate a gay man's creativity as eccentricity. They may dismiss close, loving relationships as mere "dependent mergers" and legitimate complaints about being mistreated/persecuted as paranoid fantasies. Avulsing gay behavior from its normalizing sociocultural context, they view gays who are simply being swans in their own society as the ugly ducklings of the straight world. Using a double standard, they call behaviors that they dub "normal" in straights "abnormal" should they occur in gays. Those who excuse straights for yelling too loudly at the soccer game or during the riot afterward condemn gays who make about the same amount of noise for "shrieking and screaming." They call straights who, never seeming able to get enough sex, cheat multiple times on their wives "imperfect, like most humans." But they call gays who, never seeming able to get enough sex "sexually compulsive" or even "whores." With a knowing wink, what they identify as "polygamy" in straights they call "promiscuity" in gays. They consider occasional behaviors to be frequent and rare and exotic behaviors to be common and central. Straights with outfits like construction boots, jeans, earrings, and unkempt pony tails sticking through the back of a baseball cap either go unremarked or are passed off as "dressing like the locals," while gays with the same "outlandish getups" are dubbed "fetishistic." While, as they see it, it is acceptable for straights to act like Clint Eastwood or John Wayne, they diagnose gays who act like the more outlandish gay rock sensations as having a gender identity disorder or as suffering from a more serious problem: being frankly delusional about exactly what sex they belong to.

When making a *dynamic* assessment, some reparative therapists blame gays themselves, not their homophobic or heterosexist society, for most or all of their problems. Psychodynamically inclined reparative therapists blame all gays' problems in life on an acquired developmental fixation or subsequent regression, while biologically inclined reparative therapists blame all gay men's woes on some sort of personal genetic weakness.

Therapeutically, some analytically oriented reparative therapists—after viewing homosexuality either as a sickness in its own right typically associated with other severe psychological illnesses like schizophrenia, or as the product of another, larger syndrome, typically narcissistic personality disorder, and after analyzing homosexuality as originating in the psychology of fixation, regression, conflict, and defense—attempt to reverse the processes via uncovering techniques. As Isay says, "Because psychoanalysts generally regard homosexuality as a pathological and a psychologically uneconomical solution to early conflict, they tend to believe that, whenever possible, it is in the best interest of the patient to change his sexual orientation or sexual behavior [by bringing] warring intrapsychic structures ... into greater harmony [Gay men in harmony become] less inclined to act out 'unacceptable impulses' as the[se] become increasingly tolerated by a strengthened ego and successfully sublimated[9] [Furthermore, the] literature is replete with recommendations in support of modifications of analytic technique that are deemed appropriate to the treatment of homosexual patients [such as] suggesting to a homosexual patient that he seek out women or discussing with a patient how to engage in heterosexual sex"[10] as well as behavioral (aversive) and inspirational (religious-oriented) treatments.

Reparative therapists often try to enlist the gay man's parents as surrogate therapists in the repair process. They tell the parents that it would be lifesaving if they ordered their sons to go straight and marry. They suggest that the parents use both the stick of tough love and the carrot of practical rewards to accomplish their ends, as in "I will pay your tuition to any school you might want to attend or give you the down payment on a new house and the money for your upcoming, big, very standard wedding if only you give up the gay foolishness." Effectively, it is as if these therapists are telling the parents to change their son from being left-handed to being right-handed by refusing to hand him toys to his left hand, only relinquishing the object when he grabs it the "right" way, that is, the way they want him to.

Not surprisingly, reparative therapists who set out to cure homosexuality claim numerous scientific and practical successes. But my own personal and professional experience, as well as that of patients and friends who have undergone such therapy, indicates otherwise—that reparative therapy not only doesn't work but actually does a great deal of harm. While some gay men in reparative therapy do seem to renounce their homosexuality, that doesn't mean that they go straight or that they go straight because of treatment. Too many so-called therapeutic successes evidence only the patient's capacity for abstinence, itself generally depending on and enforced by their ability to dissemble. Their so-called conversions are too often just a manifestation of their ability to cover up: the secret homosexual escapades they are having behind the therapist's back and not reporting directly during their sessions.

My reparative analyst (in those days she was called "an orthodox Boston psychoanalyst") managed to do me plenty of harm. She wasted my money and five years of my youth by laying down the rule of abstinence that kept me from living a normal life in the here and now and preparing for later happiness, as she deaffirmed who I was, a valuable individual in my own right, not an invaluable subvariety of something else: what she thought I ought to be. As I say might have described my plight, "My clinical material suggests that [efforts to make a gay man straight] may cause symptomatic depression [and alcoholism] by contributing to an already diminished and injured self-esteem, and in some cases they may produce severe social problems in later life."[11] For years, she forced me to live the sheltered life of therapy for the time it might take to change. And I submitted: first, because I wanted to be an analyst—and in those days you had to be straight to be admitted to Freudian Institutes—and, second, because I wanted a staff appointment at the hospital where I worked, and the head of the department wouldn't have queers on the staff (but did relent when my immediate superior reassured him that I would be okay because I was taking the cure). After five years of celibacy, marked by excessive drinking interspersed with one flawed attempt at heterosexuality with a prostitute and an occasional lapse where I got drunk to give myself an excuse to do something homosexual that I couldn't be held responsible for, I took off one blessed weekend for Provincetown and met "my first partner for life" (who, unfortunately, was later to die at a very young age). My analyst responded to my liberating actions by liberating me from (really, throwing me out of) analysis, then suggesting psychotherapy instead —in those days not considered to be the gold standard, at least for the striver I was. I responded by leaving Boston to go live with my new partner in a more welcoming place: New York City. And I never went back, either figuratively or literally.

Apparently, for this analyst, actuating my inner identity and attending to matters relating to belonging and enhanced personal satisfaction were not therapeutic. What she overlooked was that she was simply making my feelings of stigmatization and isolation worse and how for years my personal integrity suffered as I more and more became a self divided— between me as I actually *was* and me as I *ought* to be—until that day when I had an epiphany and, deciding to become a fully authentic person, reintegrated my divided self, now newly united because in her complete absence, I had all the room I needed to get myself properly together.

RECOMMENDATIONS (MY PRACTICE GUIDELINES)

Gay men who require therapy because they have emotional issues to contend with and resolve should consider seeking affirmative-eclectic therapy while avoiding purist affirmative therapists, such as those who sidestep the need to acknowledge/resolve personal problems by instead blaming everything on social opprobrium and its (admittedly troublesome and occasionally disastrous) negative effects. Reparative therapist and their therapy are not to be considered at all.

In my work with gay men, I neither repair what doesn't need to be fixed nor fix what doesn't need to be repaired. I do not come up with solutions to put together pieces of lives that are not shattered. Naturally, while I make every attempt to identify and cure psychopathology in homosexuals, I make no attempt to cure homosexuality, which is not psychopathological.

I neither deny emotional disorder when it exists nor conjure it up in its absence. I do not allow my positive countertransference feelings for gay men to blind me to their psychopathology. I do not believe that diagnosing behavior is the same thing as criticizing and condemning it and as a result stigmatizing those in whom it occurs. I do believe that the *DSM-IV* is a document that doesn't discriminate according to sexual orientation and so is as applicable to homosexuals as it is to heterosexuals. I make a special effort to cut through the rationalizations and cover-ups that gay men and some of their therapists use to normalize pathological behavior, such as "paraphilia = self-expression" or "having sex with three-year-old boys = acceptable because children of this age diddle themselves anyway." Mine is not a focus on my patients' sexual orientation, only a concern for any of their related and unrelated problematic (disordered) mindsets and behaviors. I know that gay life can be anxiety laden for reasons other than victimization by homophobes and hetereosexists, for I recognize that a gay man's problems can be not only due to society's disapproval of his homosexuality but also the product of his personal difficulties. Gays fall emotionally ill in the same ways and for the same reason as do straights. Like anyone else, gays can suffer from anxieties, such as a fear of success which is as much a consequence of personal terror as of social constraints, and from personality problems that determine their destiny as much as social antagonisms, stigmatizations, and deprivations. And if they stay lonely, it may strictly be not because society frowns on their personal interconnections but because they are masochistically all set to fulfill the parental, now become a personal, curse to "go forth and be miserable." And because the same psychodynamics generally apply to gays and straights, gays like straights can become emotionally crippled by cold and distant mothers and/or punitive fathers. Yet paradoxically—and as with anyone else, gay or straight—too much parental *loving* can be as detrimental as too much parental *abuse*.

Using a conventional/affirmative-eclectic approach, I combine traditional psychological mindedness and time-honored attentiveness to psychopathology with a special overarching positivity that infuses the whole. My affirmation, as Davies says, is not a replacement for but an augmentation of traditional approaches.[12] Of course, as I would with any patient, with my gay patients I will make diagnosis-based therapeutic modifications.

Thus, I treat paranoid gay men differently from how I treat depressed gay men, as I focus on reality testing with paranoids and developing insight with depressives. I do not withhold insight from all gay men in the misguided belief that all gays, each and every one of them emotional sissies, do not have the strength and flexibility they need to learn about themselves and especially about things they might find less than flattering. I certainly ask gays to play by some of the ordinary rules of life, for I believe that equality means equal responsibility as much as equal privilege. While I seriously sympathize with gay men who are oppressed because they are victims of prejudice and discrimination, I do not join in in affirming gays who are making too much of a career out of their oppression. I do not believe that setting healthy limits on certain things, such as excessive promiscuity that is ultimately a passive-aggressive way to spit in the establishment's eye, is the same thing as "my being an oppressive establishmentarian and apostle of inhibitions." I believe that setting limits is a reasonable response on my part to self-destructive, self-effacing, self-mocking behaviors that can take away all the real fun in life, mess up a career, and contribute to destroying physical health. I do not ask gays to simply gratify their whims and follow the pied piper of the moment—doing only what *feels* good while failing to keep an eye on what *is* good. Instead, I ask them to consider giving up something to get something better, to always act with consideration for the negative consequences of freedom without responsibility, and to not overworry about not living the good life while acting entirely too unconcerned about the possible downsides of too much good living.

ADVICE ON CHOOSING A THERAPIST

Your ideal therapist is emotionally healthy, well trained, and knowledgeable. He or she may be from a different socioeconomic background, race, or ethnic group than you as long as a serious lack of language skills—and the conceptual difficulties that can result—do not impede progress. He or she does not subscribe to myths, prejudices, and stereotypes about gays based on limited experience with gay men, as do some of those therapists who in their training have contact only with gay men who are sufficiently troubled to need emergency room care. He or she is sensitive to how patients who have been hurt before in real life are vulnerable to being hurt again, in exactly the same way, in therapy. Finally, he or she is technically able to monitor and handle the transference and keep both its negative and its positive aspects from defeating treatment and to monitor the countertransference and keep both its negative and its positive aspects from leading to therapeutic blunders.

Some gay men have difficulty with a therapist being *straight*. As Pinsker says, sometimes gay patients are "convinced that only a gay therapist can understand [them. But] a therapist does not have to be gay to treat gay men. Keep in mind that psychotherapy's usefulness is not limited to those life experiences or characteristics that patient and therapist share."[13] Fortunately, motivated straight therapists can learn quite enough about the gay life from friends, colleagues, patients, community events, workshops, Gay Pride Day ceremonies, and both the literature about gay men not written specifically to familiarize straights with gay life and, like Kort's book,[14] the literature dedicated to informing straight therapists how to treat gay men. Many therapists even feel that an intimate familiarity with gay life is unnecessary: because of the universal nature of emotional disorder—which does not, after all, discriminate in at least its essential details according to sexual orientation.

Other gay men, perhaps themselves self-homophobic/erotophobic, have difficulty with their therapist's being *gay*. These gay men may have a guilt-based/self-homophobic virginity complex that leads them to pick a straight over a gay therapist because they want not a doctor but an innocent. This difficulty cannot be fully eliminated, but it can—and should—be discussed up front lest it become a hidden barrier that affects all the therapy to come.

Experience with addictive disorders is important, for, as Pinsker says, "Substance abuse [and especially alcoholism] is so often part of the problem, even when not mentioned by the patient, that it should receive attention early."[15]

Never choose a punitive therapist to please your parents, to live out your self-hatred (as did one gay man who acted out his self-disgust by asking for shock therapy to punish him for getting gonorrhea), or to salve a conscience that tells you that being gay is a sin. Don't deal with your fear of any change by choosing a too-permissive therapist who lets things stay as is or one who is incompetent and as such (you hope) will have little to no effect on your life. Far too often, after getting "hooked on the transference," gay men come to view the most incompetent of therapists as expert and take in all the bad therapy they have to offer.

This happened to me when my parents forced me into treatment. To make certain that it didn't work, I chose an incompetent therapist who gave me some very bad advice—telling me which specialty to choose when he should have left that important life decision entirely up to me.

Later, I picked a hurtful therapist because I needed to keep myself from having a good life so that I could live out a need to suffer. I, at the time a highly masochistic individual, had moved to San Francisco because I was a gay psychiatrist, and as such the Boston Psychoanalytic Institute would not admit me, and I felt I had a better chance of being accepted to an institute in a gay-friendly community. Alas, the San Francisco training analyst I saw asked me, "What makes you believe that?" Fooling myself into thinking that he was not dismissing me but, in good psychoanalytic fashion, trying to find out my deepest thoughts exactly, I began psychoanalysis with the woman this man referred me to, seeing her four times a week for five years. It took me five years to be sufficiently comfortable to work up enough courage to ask her to support my application to the institute. Now she was clearer about her intentions: too late, it turns out, because she finally said in no uncertain terms, "No, impossible, you are a homosexual."

All disciplines—social workers, psychologists, psychiatrists, and nurse practitioners—have their share of individuals who are gay unfriendly either because they are themselves homophobic or because they are generically mean individuals who criticize and hurt gay men just as they criticize and hurt everyone else. In addition, all disciplines have their share of individuals who are inadequately prepared, like doctors who are trained mainly in covering the psychiatric emergency room at night (one reason besides training that hospitals have psychiatry residency programs), psychologists versed mainly in how to run controlled studies based on raw material collected from badly done telephone interviews of inherently questionable accuracy, social workers whose main training and interest lies in helping not those who are emotionally conflicted but those with reality-based environmental problems, and nurse practitioners who find it difficult to cross over from caring for the physically ill to caring for the emotionally disturbed.

Analytically oriented therapists work most effectively with gays who have innate emotional problems not primarily pegged to antigay oppression and least effectively with gays who suffer mainly from situational, reactive difficulties. Examples of the latter include gays who are depressed because, unprovoked, their lover is cheating on them; their colleagues are harassing them at work; or they were just fired from their jobs simply for being homosexual.

Conversely, each discipline in addition to its unique limitations has something special to offer the gay man. Some social workers, to their credit, quite properly depathologize what others would inappropriately condemn as grossly disturbed behavior. They view what others call "bad behavior" strictly as an understandable and appropriate response to harsh crippling reality or as part of an individual's style rather than his personal pathology. For example, when a psychiatrist stated that a gay man who had left his wife and children for a male lover was acting out by moving in with this lover to an apartment right down the hall from his estranged wife, a social worker responded that, on the contrary, she thought it was simply a matter of different people making different arrangements and approving of and objecting to different things—to say nothing of the, at the time, tight real estate market. When I confessed to a social worker that I had published a booklet of "Gay Sex Coupons" only to discover that the publisher had put my name on what I at first believed would be an anonymous production, a social worker asked me, "What is wrong with helping gay men have better sex?" When a psychiatrist suggested that gay men who cruise tearooms do so as a manifestation of emotional disorder, such as a pathological need for full anonymity that is the product of severe interpersonal avoidance, a social worker countered that in his opinion, many gay men cruise tearooms at night because their profession keeps them from being able to meet sex partners during the day in places where there is even greater danger of exposure, and because tearooms are where the sex is.

While many psychologists understand the dynamics of emotional disorder in gay men and use this understanding to impart insight, some resolutely treat only manipulatively (to their patients' overall detriment) using strict behavioral (aversive and nonaversive) techniques that are superficial in the sense that they only trick the patient into doing one's bidding. For example, one psychologist, countermanding my prescription for sleep medication for a patient suffering from severe depressive insomnia, attempted to cure this highly depressed gay patient's sleeplessness solely by the simple (and trivial) expedient of telling him to reserve his bedroom for sleeping only and to do other things, ranging from sex to reading, in another room as a way to "condition himself" to "just fall asleep every time you get into bed."

Psychopharmacologists work most effectively with seriously troubled gays who are schizophrenic or have a mood disorder, and least effectively with healthier patients when they give them medication alone without the psychotherapy they need. They are also particularly ineffective when they diagnose only that disorder with which they are most comfortably familiar and know how to treat because they at least think they have specific drugs for it, particularly when they mistake schizoaffective inappropriateness, histrionic flamboyance, or just the intense joy of coming out for full bipolar disorder.

In short, social workers, psychologists, psychiatrists, nurse clinicians, and others can all make competent therapists as long as they have warmth, empathy, and knowledgeability that includes the ability to make a proper diagnosis and a correct dynamic formulation to become the basis of a skillful, supportive, and corrective gay-aware approach to treatment.

Here is a testimonial from a thankful gay man who found therapy properly done along the recommended lines to be a positive life-changing experience:

Dear Dr. Kantor,

I am a gay man that realized at puberty that I preferred my fellow man, not woman. I went thru the possible cure of marriage to a woman, didn't work. Finally, for my own mental health, I came out at 30 years old post divorce from my wife. I know that you have heard similar stories before.

I am at the ripe old age of 46 someone who sowed my wild "gay" oats, and have been spared HIV (test every 6 months). Now I am ready for that dreaded word, relationship. I have had about 3 serious, over 2 years, lovers over the past 25 years. Therapy really helped me know that there is hope regarding a future love for me out there. Had to write to thank you, and all my therapists, for sharing their knowledge with me, and to ask them to keep up their good work.

Most sincerely,
Rolf.

Appendix

Origins

The following is a presentation, without suggesting endorsement, of outlines of some of the main, generally psychopathologically oriented descriptive and dynamic theories that others have advanced to explain homosexuality. My discussion is based in some measure on material in the website "Born Gay,"[1] to which I have also contributed. My attempt to unravel the origins of homosexuality does not imply that I feel that because we can understand homosexuality, we can treat it, doing so just "as we treat other psychopathological conditions."

No one knows for certain what "causes" homosexuality. Homosexuality just happens (it could be a bumper sticker). Men don't make a choice to be gay; they just feel naturally attracted to other men, spontaneously and personally as well as sexually, just as heterosexual men feel naturally attracted to women, spontaneously and personally as well as sexually. Being gay is an inclination, simply an "orientation," a variation of normal, by analogy an isomer of heterosexuality: constructed in much the same way, only in its mirror image, and opposite in direction but otherwise structurally the same. As one patient put it, comparing being gay to the gift of creativity, "I feel about men like Mozart must have felt about the piano when first he saw one: he knew exactly what it was for."

A patient traces his homosexuality back to a time before he was four years old when he remembers lulling himself to sleep with fantasies of spanking a male friend's bare bottom. Around that time, he was also having nightly bedtime fantasies of being part of a loving ménage à trois—at times with the comic book characters Batman and Robin and at times with the comic book characters the Human Torch and Toro. With those couples, he was fully appreciated and loved by the older men—his heroes, whom he adored not only for their accomplishments but also because they were as much unlike his father as he could possibly make them. Other strong persistent memories retained from this early time involved pleasurable feelings of warmth and love toward an older man who was a puppeteer he had seen in his skivvies and a recurrent frightening dream consisting of "I am running in fear from an unknown terror I believe was the stick that in reality, when I was very young, my mother beat me with when I did something heterosexual that displeased her—playing doctor with the little girl next door. Then I came to a fork in the road and chose the safe over the dangerous path, which I later came to understand represented being gay over being straight." True to pattern, his adult homosexuality was later to emerge fully formed "like Athena emerging whole from the head of Zeus." At first, his homosexuality resided entirely and ruled completely unopposed in a part of his brain devoted entirely to his biological/sexual instinct. Only later and secondarily did it become juxtaposed with involuntary and voluntary cognition and, as such subjected, to psychological conflict so that after being gay first, he became a conflicted homosexual next.

PSYCHOLOGICAL THEORIES

First, homosexuality is not a different or an alternative but a lesser, incomplete form of sexuality, so homosexuals are multidimensionally "inferior" to heterosexuals and, by extension, deserving less parity with and instead scorn and stigmatization by heterosexuals—its practitioners properly socially deprived, for religious, civil, and moral reasons, of equal rights and full opportunity.

Second, homosexuality is an active choice—not a sexual orientation laid down in childhood but a conscious selection made by the individual "to be gay." This theory doesn't always specify when or how the choice is made, but since so often homosexuality goes way back, this choice would have to be made very early in life yet at a time when, as I believe, children are way too young to make such weighty, conscious selections.

It is true that *opportunistic* homosexuality can be a choice, at least for those who are bisexual. (Heterosexuality can also be opportunistic, as when a bisexual chooses "being" straight in order to have children and heirs or for professional reasons. In my experience, most bisexual individuals making heterosexual choices can generally maintain their chosen behavior for only a short while before "relapsing"—as did a gay buddy I had who "went straight" long enough to have children, all the while maintaining a secret gay marriage on the side, only later to divorce his wife so that he could, at last, once again become openly gay.)

Reparative therapists often cite opportunistic homosexuality as an example that proves that all homosexuality is a choice, meaning that they are on the right track when they to try to save gays from themselves by getting them to rethink their selection. But these therapists are best advised to make another choice of their own: to urge gays not to go straight but to leave them alone or, if they need therapy, to treat them for something else: helping them shift in the direction not of becoming straight but of achieving the goal of being as worthy a person and as good a citizen as they possibly can be.

I myself had few, if any, heterosexual leanings my entire life. I did have heterosexual romantic (but not sexual) feelings into adulthood—and even formed a number of romantic relationships with women that, however, generally arose out of my motivation to live a "married lifestyle" with a wife and children (but without having intercourse). In my entire life, I tried heterosexual intercourse only once: with a prostitute who was to be the magic pill I took because I believed that the experience would catalyze my "recovery to heterosexuality through psychoanalysis." Ultimately, even my romantic heterosexual feelings faded in the face of homosexual desire surfacing and surging during puberty. Après le deluge, being straight was no longer even a remote option. Clearly, I was gradually falling in line with who and what I was. But my analyst, toward the end, just before I gave up on her, suggested I was making a bad choice to be a gay man and doing that deliberately while sticking with my choice defiantly in the face of every opportunity she gave me to change back and go straight—spitefully refusing to do what she thought I ought and instead, like a stubborn obsessional, doing the opposite of what she wanted me to do just because she wanted me to do it.

Third, homosexuality develops out of bisexuality as the straight (mature) instincts (somehow and for unknown reasons) regress and the gay (immature) instincts assume dominance. To some extent, this happens because homosexuality represents a spreading phobia of heterosexuality (and therefore responds to the same behavioral remedies that prove useful to "cure" social phobia, particularly negative conditioning).

Fourth, homosexuality is a psychological/developmental problem, due to a pathological mother complex, where the man identifies and binds with his mother because she is the powerful, controlling, alluring one and/or due to a pathological father complex where the man avoids identifying with a father because the father is remote, absent, aesthetically displeasing, or punitively castrative. In the latter case, the frightened, traumatized boy attempts to master his fearful traumata at Dad's hands by running to (and identifying with) Mom or by seeking a new, good man-mother to suckle him—a more appealing/available/loving father he hopes to give him the latter-day positivity, caring, and emotional support he never got then and for which he deeply yearns now.

Far too many of these theories gratuitously/incorrectly imply/state that one should blame one's parents for making one gay. I believe that if parents do participate in a process of "homosexualization" of a boy at all, it is only in a peripheral way. They don't make him queer. But they can help determine secondary aspects of his homosexuality, such as whether he becomes a politically conservative or a liberal thinker, an effeminate or a masculine man, a guilty or a guilt-free homosexual, or a homosexual who is merely sexually disinterested in women or actively afraid of them—as if there is occasional truth in the "classical" (psychoanalytic) formulation that all gays see all women as having a "vagina dentata" poised, like a bloodthirsty crocodile, "to snap."

As was true in my case, my parents influenced my homosexuality only secondarily and in its more superficial manifestations. Just before I was born, my mother had lost her father. From third-party reports as well as clues obtained from my reasoning as an adult back to what must have gone on in my childhood, I inferred that during my first, formative months or years, my mother was seriously depressed and perhaps so much so that she was unable to fully give me the love and warmth that a newborn requires, and I hypothesized that for the first years of my life, she was a very angry woman who took her anger at her fate out on me along the lines of "your being here reminds me that I lost my father." I believe that her depression and its attendant anger lasted for a long time—and I misinterpreted it as being a response to my sexuality (sexuality that would have been obvious to her even at that time), for "why else," I asked myself, "could she possibly hate me?" My analyst suggested that I became a homosexual as a result of this early interactive process. But I believe that I was a homosexual first and that these issues "merely" secondarily resulted in my becoming a certain kind of homosexual—during the early years of my being out, one with pervasive guilt about being gay and result-ant low self-esteem first about my sexuality and then, second, spread-ing to be about other nonsexual, areas of my life.

Most psychological theories about the cause of homosexuality tend to unfortunately confound cause with consequence. Thus, mother fixation theories at least to some extent reflect how the boy is overly attracted to his mother at a very early age because, already a homosexual, he finds her more simpatico than father, and theories of a castrative father/vagina-dentata mother simply reflect the fantasies of a boy who views his parents (and many people beside them) as castrative ball busters because having been traumatized when was a babe, he has already, when still very young, developed a well-established "sensitivity to" or even "innate paranoia" about being abused—for other things, being gay just being one of them. I also believe that phobic theories advanced to explain the cause of homosexuality (e.g., along the lines of a fear of women) actually tell us not that the homosexual boy fears women but that he, early on, already simply favors men.

BIOLOGICAL THEORIES

Here is a representative sampling of the biological theories of the cause of homosexuality:

- The fetus is potentially both gay and straight, but, in utero, the gay aspect develops, while the straight regresses and becomes atretic (withered). Abnormal intrauterine hormonal factors, such as a deficit of testosterone, are paramount and determine this outcome.
- There is a flaw in the egg or sperm so that the parental seed is weakened, leading to the creation of the "inferior homosexual."
- The entire process is determined by homosexual genes.
- Homosexuality is due to an infection, thus paralleling the "mental changes of syphilis."
- Homosexuality is temperament (e.g., feminine passivity) lived out sex-ually. And temperament is, as we all know, at least partly innate (e.g., "biologically based").

COMBINED THEORIES

I believe that homosexuality is primarily inborn/biologically based (e.g., residing in genetic/uterine environmental/hormonal factors) and only secondarily, in its peripheral manifestations and thus superficially, influenced by experience (individual and social development.).

Both primary and secondary influences can determine specific superficial aspects of *homosexual destiny*. In the realm of the primary factors, possibly those who become homosexual because of genetic factors are more or less likely to have signs of cross-gender traits and more or less likely to seek SRS (Sex Reassignment Surgery) than those who become homosexual because of an intrauterine "hormonal bath." Upbringing certainly determines personality and personality-specific homosexual "lifestyle." That can also tip the balance one way or the other for those who are bisexual.

RECOMMENDATIONS

Gay men should not feel guilty about being gay for any reason and certainly not because they believe that they are bad for having chosen to be homosexual and worse for refusing to change back. As a corollary, instead of wishing you weren't gay, just accept it as being "you, in your bones." Now get over any qualms you might have about that and get on with your life. Simultaneously, ignore people who deaffirm you by expecting you to change on your own or through treatment and instead seek people who affirm you just as you are, without expecting you to significantly alter your personality and behavior.

Freud, according to Jones, said, when referring to the talking cure, that he could not "abolish homosexuality and make normal heterosexuality take its place. . . . In a certain number of cases we succeed in developing the blighted germs of heterosexual tendencies which are present in every homosexual [but] in the majority of cases it is [not] possible."[2] Accept this, then avoid people who nag you to be different and instead stick with people who help you lead a happier, more productive life by helping you solve the realistic problems that can be secondarily associated with being gay. These include problems around coming out, prejudice and discrimination, gay marriage and parenting, and thorny sexual problems not primarily related to your being homosexual but a product of your being unable to perform adequately sexually/homosexually because of sexual dysfunctions, such as erectile dysfunction or "ejaculatio tarda" (an inability to come to orgasm in a timely fashion).

Notes

INTRODUCTION

1. J. Kort, *Gay Affirmative Therapy for the Straight Clinician: The Essential Guide* (New York: Norton, 2008), 1.

CHAPTER ONE

1. B. Denizet-Lewis, "Coming Out in Middle School," *New York Times*, September 27, 2009, 54.

CHAPTER TWO

1. J. Kort, *Gay Affirmative Therapy for the Straight Clinician: The Essential Guide* (New York: Norton, 2008), 278.
2. *Gilda* (1946). From Wikipedia, the free encyclopedia. Retrieved 1/31/2011 from http://en.wikipedai.org/wiki/gilda.

CHAPTER THREE

1. M. Kantor, *Distancing: Avoidant Personality Disorder Revised and Expanded* (Westport, CT: Praeger, 1993), 234.
2. B. Beck, "Rules of the Gay" (2002), retrieved November 25, 2010, from http://wweek.com/editorial/2002/07/24/rules-of-the-gay.

CHAPTER FOUR

1. E. Coleman and B. R. S. Rosser, "Gay and Bisexual Male Sexuality," in *Textbook of Homosexuality and Mental Health*, ed. R. P. Cabaj and T. Stein (Washington, DC: American Psychiatric Press, 1996), 708.

2. Ibid., 711.

3. Ibid., 710.

4. S. Froias, *Demystifying the 'Radical' Gay Agenda: Got AIDS?*, tri-*CityNews*, April 15, 2010, 12.

5. Coleman and Rosser, "Gay and Bisexual Male Sexuality," 710.

6. R. C. Fox, "Bisexuality: An Examination of Theory and Research," in Cabaj and Stein, *Textbook of Homosexuality and Mental Health*, 150.

7. Ibid.

8. Ibid., 149.

9. Ibid., 152.

10. Ibid., 148.

11. S. B. Levine, "Hypoactive Sexual Desire Disorder in Men: Basic Types, Causes, and Treatment," *Psychiatric Times* 27, no. 6 (June 2010): 40.

12. D. Davies, "Working with People Coming Out," in *Pink Therapy: A Guide for Counselors and Therapists Working with Lesbian, Gay and Bisexual Clients*, ed. Dominic Davies and Charles Neal (Buckingham: Open University Press, 1996), 83.

13. J. Kort, *Gay Affirmative Therapy for the Straight Clinician: The Essential Guide* (New York: Norton, 2008), 189–90.

14. B. Beck, "Rules of the Gay" (2002), retrieved November 25, 2010, from http://wweek.com/editorial/2002/07/24/rules-of-the-gay.

15. American Psychiatric Association, *Diagnostic and Statistical Manual of Mental Disorders* (4th ed.) (Washington, DC: American Psychiatric Association, 1987).

16. Levine, "Hypoactive Sexual Desire Disorder in Men," 41.

17. Ibid.

18. S. Simon, "A New Therapy on Faith and Sexual Identity," *Wall Street Journal*, August 6, 2009, A9.

CHAPTER FIVE

1. PDM Task Force, *Psychodynamic Diagnostic Manual* (Silver Spring, MD: Alliance of Psychoanalytic Organizations, 2006), 125–32.

2. American Psychiatric Association, *Diagnostic and Statistical Manual of Mental Disorders* (4th ed.) (Washington, DC: American Psychiatric Association, 1987), 526.

3. Ibid., 525.

4. Psychology Wiki, "Regression in the Service of the Ego," retrieved November 25, 2010, from http://psychology.wikia.com/wiki/Regression _in_the_service_of_the_ego.

5. D. Seil, "Transsexuals: The Boundaries of Sexual Identity and Gender," in *Textbook of Homosexuality and Mental Health*, ed. Robert P. Cabaj and Terry S. Stein (Washington, DC: American Psychiatric Press, 1996), 743.

6. American Psychiatric Association, *Diagnostic and Statistical Manual of Mental Disorders*, 536.

7. Seil, "Transsexuals," 749.

8. Ibid.

9. American Psychiatric Association, *Diagnostic and Statistical Manual of Mental Disorders*, 537–38.

10. Ibid., 538.

11. Ibid., 537.

12. Ibid., 533.

13. Seil, "Transsexuals," 748.

14. Ibid., 749.

15. Ibid., 746.

16. Ibid.

17. Ibid.

18. Ibid., 747.

19. Ibid., 753–54.

20. Ibid., 751.

21. Ibid.

22. Ibid., 747.

23. Ibid.

24. Ibid.

25. American Psychiatric Association, *Diagnostic and Statistical Manual of Mental Disorders*, 534.

26. Seil, "Transsexuals," 758.

27. Ibid., 755.

28. Ibid., 756–57.

29. Ibid., 757.

30. Ibid.

31. Ibid.

32. Ibid., 758.

CHAPTER SEVEN

1. R. M. Kertzner and M. Sved, "Midlife Gay Men and Lesbians: Adult Development and Mental Health," in *Textbook of Homosexuality and Mental Health*, ed. Robert P. Cabaj and Terry S. Stein (Washington, DC: American Psychiatric Press, 1996), 292.

CHAPTER TWELVE

1. S. Froias, *Rainbow Room: Demystifying the Radical Gay Agenda: Tyler Clementi, triCityNews*, October 7, 2010, 12.

CHAPTER THIRTEEN

1. Wikipedia, "Candide," retrieved November 26, 2010, from http://en.wikipedia.org/wiki/Candide.
2. American Psychiatric Association, *Diagnostic and Statistical Manual of Mental Disorders* (4th ed.) (Washington, DC: American Psychiatric Association, 1987).
3. H. Pinsker, *A Primer of Supportive Psychotherapy* (Hillsdale, NJ: The Analytic Press, 1997), 42.
4. J. Kort, *Gay Affirmative Therapy for the Straight Clinician: The Essential Guide* (New York: Norton, 2008), 47.
5. G. Kowszun and M. Malley, "Alcohol and Substance Misuse," in *Pink Therapy: A Guide for Counselors and Therapists Working with Lesbian, Gay and Bisexual Clients*, ed. Dominic Davies and Charles Neal (Buckingham: Open University Press, 1996), 173.
6. Kort, *Gay Affirmative Therapy for the Straight Clinician*, 138.
7. R. Isay, "On the Analytic Therapy of Homosexual Men," in *Affirmative Dynamic Psychotherapy with Gay Men*, ed. Carlton Cornett (Northvale, NJ: Jason Aronson, 1993), 23–24.
8. J. Krajeski, "Homosexuality and the Mental Health Professions: A Contemporary History," in *Textbook of Homosexuality and Mental Health*, ed. R. P. Cabaj and T. Stein. (Washington, DC: American Psychiatric Press, 1996), 19.
9. Isay, "On the Analytic Therapy of Homosexual Men," 25.
10. Ibid., 28.
11. Ibid., 29.
12. D. Davies, "Towards a Model of Gay Affirmative Therapy," in Davies and Neal, *Pink Therapy*, 25.
13. Pinsker, *A Primer of Supportive Psychotherapy*, 35.
14. Kort, *Gay Affirmative Therapy for the Straight Clinician*.
15. Pinsker, *A Primer of Supportive Psychotherapy*, ix–x.

APPENDIX

1. "Born Gay," retrieved November 29, 2010, from http://borngay.procon.org.
2. E. Jones, *The Life and Works of Sigmund Freud*, 3 vols. (New York: Basic Books, 1957), 3:195.

Index

ostracized from, 14, 15, 16. *See also*
  Parents
Family therapy, 197
Fear, as lack of desire, 41. *See also*
  Paranoia
Feminine identity, 94, 138. *See also*
  Gender identity
Fetishes, 60, 87; transvestic fetishists, 87,
  91, 93–95, 105
Fetishism, 90–91
Fidelity, in relationships. *See* Infidelity
  and cheating; Monogamous
  relationship
Flamboyance, 133, 165, 191. *See also*
  Hypomania
Fox, R. C., 66–67
Freud, Sigmund, 67, 122–23, 134, 201,
  214
Friends, 57; aging and, 112; identity crises
  and, 106; lifestyle and, 27–28; parents
  and, 120–22; peer pressure, 80, 97, 104;
  substance abuse and, 150; support of,
  159–60, 161. *See also* Relationships
Froias, Steven, 178
Frotteurism, 91

Gay identity, 128. *See also* Identity/
  disorders of identity
Gay life, enigma of, ix–x. *See also*
  Lifestyle
Gay love, 81–82
Gay marriage, 29–30, 31, 41, 128;
  cheating in, 35, 53, 54–55; difficulties
  in, 52–55; end-of-life decisions in,
  35–37; example of successful, 32–37;
  paranoia and, 53–54. *See also*
  Monogamous relationship
Gay pride, 151–52, 158, 168
Gay subculture, 108, 154, 163
Gender dysphoria, 101
Gender identity, 21, 176
Gender identity disorder (GID),
  97–101; transsexualism, 85–86,
  94, 98–100
Gentrification, 162
Geographic solution, to homophobia, 161,
  193–94
GID. *See* Gender identity disorder

Grief, suicide and, 171–75; levels of grief,
  171–72; prevention and treatment of,
  181–83
Group therapy, 181, 183, 187
Guilt and shame, 111, 213; cognitive
  distortions, 157–58; coming out and, 3,
  5, 10; erotophobia and, 74; fear of
  rejection and, 157; friends and, 159–60;
  gay pride and, 151–52; grief and, 172;
  homophobia and, 153–57, 168;
  infidelity and cheating, 61, 66; low
  self-esteem and, xvii, 151–66; paraphilias and, xv–xvi; parents and, 119;
  survivor guilt, 114, 163
Gynemimesis, 100

Heterosexism, 152, 156, 192, 199
Histrionic personality disorder, 127, 133,
  147, 198
HIV/AIDS, 171, 172
Homophobia, 20, 63, 162; bitchiness as,
  29; bullying and, 167, 168, 177–78;
  emotional disorders and, 134, 136, 138;
  external, 153–56; geographical solution
  to, 161, 193–94; internalized, 131–32,
  156–57; paranoia and, 156, 157–58;
  politics and, 23; retaliative outing, 9;
  stress from, 128, 143; therapist and,
  205; therapy and, 191–93, 192;
  violence and, 154–55; at work,
  143–44
Homosexuality, theories on, xviii,
  209–14; biological, 213; psychological,
  210–13; recommendations, 214
Hopelessness, suicide and, 169, 171
Hypersexuality, 153. *See also* Promiscuity
Hypoactive sexual desire disorder
  (HSDD), 74, 77–80
Hypomania, 72, 132–33, 138, 153;
  coming out and, 4; denial and, 174;
  loneliness and, 168

Ideal self, 122–23. *See also under* Self
Identity/disorders of identity, xvi, 44,
  102–7, 131; coming out and, 4, 7;
  divided self, 201; fetishism and, 90;
  gender, 21, 176 (*See also* Gender
  identity disorder); identity crises,

Psychotherapy, 187; indications for, 189.
See also Therapy and therapists
Psychotic delusions, 170. *See also*
Paranoia
PTSD. *See* Posttraumatic stress disorder

Rage. *See* Anger and rage
Reactive disorders, 128
Rejection, fear of, 12, 109, 145, 193;
erotophobia and, 75; low self-esteem
and, 157; relationships and,
49–52; trauma aversion and,
167, 169, 181
Relationships, xiv–xv, 31–57;
compatibility in, 43, 52; anxiety about,
159; avoiding Mr. Wrong, 37–40;
compulsive sexuality and, 69;
destructive ambivalence in, 44;
evaluations of, 180; excessive
perfectionism and, 41–42, 180; fear
rationalized as lack of desire, 41;
flexibility about type, 47–48; infidelity
and cheating in, 195; need rationalized
as attraction in, 40; negative mindsets
that interfere with, 40–45; paraphilias
and, 85; positivity in, 48–49, 51, 78,
115; prioritizing, 45–47; rejection and,
49–52; self-disavowal in, 44–45; sexual
compulsives and, 72–73; taking others'
advice on, 55–57; trauma inflicted in,
140–41. *See also* Gay marriage;
Monogamous relationship; Partners and
partnering
Religion, lifestyle and, 21–22
Reparative therapy, 11, 13, 197–201, 211
Retaliative outing, 9
Rosser, B. R. S., 60, 63

Sadists, 38, 85, 87, 106, 148, 156;
therapists as, 197, 198
Sadomasochism, 84, 85, 91–92, 149;
causes of, 88–89; coming out and, 4;
degrees of, 87; fisting and, 92;
substance abuse and, 147. *See also*
Masochism
Sadomasochistic personality disorder, 4,
134–36
Safe sex, 64. *See also* Unsafe sex

Same-sex partnering. *See* Gay marriage;
Partners and partnering
Schizophrenia, 199
Self-acceptance, 137; aging and, 113, 115;
coming out and, 3, 9–10, 16; midlife
crisis and, 109; relationships and,
31–32. *See also* Self-esteem
Self-affirmation, 49, 133, 152
Self-confidence, 151
Self-control, 69, 73, 80, 194
Self-disavowal, 44–45
Self-esteem, 53, 77, 127, aging and, 114;
coming out and, 158–59; compulsive
sexuality and, 69, 72; conquering low,
158–66; denial and, 174; depression
and, 131; internal homophobia and,
156; negativity and, 163–164, 168;
shame, guilt, and, xvii, 151–66, 213;
therapy and, 194, 201. *See also* Self-
acceptance
Self-expression, 81
Self-hatred, 16, 204; grief and, 173; internalized homophobia, 131–32, 156–57
Self-help groups, 183. *See also* Group
therapy
Self-image, 6, 90, 160, 163; grief and,
171; ideal self, 122–23. *See also*
Identity/disorders of identity
Self-knowledge, 190
Self-realization, lifestyle and, 26, 27
Self-support, loss of, 172, 173
Sex and sexuality, xv, 58–82, 206;
abstinence, 81, 146, 152, 165, 200;
bisexuality, 66–68, 105, 131, 210–211;
compulsive sexuality, 68–73, 80, 131,
199; dysfunctions, 74–81; gay love,
81–82; key aspects of, 59–60; medical/
mechanical complications, 73;
monogamy and, 33, 55; monogamy *vs.*
promiscuity, 60–66; unsafe, 133, 135,
178. *See also* Erotophobia; Paraphilias
Sex guides, 78
Sex reassignment surgery (SRS), 97, 101
Sexual compulsion. *See* Compulsive
sexuality
Sexual dysfunctions, 74–81; hypoactive
sexual desire disorder, 74, 77–80. *See
also* Erotophobia

About the Author

Martin Kantor, MD, is a Harvard psychiatrist who has been in full private practice in Boston and New York City and active in residency training programs at several hospitals, including Massachusetts General and Beth Israel in New York. He also served as assistant clinical professor of psychiatry at Mount Sinai Medical School and as clinical assistant professor of psychiatry at the University of Medicine and Dentistry of New Jersey—New Jersey Medical School. He is now writing fulltime and is the author of numerous other books, including *The Essential Guide to Overcoming Avoidant Personality Disorder* (Praeger, 2010); *Homophobia, Second Edition: The State of Sexual Bigotry Today* (Praeger, 2009); *Uncle Sam's Shame: Inside Our Broken Veterans Administration* (Praeger, 2009); *Lifting the Weight: Understanding Depression in Men, Its Causes and Solutions* (Praeger, 2007); *The Psychopathy of Everyday Life: How Antisocial Personality Disorder Affects All of Us* (Praeger, 2006); *Understanding Paranoia: A Guide for Professionals, Families, and Sufferers* (Praeger, 2004); *Distancing: Avoidant Personality Disorder, Revised and Expanded* (Praeger, 2003); *Passive-Aggression: A Guide for the Therapist, the Patient, and the Victim* (Praeger, 2002); *Treating Emotional Disorder in Gay Men* (Praeger, 1999); and *Homophobia* (Praeger, 1998). He has also authored *My Guy: A Gay Man's Guide to a Lasting Relationship* (2002); *Together Forever: The Gay Man's Guide to Lifelong Love* (2005, nominated for a Benjamin Franklin Publisher's Marketing Association award); and *Hot Gay Sex Coupons* (2004).